Economic Dimensions of
COVID-19
in Indonesia

Economic Dimensions of
COVID-19
in Indonesia

Responding to the Crisis

EDITED BY

BLANE D. LEWIS
FIRMAN WITOELAR

ISEAS YUSOF ISHAK
INSTITUTE

First published in Singapore in 2021 by
ISEAS Publishing
30 Heng Mui Keng Terrace
Singapore 119614

E-mail: publish@iseas.edu.sg
Website: http://bookshop.iseas.edu.sg

The responsibility for facts and opinions in this publication rests exclusively with the authors and their interpretations do not necessarily reflect the views or the policy of the Institute or its supporters.

ISEAS Library Cataloguing-in-Publication Data

Name(s): Lewis, Blane D., editor. | Witoelar, Firman, editor.
Title: Economic dimensions of COVID-19 in Indonesia : responding to the crisis / edited by Blane D. Lewis and Firman Witoelar.
Description: Singapore : ISEAS – Yusof Ishak Institute, 2021. | Includes bibliographical references.
Identifiers: ISBN 9789814951456 (hard cover) | ISBN 9789814951463 (pdf) | ISBN 9789814951470 (epub)
Subjects: LCSH: COVID-19 pandemic, 2020 — Economic aspects — Indonesia. | Indonesia — Economic policy.
Classification: LCC HC450 H43E19

Cover photo: President Joko Widodo visits the office of the COVID-19 Response Acceleration Task Force at the National Disaster Management Agency, 10 June 2020.
Image used with permission from the Secretariat Office of the President of the Republic of Indonesia. Photo by Muchlis Jr, BPMI Setpres.

Edited, typeset and indexed by Tracy Harwood, Canberra
Printed in Singapore by Markono Print Media Pte Ltd

Contents

Tables and figures

Tables (continued)

Figures

Contributors

Abdurohman, Senior Researcher, Badan Kebijakan Fiskal (Fiscal Policy Agency), Finance Ministry, Government of Indonesia, Jakarta

Vivi Alatas, Chief Executive Officer, Asakreativika, Jakarta

Felippa Amanta, Head of Research, Centre for Indonesian Policy Studies, Jakarta

Sharon Bessell, Professor of Public Policy and Director, Gender Equity and Diversity, Crawford School of Public Policy, College of Asia and the Pacific, Australian National University, Canberra

Angie Bexley, Senior Research Fellow, Crawford School of Public Policy, College of Asia and the Pacific, Australian National University, Canberra

Masyita Crystallin, Special Advisor to the Minister of Finance for Macroeconomics and Fiscal Policy, Government of Indonesia, Jakarta

Stephen Grenville, Nonresident Fellow, Lowy Institute, Sydney

Hal Hill, HW Arndt Professor Emeritus of Southeast Asian Economies, Crawford School of Public Policy, College of Asia and the Pacific, Australian National University, Canberra

Milda Irhamni, Associate Director of Research, Abdul Latif Jameel Poverty Action Lab (J-PAL) Southeast Asia, Jakarta

Blane Lewis, Senior Fellow and Head, Indonesia Project, Crawford School of Public Policy, College of Asia and the Pacific, Australian National University, Canberra

Chris Manning, Honorary Fellow, Indonesia Project, Crawford School of Public Policy, College of Asia and the Pacific, Australian National University, Canberra

Riyana Miranti, Associate Professor, National Centre for Social and Economic Modelling, Faculty of Business, Government and Law, University of Canberra

Ruth Nikijuluw, PhD candidate, Arndt-Corden Department of Economics, Crawford School of Public Policy, College of Asia and the Pacific, Australian National University, Canberra

Arianto Patunru, Fellow, Arndt-Corden Department of Economics, Crawford School of Public Policy, College of Asia and the Pacific, Australian National University, Canberra

Roland Rajah, Lead Economist, International Economics Program, Lowy Institute, Sydney

Budy P. Resosudarmo, Professor, Arndt-Corden Department of Economics, Crawford School of Public Policy, and Deputy Head, Poverty and Inequality Research Centre, Australian National University, Canberra

Firman Witoelar, Fellow, Indonesia Project, Crawford School of Public Policy, College of Asia and the Pacific, Australian National University, Canberra

Acknowledgments

We thank Australian National University (ANU) Vice Chancellor Professor Brian Schmidt and the Australian Government's Ambassador to Indonesia the Honourable Gary Quinlan for their inciteful opening remarks at the conference *Economic Dimensions of COVID-19 in Indonesia: Responding to the Crisis*, on which this volume is based. The editors would also like to acknowledge the financial and in-kind support of the Australian Government Department of Foreign Affairs and Trade and the ANU Crawford School of Public Policy.

We thank the conference session chairs and speakers and our numerous ANU graduate student volunteers, without whom the smooth execution of the conference would not have been possible. We also convey our deep gratitude to Indonesia Project staff for their valuable assistance in putting the conference together and for their unwavering support to the Project in general: Kate McLinton, Lydia Napitupulu, Nurkemala Muliani and Bhaskara Adiwena.

We are especially grateful for the considerable efforts our chapter authors have undertaken and for the high quality of their work published here. Finally, we express our immense gratitude to this book's editor, Tracy Harwood, for her superb and expeditious work.

Blane Lewis and Firman Witoelar
Canberra, February 2021

© Australian National University
Base map CAP 12-215a

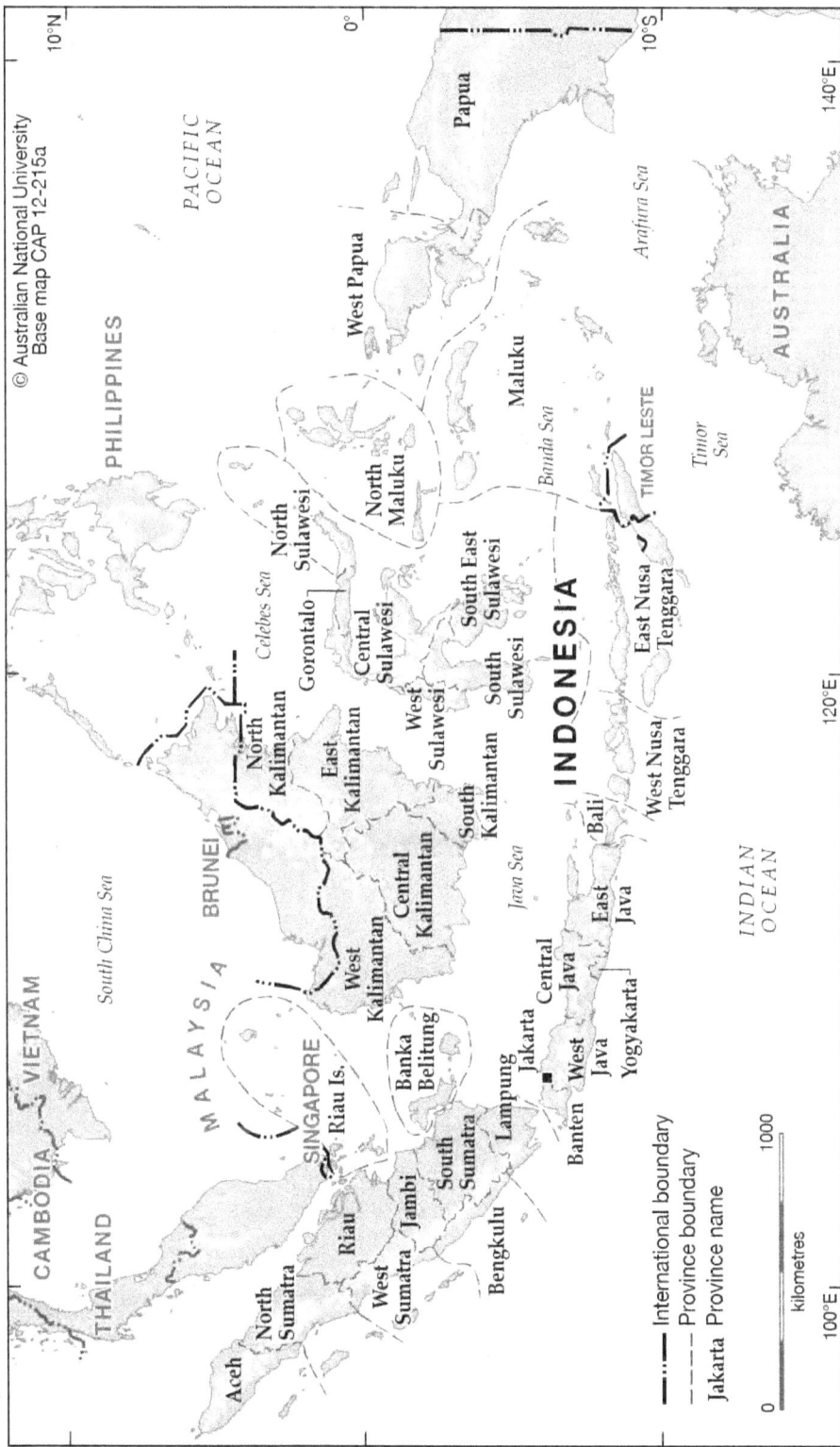

THAILAND

CAMBODIA

VIETNAM

PHILIPPINES

South China Sea

PACIFIC OCEAN

MALAYSIA

BRUNEI

SINGAPORE

Celebes Sea

North Kalimantan

North Sulawesi

Gorontalo

North Maluku

Central Sulawesi

West Papua

Papua

Aceh

North Sumatra

Riau

West Sumatra

Jambi

Riau Is.

Banka Belitung

East Kalimantan

West Sulawesi

South East Sulawesi

South Sulawesi

Maluku

Arafura Sea

Bengkulu

South Sumatra

Lampung

West Kalimantan

Central Kalimantan

South Kalimantan

Java Sea

Jakarta

Banten

West Java

Central Java

Yogyakarta

East Java

Bali

West Nusa Tenggara

East Nusa Tenggara

TIMOR LESTE

Banda Sea

Timor Sea

INDONESIA

INDIAN OCEAN

AUSTRALIA

10°N

0°

10°S

100°E

120°E

140°E

International boundary
Province boundary
Jakarta   Province name

kilometres
0   1000

1 Introduction: The impact of COVID-19 in Indonesia

Blane D. Lewis and Firman Witoelar

Beginning in December 2019 the novel coronavirus swept quickly through all regions of the world. COVID-19 has wreaked social, political and economic havoc everywhere and has shown few signs of entirely abating. The recent development and approval of new vaccines against the virus, however, now provides at least some reasonable hope that we may be coming to the beginning of the end of the pandemic. This volume collects papers from a conference organised by the Australian National University's Indonesia Project titled Economic Dimensions of COVID-19 in Indonesia: Responding to the Crisis, which was held 7–10 September 2020. It constitutes the first thorough analysis of the impact of the pandemic in Indonesia and government's initial response to its deleterious effects.

Collectively, the chapters in this volume focus for the most part on the economic and socioeconomic elements of COVID-19 in Indonesia. After the overview, the remaining chapters can be usefully organised according to three broad topics: monetary and fiscal affairs; trade, labour and poverty; and health, human capital and gender. We begin this introductory chapter by summarising the main points of each chapter. We conclude with a brief discussion of Indonesia's path ahead.

Overview

Hal Hill emphasises that the pandemic represents one of the most serious challenges faced by Indonesia in its 75-year history as a nation. While the country's health system has struggled to respond successfully, macroeconomic policy has been reasonably adept. COVID-19's impact on poverty and unemployment has been generally significant but varied in its severity across Indonesia's vast geography. Overall—thanks to good luck and effective management—negative economic effects have been restrained, at least as compared to those of other countries in the region. Hill argues it is unlikely that the crisis will force the Widodo administration to change its general policy direction in any fundamental way.

Monetary and fiscal affairs

Stephen Grenville and Roland Rajah discuss the two main tasks for monetary policy in the context of the ongoing pandemic: to mitigate short-term portfolio outflows and to help finance the budget deficit. The authors demonstrate that financial outflows, which rose considerably at the beginning of the crisis, quickly stabilised thanks to government intervention in the currency and bond markets. They then examine Bank Indonesia's unaccustomed role in financing the deficit through the purchase of government bonds. While 'money printing' has obvious macroeconomic risks, it is clearly justified by the current conditions. The authors call on Bank Indonesia to develop a sound exit strategy from its government bond–buying program.

Masyita Crystallin and Abdurohman explore the early negative impact of the crisis on economic growth and examine the details of the government's multifaceted fiscal policy response. The authors conclude that government's comprehensive approach has been largely effective, while emphasising the difficult challenges facing program implementation, particularly funds disbursement. They stress that the pandemic has highlighted the need for continued fiscal reforms, especially regarding government mobilisation of public revenues.

Blane Lewis and Ruth Nikijuluw investigate the potential effects of COVID-19 on district government revenues and spending, household spending, and ultimately local public service access. The authors find that although declining district revenue from intergovernmental transfers and supply shock–induced decreases in household spending are considerable, the overall impact on local public service access is unlikely to be very severe via these channels. They argue that increasing central transfers to local governments would be unwise, given the longstanding ineffectiveness of districts in using their fiscal resources to enhance service delivery.

Trade, labour and poverty

Arianto Patunru and Felippa Amanta consider the impact of the pandemic on Indonesia's food security. They argue that forced mobility restrictions related to the country's COVID-19 response have constrained food production, distribution and trade. These disruptions are likely to result in food shortages, price spikes and/or price volatility, which will in turn negatively affect the livelihoods of people working in food supply chains and threaten long-term food security, especially among the poor. Patunru and Amanta highlight needed reforms, including increased investment in agriculture, diversification of food supplies, easing food trade flows, and enhancing international cooperation to ensure regional food security.

Chris Manning examines the effects of the crisis on jobs, noting that the informal sector, tourism, labour-intensive manufacturing, construction and transport have been especially hard hit. He argues that Indonesia has avoided the more severe labour market disruptions experienced by other countries in the region, perhaps because extensive use of the internet has facilitated work from home and the new pre-employment card has enabled continued skills development, among others. He observes that some provisions in the recent 'omnibus law' have the potential to create better jobs during recovery.

Vivi Alatas investigates Indonesia's social assistance targeting methods in the context of the pandemic. She determines that COVID-19 has aggravated major political and technical challenges to targeting assistance to those in need. Alatas maintains that targeting accuracy can only be improved by collecting better data on poor households and by enhancing beneficiary selection based on those data.

Health, human capital and gender

Firman Witoelar and Riyana Miranti discuss the impact of the crisis on non-communicable diseases (NCDs), including mental disorders, maternal health problems, and infectious and nutritional illnesses, among others. The authors observe that NCDs have become increasingly burdensome in recent years in Indonesia and that the pandemic has exacerbated health and economic costs associated with such illnesses. The direct negative short- and long-term health effects of COVID-19 are more acute for those who suffer from NCDs. And declining nutritious food intake and reduced insurance coverage, both indirectly caused by job and income loss during the crisis, may be felt more strongly among people with NCDs.

Budy Resosudarmo and Milda Irhamni examine the effects of the crisis on human capital. They first demonstrate that the number of COVID-19 cases and related deaths in Indonesia are likely to be several times higher than reported. The authors then develop a conceptual framework that can be used to analyse the myriad and complicated channels through which the pandemic affects human capital development, focusing on health and educational performance, over both the short and long term. Drawing on the history of other pandemics, they show the effects of COVID-19 are likely to have deep and lasting impacts on the stock of human capital in Indonesia.

Sharon Bessell and Angie Bexley focus their chapter on investigating the heterogeneous impact of the crisis on the poor and other vulnerable groups. They advocate the use of multidimensional poverty measures to assess the impact of the pandemic on individuals, as opposed to households, and draw on evidence from the previous employment of such methods in South Sulawesi. The authors highlight the likelihood of particularly negative impacts of the crisis on women, especially as regards expanding time burdens and rising domestic violence.

The path ahead

A challenge faced by all authors of chapters in this volume concerns difficulties in accessing quality and timely information on the impact of the pandemic and government responses to the crisis. Since the onset of the crisis, the absence of a uniform standard in terms of reporting the cases and the lack of transparency about the data have complicated management of the pandemic and efforts to study it. While such information obstacles are often present in Indonesia, the rapidly changing nature of crisis effects and reactions has intensified the usual complications. As more and better data become available, extended and enhanced analyses of the issues considered here and others can take place. Many of the chapter authors are committed to continuing to research the impact of coronavirus in Indonesia over the longer term.

Regarding the pandemic itself, the latest available information suggests that COVID-19 cases and deaths are still experiencing sharp increases in Indonesia. Many of the concerns discussed in several chapters in this volume regarding the management of the pandemic are still unresolved. Large gaps in the implementation of contact testing, contact tracing and isolation of suspected cases remain. The government continues to struggle in delivering a consistent message between enforcing strict public health measures and encouraging economic activity that increases people's mobility such as domestic tourism.

On a more positive note, the government expects to begin rolling out its coronavirus vaccination program in early January 2021. People between the ages of 18 and 59 years will comprise the initial target group. Vaccines will be made available free of charge. There will still be challenges in the logistics of the vaccine delivery and acceptance of the vaccine, as well as surveillance and monitoring of the vaccination program. Public health experts warn that the vaccine alone will not stop the pandemic; public health measures will still need to be enforced. While Indonesia is not out of the woods yet there is reason to be cautiously optimistic that recovery is underway.

2 Indonesia and the COVID-19 crisis: A light at the end of the tunnel?

Hal Hill

Abstract

The COVID-19 crisis is one of the most serious challenges in Indonesia's 75-year history. It is testing all aspects of government and society, from health and social security systems to macroeconomic management and administrative capacity. The country's health system has struggled, owing to past underinvestment and inconsistent management during the crisis. Macroeconomic management has been more sure-footed, although the fiscal stimulus has been comparatively small and initially slow to reach its intended recipients. The social impacts are still unfolding, reversing the past decades of declining poverty and unemployment. Nevertheless, through a combination of good luck and effective management, the overall economic impact on Indonesia is considerably less than most of its middle income Asian neighbours. The economic decline in 2020 is also much smaller than that experienced during the Asian financial crisis. Predictably, there have been substantial subnational variations in socioeconomic impacts, ranging from the steep decline in tourism-dependent Bali to much smaller impacts in more remote, lightly settled regions. There is so far little evidence that the Widodo administration will change policy directions in any fundamental way as a result of the crisis.

1. Introduction

The COVID-19 crisis is a defining event for the world. It is the most serious pandemic in a century, and the sharpest peacetime global economic contraction in 90 years. It is truly global, it was unanticipated (at least in the form that it took), and it is everywhere testing all aspects of government and society, from macroeconomic management and health systems to societal resilience and personal wellbeing. It is also occurring at a troubled time for the world, with the rise of populism, authoritarian leaders, democratic regression and a serious dispute between the world's two economic superpowers, and a concomitant weakening of cooperative global institutions and coordinated action to address pressing global economic, political and environmental challenges.

The COVID-19 crisis is also a perfect illustration of the phenomenon of John Kay and Mervyn King's (2020) 'radical uncertainty', of 'unknown unknown' events that are inherently unpredictable. Writing in the midst of the crisis (October 2020), with no immediate end in prospect, is a perilous exercise. We don't yet know when an effective vaccine will become available, or even if, as with the great pandemic of 1918–1920, it will eventually fade into insignificance after causing great carnage. We don't yet have an accurate picture of the pandemic's economic costs in the short run, let alone the longer term. The social costs, particularly poverty incidence in poor countries, are still at best guestimates based on useful but hasty surveys and small samples. The political ramifications are still unfolding. It is still not clear whether the crisis will embolden governments to undertake politically sensitive policy reform or push leaders further down the path of unproductive populism. We also have at best an imperfect understanding of the reasons for the very large differences in country responses, from the quick and adept to fumbling incompetence. Across the world, the only real certainty to date is that the rich/poor country divide has been accentuated, as evidenced by the massive fiscal support programs that rich countries have been able to mount.

Against this backdrop, this chapter addresses the COVID-19 crisis and response in Indonesia. Emphasising the high degree of uncertainty, Section 2 briefly compares this event to previous major crises, while Section 3 provides an overview of the government's response. Section 4 summarises the economic impacts, while Section 5 looks at the health sector management. The next three sections investigate various aspects of macroeconomic management before and during the crisis. Section 9 considers the social impacts. Section 10 sums up and asks what broader lessons have been learned or at least will be on the public policy agenda in the near term and possibly beyond.

To set the scene, Table 2.1 provides a summary of the COVID-19 impact in Indonesia and selected Asian middle income countries to date. I focus on three key indicators: COVID-19 cases and fatalities (both per million population) and the International Monetary Fund's latest economic growth forecasts for the year 2020. I will discuss these data, and their limitations, in more detail below. Here it is useful to highlight two salient aspects as they relate to Indonesia. First, although the COVID-19 statistics are very approximate, Indonesia's reported COVID-19 incidence, as measured by the fatality rate, appears to be about one-third of the global average. It is similar to India and the Philippines, which have also both struggled to contain the virus, and well short of the exemplary record of China, Thailand and Vietnam. Second, thus far the economic impacts for Indonesia have been much milder than most comparators. Indonesia's forecast economic decline in 2020, of 1.5 per cent, is about one-third of the global figure. It is well below that of India, the Philippines and Thailand, although China and Vietnam have clearly benefited from more effective containment strategies. But the main conclusion nevertheless holds: through a combination of good luck and some good management, to date Indonesia appears to have escaped the worst of the crisis.

Table 2.1 The COVID-19 crisis: Indonesia and neighbours, October 2020

Country	COVID-19 cases	COVID-19 fatalities	GDP growth 2020 (%)
Indonesia	1,228	45	−1.5
China	60	3	1.8
India	5,369	82	−10.3
Thailand	53	<1	−7.1
Vietnam	12	<1	1.6
Philippines	3,198	59	−8.3
World	5,077	142	−4.4

Note: COVID-19 statistics per million population, as at 15 October 2020.

Source: Worldometer for COVID-19 data (www.worldometers.info/coronavirus/); World Economic Outlook Database for GDP estimates (www.imf.org/en/Publications/WEO/weo-database/2020/October).

2. A major crisis

This is a major crisis event for Indonesia, in its own way perhaps as serious as the three other major events that have tested the Republic, namely the independence struggle of 1945–1949, the political turmoil and regime change of 1965–1966, and the Asian financial crisis (AFC) and regime change of 1997–1998. The socioeconomic impacts are likely to be at least as serious as the first two events, though not (yet) anywhere on the scale of 1997–1998. Reflecting its economic success in the modern era, prior to 2020 Indonesia had recorded just one year of negative economic growth since the late 1960s (–13 per cent in 1998). Also excluding 1998, it is the first year that there has been an appreciable increase in head count poverty incidence since 1976, when poverty began to be measured on a regular basis.

In contrast to the other three events, this crisis has occurred against the backdrop of a global crisis, with the result that international assistance measures have been limited, exacerbated by pre-existing weaknesses in the global economic and political architectures. The implication is that absent on this occasion is the global goodwill that accompanied the cessation of hostilities in 1949, the major international economic support program that got underway in 1967, and the opportunity that Indonesia and other AFC-afflicted economies grasped to export their way out of the crisis in 1998–1999, facilitated by a sharp depreciation of the currency and a buoyant global economy.

The potential political ramifications of the COVID-19 crisis are still to unfold. But perhaps this will illuminate one of contemporary Indonesia's strengths, namely that its settled, democratic polity and regime legitimacy will greatly enhance the ability of the country to navigate its way through the crisis.

3. The government's response: An overview

Unlike most crises, COVID-19 is testing practically every aspect of government: the health system, emergency social supports, communication strategies, enforcement of temporary restrictions on personal mobility and freedoms, quick-acting fiscal and monetary measures, the closure and policing of international borders, food supplies, interjurisdictional cooperation and coordination, trust in public institutions and above all else national leadership.

The crisis originated in the health sector, and control of the virus has therefore been central to the crisis management response. In the words of Anne Krueger:

The lesson from day one still holds: until the virus is defeated, there can be no return to normal … The twin goals of defeating the virus and reviving the economy are one and the same … And it is the public's adherence to preventive measures that will determine the pace at which the virus is defeated. (Krueger 2020)

This has therefore been the first marker of country success. It is also one that defies a priori hypothesising. The richest and most powerful country on earth, the United States, has the world's highest-reported case incidence and mortality, while some relatively poor countries have been able to respond quickly and effectively. Take the case of Vietnam, which has had one of the lowest infection and mortality rates. Its success is reportedly explained by at least five factors: it had learnt from its earlier experience with the SARS epidemic; it closed its international borders quickly; it has a strong central government that quickly instituted a clear and consistent communication strategy; the country has a reasonably comprehensive if rudimentary public health system, aided by near universal literacy; and its test, trace and quarantine procedures in response to local outbreaks have generally been quick and effective. Table 2.1 indicates the resultant economic dividend the country has enjoyed. As we shall see, Indonesia's early responses differed from those of Vietnam in several respects.

The next line of defence has been an economic one. Mobility restrictions and commercial shutdowns necessitated prompt and large-scale government interventions. Nervous financial, debt and foreign exchange markets had to be reassured, especially in countries like Indonesia that had experienced a deep economic and financial crisis in recent memory. Moreover, the response had to be comprehensive, embracing all arms and tiers of government: the monetary response had to stabilise currencies, reassure creditors (particularly foreign creditors) and ensure financial lines of credit remained open. The health system required an urgent injection of resources to manage the sharply rising caseload. The enterprises that were forced to close required emergency support, and relief from creditors. The workers and households that were denied income-earning opportunities needed temporary fiscal support through quick-release tax-and-transfer measures. While most of these responses were economy-wide in nature, some had to be fine-tuned and directed to groups of people and communities particularly affected. Urban, IT-connected white-collar professionals with access to good health care have been much less affected by the crisis than the homeless and workers in the hospitality sector. Tourism-dependent Bali has been worse affected than some of the more remote agrarian communities. Logistics and transport networks needed to be maintained, particularly for the delivery of food, medical equipment and pharmaceuticals, and other essential supplies. More broadly, as consumption fell sharply and investment collapsed, governments needed to resort to old-fashioned Keynesian stimulus measures to ameliorate the economic decline.

As we shall see in the following sections, Indonesia has managed some dimensions of the crisis response quite effectively, while in other respects it has struggled. These outcomes reflect what was already well known about the Indonesian government: competent professionals running the central bank and the Ministry of Finance alongside many cabinet-level political appointees, crucially including the health minister on this occasion. In addition, interjurisdictional coordination between the national and regional governments has been variable, with the president and provincial governors sometimes issuing conflicting edicts. Not unlike other major international figures, President Joko Widodo (Jokowi) himself has vacillated between lockdown and opening up, in his assessment of the severity of the pandemic, in his resort to and reliance on the scientific expertise, and in his excessively optimistic predictions concerning the availability of a (Chinese) vaccine. The result has been his 'zig-zag response' throughout the year (Fealy 2020).

4. Economic impacts: An overview[1]

Despite the sometimes muddled government response, Indonesia's economic contraction in 2020 has been comparatively mild, as Table 2.1 shows. Why? Three general sets of factors explain the variable economic outcomes across countries: how effectively the virus has been controlled, the size of the emergency fiscal and monetary stimulus, and the general economic/demographic structure. Each of these factors encompasses a wide range of subsidiary variables. For example, the first one includes the government's capacity to move quickly in formulating and implementing defensive measures, including 'smart' lockdown strategies, and the pre-existing state of the health system. The second includes pre-crisis macroeconomic health, and the capacity to quickly institute emergency monetary stabilisation and targeted spending measures. The third includes a range of variables. For example, an economy's dependence on services that require people to cross international borders to deliver or receive them, such as tourism, increases its vulnerability. Conversely, a larger agricultural sector and a more youthful population, both features of developing countries, are likely to enhance coping strategies.

---

1 For detailed economic analyses of the crisis and its impacts, see Olivia et al. (2020) and Sparrow et al. (2020).

This framework facilitates an understanding of the economic impact of COVID-19 on Indonesia. With regard to the first factor, the government has struggled to institute effective test-and-trace facilities and the public health sector has been overwhelmed. By comparison, the Vietnamese success story is underscored by the fact that its 2020 growth is forecast to be similar to that of China. Nevertheless, Indonesia's lockdown strategy has not been as stringent or as severe as most developing countries, allowing economic activities to resume (at a cost) more quickly.[2] On the second, the monetary stabilisation measures have to date been effective, while the fiscal stimulus measures have been rather small in aggregate and slow to impact. For the third factor, the country has benefited from its still sizeable agrarian sector,[3] while it is less dependent than some of its neighbours on shrinking tourism and international remittances.[4]

Indonesia's national and regional accounts data released through to the second quarter of 2020 confirm these general observations. Agriculture has been the most resilient of the major sectors, after returning to stronger growth in the second quarter of the year. Some service sectors have been growing strongly, notably telecommunications, while others such as accommodation and restaurants have contracted sharply. The expenditure accounts suggest that so far there has been surprisingly little consumption smoothing, in that household saving has fallen at a similar rate to the economy as a whole. The inference is that households are spending less either because of declining income or as a precautionary saving strategy. Predictably investment has collapsed. The one puzzling feature is that government consumption has also declined, a point discussed below. At the regional level, not surprisingly tourism-dependent Bali has been very hard hit, as has Yogyakarta, a major provider of education services. By contrast, the economic impacts have been lighter in some of the more remote agrarian regions.

---

2 For example, according to the Oxford COVID-19 Government Response Tracker, the Indonesian figure never exceeded 65 (in a range from 0 to 100), and was almost always lower than that of the countries listed in Table 2.1. See https://COVID-19tracker.bsg.ox.ac.uk/

3 Agriculture is the primary sector of employment for almost 30 per cent of the Indonesian workforce.

4 By comparison, the tourism-dependent Thai economy and the remittance-dependent Philippine economy are forecast to decline by around 7 and 8 per cent, respectively, in 2020 (Table 2.1). This is despite diverging virus containment strategies, effective in Thailand, while similar to Indonesia in the case of the Philippines.

5. The health management system

The health system is central to the management of the COVID-19 crisis. The observation that 'we are only as strong as our weakest link' is central to understanding health outcomes. A country (such as the United States) may have the world's most advanced health know-how, but if a significant minority of the population does not have access to high-quality health facilities, the pandemic can quickly spread throughout the community, including to more affluent households.

In this context what is relevant is the health system in its entirety—the supply and quality of the full range of health professionals (from frontline nursing staff to highly specialised epidemiologists), the medical services (from daily providers such as Indonesia's health clinics, the *puskesmas* and *posyandu*, to advanced specialist hospitals), the availability of pharmaceutical and health equipment supplies, the access to these services regardless of socioeconomic status (in which public health facilities are the key agent) and the overall administration of the health sector. The last factor is relevant since the pandemic is a national phenomenon but much of the Indonesian health service provision was decentralised in 2001.

At first glance, Indonesia appears to have managed the pandemic relatively well. As of mid-October 2020, it had recorded 1228 cases and 45 fatalities per one million population. This is less than one-quarter of the global case rate and about one-third of the global fatality rate. The numbers are high compared with the well-managed developing East Asian jurisdictions,[5] but substantially lower than both India and the Philippines, and much lower than the United States.

Five general observations are relevant to understanding Indonesia's management of the health crisis. First, history is relevant. Indonesia has made great advances in health outcomes over the past half century. Life expectancy has risen by about 20 years, while infant mortality is less than one-sixth that of the 1960s. Nevertheless, Indonesia has not invested heavily in the health sector, with government spending in the sector amounting to little more than 1 per cent of GDP, while total (public plus private) spending is about 3 per cent, well below that of India, the Philippines and Thailand. The supply of medical doctors, currently about 4.3 per 1000 population, also lags these comparators. Third, as is the case in most developing countries, the relevant COVID-19 statistics are highly approximate. For example, according to informed epidemiological

---

5 To which in Table 2.1 could be added Hong Kong, Singapore, South Korea, Taiwan, and arguably Japan and Malaysia.

opinion, including various 'excess mortality' estimates,[6] the actual COVID-19 incidence, both cases and fatalities, could be up to three times higher than the official estimates. This is partly because Indonesia has one of the lowest testing rates in East Asia (see Resosudarmo and Irhamni, this volume).

Moreover, fourth, the COVID-19 mortality statistics need to be interpreted alongside other major health challenges. For example, according to official estimates, through to mid-October approximately 12,500 Indonesians had died as a result of COVID-19. This can be compared to other endemic health conditions such as tuberculosis, for which the estimated annual mortality is thought to be about 100,000, in addition to several thousand more from malaria. There are obviously major comorbidities in all these cases, in addition to the fact that vulnerable populations generally have had more limited access to health services during the COVID-19 crisis.

Fifth, while the national Ministry of Health has many well-qualified professional staff, the quality of ministerial appointments has varied considerably during the democratic era. Unlike, for example, the Ministry of Finance, where high-quality professionals have been the ministerial norm, health ministers have varied from the most highly qualified professionals to political appointees unable to manage a complex department. While the current minister is a medical doctor, the general perception is that his communication and leadership has been found wanting in the crisis. Exhortations to prayer hardly constitute sound health advice.

For all these reasons, the Indonesian health system has struggled to contain the virus. Unlike financial crises, health crises are not easily amenable to 'quick fix' approaches. Just as the AFC led to macroeconomic and social policy reform, health sector reform will surely be a major policy priority in the post–COVID-19 era.

6. Macroeconomics I: Resilience and vulnerability

There are well-developed bodies of knowledge that identify vulnerability to financial and political crises. But there is little guidance about pre-existing capabilities in the face of a massive pandemic. By definition, the state of the health system, macroeconomic health, and general government and institutional capacities (including public trust) are all

---

6   That is, mortality estimates for specified jurisdictions in 2020 compared to the same period in recent years, with the presumption that the difference may be attributed to COVID-19 fatalities.

relevant. Indonesia's health system was surveyed in the previous section. The various measures of 'government effectiveness' and 'societal trust' have proven to be of very little predictive value.[7]

Macroeconomic vulnerability indicators are relevant because pandemics typically morph quickly into economic crises, as has clearly been the case with COVID-19. On this yardstick, Indonesia entered the crisis in a position of relative strength. It had not had an economic crisis since the AFC and, before that, the mid-1960s. It weathered the 2008–2009 global financial crisis comfortably, partly owing to the fact that successive governments had learnt bitter lessons from the AFC experience. It had a professional, independent and well-regarded central bank. The floating exchange rate regime was working well, inflation was moderate and banking sector prudential regulation has greatly improved. Public debt was modest, following the dramatic fiscal consolidation after the AFC, and the government was strictly adhering to the provisions of the 2003 Fiscal Law, which limited fiscal deficits to 3 per cent of GDP. Among developing country comparators, its macroeconomic indicators were robust.[8]

Nevertheless, there were several potential pre-crisis macroeconomic challenges. One was the country's low tax effort (about 12 per cent of GDP) and the associated limited fiscal space, especially since about one-third of the national budget flows directly to the subnational governments. A second consideration, once the crisis hit, was how to finance the increased expenditure as part of any fiscal stimulus measures. Apart from the special case of Bank Indonesia bond purchases, discussed below, each form of debt-financing might pose risks. Although Indonesia's savings rate is quite strong, there are limited long-term financial instruments available domestically, principally owing to the relatively small bond market. Internationally, Indonesia still faces a higher country borrowing spread than most of its neighbours, and this 'risk premium' actually rose further in the early stages of the COVID-19 crisis as foreign holders of government securities deserted the market (see Grenville and Rajah, this volume), as they did during the 2013 'taper tantrum' episode. The depreciating rupiah

---

7 For example, the World Bank's Worldwide Governance Indicators category 'government effectiveness' scores countries from highest to lowest in the range 2.5 to –2.5. In 2019, the United States scored 1.49 while Vietnam was 0.04. Indonesia was 0.18. The United States' mortality rate to date is 691 per million, far above the mortality rates for Indonesia and Vietnam, even if the latter two are multiplied upwards by a factor of three.

8 See, for example, the *Economist's* (2 May 2020) ranking of 66 developing economies according to four criteria: public debt, foreign debt (both as a percentage of GDP), cost of borrowing and reserve cover. Indonesia was ranked 16th highest in the group.

further heightened the risk of these foreign currency–denominated borrowings. The international financial institutions have made some funding available, but realised disbursements are relatively small and often fall well short of the announcements. US Fed swaps were also not available. Finally, Indonesia essentially operates without any international financial safety nets, since it is evident that resorting to an International Monetary Fund program is politically unacceptable, while the regional support mechanism, the Chiang Mai Initiative Multilateralization, has never been used in its ten years of existence, and it now seems likely that it never will be, in part because any significant support program requires International Monetary Fund involvement.

7. Macroeconomics II: The monetary response

As the COVID-19 crisis began to unfold, the financial markets reacted promptly and negatively in many emerging economies. In the case of Indonesia, there was a sudden exodus of capital. In the four quarters of 2019, net portfolio investment inflows were in the range US$4–7 billion per quarter, peaking at US$7.3 billion in the December quarter. However, there was a dramatic reversal in the March 2020 quarter, with net outflows of US$6.1 billion, in other words a reversal of over US$13 billion. In response, with an open capital account and a floating rate regime, the rupiah declined by about 20 per cent at the height of the outflow in early April. As in the 2013 taper tantrum episode, Indonesia's country spread (or risk premium) was higher than neighbouring economies and consequently its exchange rate depreciation was greater. With memories of the 1997–1998 currency collapse still uppermost in policymakers' minds, and concern about the implications for the country's unhedged foreign currency–denominated debt, this was the country's most immediate economic challenge.

Bank Indonesia acted swiftly and effectively, in concert with major central banks around the world, and calm was restored. Part of the stabilisation measures included support for the rupiah, as evidenced by the fact that foreign currency reserves fell by US$8 billion in the March quarter. There was also only limited monetary policy easing, with the result that capital in search of positive yields began to return quite quickly, resulting in a strengthening of the currency.[9] In fact, the outflows in the March quarter were more than reversed in the June quarter,

---

9 Thus far, Bank Indonesia has lowered its official interest rate in four steps by 100 basis points during the crisis. But at 4 per cent, or about 2 per cent in real terms, it is one of the few G20 economies where government-guaranteed positive real rates are available.

when net inflows of US$9.8 billion were recorded. Meanwhile, foreign direct investment inflows remained stable and positive over this period, reflecting the fact that the decision-making horizons are longer and the commitments would have predated COVID-19. This episode served as yet another reminder that, in times of crisis, different types of capital flows behave very differently. Moreover, it reinforced policymakers' concerns that funding budget and balance of payment deficits through short-term capital flows increases a country's vulnerability to sudden changes in investors' risk perceptions. As a corollary, since Indonesia's savings rate is quite buoyant, the challenge—frequently discussed but yet to be substantially addressed—is to deepen its capital market by developing longer-term financial instruments.

There have been two additional, controversial elements of the Bank Indonesia rescue strategy, which I will examine in the following sections. First, as part of a 'burden-sharing' agreement with the government, Bank Indonesia announced it would support the government's fiscal measures by purchasing government securities (see also Grenville and Rajah, and Crystallin and Abdurohman, this volume). This it commenced doing in early August 2020. Second, a draft bill submitted to the House of Representatives (Dewan Perwakilan Rakyat, DPR) in September proposed the establishment of a monetary board headed by the Minister of Finance to oversee Bank Indonesia's operations. Both measures undermine the 1999 law guaranteeing the bank's independence.

8. Macroeconomics III: In search of Keynes

Whereas the government's monetary policy response was swift and bold, the fiscal response has been hesitant and cautious. In part this reflects the nature of these two key instruments of economic policy. Central banks can instantaneously change official interest rates and quickly undertake foreign exchange transactions. Finance ministries can develop a plan for emergency fiscal measures, but they need to be costed (at least approximately) and then implemented.

The first decision has to be whether fiscal measures take the form primarily of tax cuts or additional expenditure. In the case of the former, the first consideration is whether consumers will spend or save their increased income. The outcome is uncertain since precautionary savings often increase in times of crisis, at least among more affluent households, the likely major recipients of any tax cuts. (This appears to be the case for Indonesia during COVID-19.) Second, the taxation authorities need to have a comprehensive online database that facilitates the rapid transfer of tax relief measures. This is problematic in Indonesia owing to incomplete taxation records, as evidenced by the low fiscal effort.

Alternatively, the fiscal measures may take the form of additional direct expenditure, which guarantees at least a first-round stimulus effect. This requires coordination with the relevant spending agencies of government, at both the national and local levels, and a well-functioning bureaucracy. In other words, apart from the special case of emergency cash transfers, a technically proficient Ministry of Finance can move only as fast as a sometimes slow-moving bureaucracy.

These considerations help explain the paradox that, although the Indonesian government entered the crisis in a fiscally sound position with quite ample resources at its disposal, the fiscal stimulus has been comparatively small and at least through until mid-2020 little of the allocated funds had been spent.

To recap, the government's pre-crisis fiscal position was bolstered by four factors. First, public debt was modest.[10] Second, the Ministry of Finance had a well-deserved reputation for fiscal prudence over several decades, on the basis of its hard-won fiscal consolidation after the AFC, and earlier through its adherence to the so-called balanced budget formula during the Soeharto era. Third, the government announced a temporary relaxation of the 2003 Fiscal Law stipulation of a 3 per cent maximum deficit for the years 2020–2022. Fourth, there was Indonesia's version of unconventional monetary policy through Bank Indonesia purchases of government securities, which in 2020 may account for as much as 60 per cent of the government's planned fiscal deficit.[11] Supplementary funding from a range of international financial institutions and bilateral donors has also been announced. Nevertheless, as noted, the government was constrained by its low fiscal effort (and hence fiscal space), its reliance on potentially flighty foreign holders of public debt, the absence or ineffectiveness of global and regional financial safety nets, and a general predisposition towards fiscal caution in times of global economic volatility.

In a series of packages announced through the year, the additional spending measures have been forecast to increase the fiscal deficit by

---

10 That is, the official estimate equivalent to about 30 per cent of GDP, to which should be added public enterprise debt and any unknown but probably modest crisis-related contingent liabilities.

11 In early August, Bank Indonesia announced it had commenced buying government securities, with purchases of Rp 82 trillion (US$5.6 billion) (Grenville and Rajah 2020). The major domestic banks were also buying in the market. Three of the four majors are state owned, and may have been subject to informal 'guidance'.

about 4 percentage points of GDP. This is a small number by global and even regional standards, where stimulus measures equivalent to 10–20 per cent of GDP and more are common.[12] Moreover, early estimates suggest that 'automatic stabilisers', mainly falling government revenue as the crisis hit, account for a little over half of the envisaged stimulus. The additional spending, envisaged to be Rp 695 trillion in 2020, is being allocated to the government's priority areas and resembles those in other countries: health sector (Rp 88 trillion), social protection (Rp 204 trillion), tax incentives (Rp 121 trillion), support for small and medium enterprises and state-owned enterprises (Rp 177 trillion), and public and regional administration (Rp 106 trillion).

Why has the release of these emergency public expenditures been slow, to the point where the minister herself has publicly expressed concern? There appears to be no single explanation. The Indonesian bureaucracy is slow moving at the best of times. Bureaucrats are fearful of the still-powerful Corruption Eradication Commission (Komisi Pemberantasan Korupsi, KPK), especially when 'non-routine' expenditures and procedures are required. There are evidently particular bottlenecks in the Ministry of Health. And while some social support programs appear to be working well, such as the ministry's favoured Family Hope Program (Program Keluarga Harapan, PKH), others such as enterprise support and labour market programs have struggled. Emergency support measures during the global financial crisis were also slow to release, but on that occasion they weren't needed in the end. Perhaps the spending will accelerate towards the end of 2020. In the same way that the AFC was the trigger for a concerted effort to build a national social safety net, the slow spending response will no doubt be subject to major 'after-the-event' analysis.

9. Social impacts

In the two decades before the crisis, Indonesia had achieved steady social progress: poverty incidence and unemployment had declined in most years, while education, health and most other social indicators have been improving. A modest but well-targeted social welfare net had been constructed in the wake of the AFC, drawing on major policy-oriented research programs and a reasonably comprehensive database. Nevertheless, daunting social policy challenges persist: many of the

---

12 For comparative data see, for example, the Asian Development Bank's COVID-19 website: https://COVID-1919policy.adb.org/

'non-poor' are only marginally or precariously above the poverty line,[13] inequality has risen substantially since 2000, in most dimensions the gender gaps remain significant, not enough jobs are being created in the formal labour market, and child stunting and wasting continue to be serious problems.

We have as yet an incomplete picture of the social impacts, as the major social surveys such as Susenas (Survei Sosio-Ekonomi Nasional, National Socioeconomic Survey) have yet to be undertaken or analysed. The data may in any case be incomplete, as COVID-19 has seriously interrupted field survey work. But several innovative quick-release, high-frequency surveys, based mostly on repeat telephone interviews beginning in early May conducted by the World Bank, Smeru, TNP2K and other leading research agencies, do provide an early picture, and one that mostly accords with priors.[14]

As Suryahadi and colleagues' (2020) forward-looking analysis shows, over the longer term, trends in poverty incidence closely follow changes in GDP. But in the short run, with a substantial vulnerable non-poor population, employment, health and food shocks can quickly push people into poverty. For example, it appears that up to one-quarter of breadwinners had stopped working by early May, although many had returned to the labour market by August as the lockdowns eased. Among those who have lost their incomes, urban dwellers, women and lower-skill workers appear to have been the most adversely affected. Most households have been able to access at least some basic health services, while online facilities have maintained basic schooling services, at least for pupils in regions and households with adequate internet access. Reassuringly, some 90 per cent of the 'bottom 40 per cent' of households report receiving some social assistance, although the magnitudes are imprecise. Child stunting has likely risen, reversing recent progress, while more than 20 million people have reported food insecurity.

It is still too early to determine the overall effects on inequality. During the AFC, inequality actually fell, as the incomes of urban, modern-sector households fell faster than those of the poor. As in the AFC, agriculture

---

13 For example, head count poverty in 2017 was estimated to range from 5.7 per cent at the World Bank's US$1.90 purchasing power parity ('destitution') poverty line to 58.7 per cent at the US$5.50 purchasing power parity ('middle class') line. The official Statistics Indonesia standard was 10.1 per cent.

14 Much of this analysis has yet to be publicly released. Several highly informative ANU Indonesia Project webinars have addressed these issues; see www.covid19indonesia.net/. For some early official analysis, see the website of the government research agency TNP2K: http://tnp2k.go.id/acceleration-policies/COVID-19-outbreak-response

has been the most resilient of the major sectors, and since the poor are disproportionately located in this sector inequality may also have declined during the COVID-19 crisis. Nevertheless, richer households have better access to high-quality health services, and their superior IT access has provided greater protection from the pandemic through work-from-home, food delivery and other strategies. So judgement will have to be suspended on the inequality issue pending the release of more data.

10. Summing up, lessons learned, policy implications

It is too early to make definitive judgements on the impact of COVID-19 on Indonesia. The most that can be said at this juncture is that, through a combination of good luck and adept management, Indonesia has thus far avoided the worst of the pandemic. Notwithstanding the fact that the well-known gaps in the health system have been exposed, that the government has struggled with its messaging, that the COVID-19 containment measures have performed indifferently, and that the fiscal stimulus measures have been limited, the overall socioeconomic impacts could have been much worse. Indonesia has not managed the crisis as effectively as China and Vietnam, for example, but its likely socioeconomic effects are less severe than in India and the Philippines. Although poverty and destitution have undoubtedly increased, the political system and societal fabric have generally remained intact. The rapid monetary stabilisation measures have ensured that there has (so far) not been a financial or foreign exchange crisis. Although the emergency social support measures are small in aggregate, they mostly appear to be reaching their targeted recipients.

The first and most important task of governments in times of crisis is to protect their citizens. But crises can also embolden governments, and enable them to undertake otherwise difficult and unpalatable reforms. Leaders can turn adversity into opportunity. There is an extensive international literature on the nexus between crises and reforms, and one which is amply illustrated in Indonesia's economic and political history. Witness the bold economic reforms of the late 1960s, the mid-1980s and the late 1990s (Basri and Hill 2020), in addition to the dramatic political reforms of 1998–1999 and the Aceh peace settlement in the wake of the devastating 2004 Indian Ocean tsunami.

Will the COVID-19 crisis also be a trigger for a bolder, reform-oriented second-term Jokowi presidency? The president has hinted that it could be. He has spoken of the need 'to reboot [the] economy', and to 'turn the crisis into an opportunity to make great leaps' (Fealy 2020). Yet the evidence so far is mixed. In early October 2020 the DPR passed the government's comprehensive omnibus law, which in principle contains some positive steps forward (such as diluting some stifling and counterproductive labour market regulations), although concerns have been raised about the environmental measures. The omnibus Bill had been proposed before the crisis and initially it was not clear that it would receive parliamentary approval. So its passage could be regarded as a positive achievement. Nevertheless, as with the sixteen reform packages of Jokowi's first term, much will depend on their implementation. Moreover, the government has yet to deliver persuasive public argumentation in support of the Bill, resulting in vigorous protests (see also Manning, this volume).

Two other policy developments during the COVID-19 era deserve mention. First, it is possible that the controversial new capital city proposal will be abandoned. Although Jokowi clearly regards this project as one of his signature visions, critics would welcome this development. The new capital would probably have been a costly and dysfunctional white elephant, while Jakarta's obvious environmental and congestion ills could be addressed much more economically by stronger urban management, and possibly also (like Malaysia) by a gradual relocation of key government activities to the city's rural hinterland. Secondly, there is the proposal to reconstitute the governance structure of Bank Indonesia through the imposition of a governing council to preside over the independent governor and monetary board. The concern in this case is that the hard-won independence of Bank Indonesia would be jeopardised, and that it could open the door to permanent Bank Indonesia deficit-financing arrangements. At the time of writing the bill had not received DPR approval, and it appears that it may be shelved.

Once the immediate crisis is overcome policymakers will be able to address some of the lessons learned during this episode. The first is obviously that Indonesia's macroeconomic policy framework has held up well, and that its key regulatory provisions—an independent central bank and restrictions on deficit financing—need to be maintained. But there will need to be a more robust tax system that enables the government to meet the community's need for more and better services. Financial development issues will also need to be addressed, particularly more effective mobilisation of national savings and improved international access to longer-term financial resources.

A second priority area will likely be social and health policy. The framework for social safety nets was established in the early 2000s. It now needs to be funded more generously, with broader reach (see, for example, Basri et al. 2020). Improved public health facilities, a genuinely national health insurance scheme, and stronger training and research and development health facilities will no doubt also be priorities.

Third, trade and industry policy will continue to be a priority area. Understandably, the COVID-19 crisis has strengthened anti-globalisation sentiments, as countries that are particularly reliant on international tourism have been among the worst affected. There are renewed calls in Indonesia and elsewhere for 'strategic import substitution', not only for vaccines and pharmaceutical products but more generally. As always, the challenge is to manage globalisation, to enjoy the benefits while introducing safeguards. Indonesia will likely want to develop a stronger pharmaceutical sector and more rigorous screening of arriving international travellers. Perhaps the tourism-dependent Balinese economy will permanently lose some of its dynamism. But the upsides of globalisation should not be forgotten. International merchandise trade fell sharply in the first quarter of 2020, but by mid-year it was beginning to recover. China is central to Indonesia's economic recovery, and already it is the best-performing major economy. Tourism will recover when it is obviously safe to travel again. And the 'old' industry policy challenges for Indonesia are just as important as ever, from missing out on global production networks to creating an efficient, business-friendly commercial environment. The crisis has also highlighted the centrality of an efficient and nationally inclusive IT system, where Indonesia could improve both its equitable development and its international attractiveness through a combination of judicious public investments alongside policies that promote greater competition among IT providers.

Finally, the crisis has highlighted the need for major public sector reform. The bureaucracy needs to be more responsive to national aspirations, in this case the need for quick-release, targeted spending. This will require fundamental reform of the civil service towards a more meritocratic, incentivised group of professionals. Relations between the central and regional governments will always to some extent be contested space. But it is now twenty years since the bold, 'big bang' decentralisation was introduced. There has since been much careful analysis of the outstanding regional policy agenda. The crisis has served as a reminder of the need to assign more clearly the relevant revenue and expenditure responsibilities across jurisdictions, and to ensure smoother coordination of jointly provided services.

Immediately prior to COVID-19 Indonesia had joined the ranks of upper middle income developing economies. Jokowi articulated the feasible goal of Indonesia becoming a developed economy by 2045 (and by extension the world's fourth-largest economy). In the coming decade it could well face a sluggish, heavily indebted global economy and a politically polarised international community. Such an outlook highlights more than ever the importance of the proposition that reform begins at home. Indonesia's reform agenda is well known and clearly articulated. Even in difficult circumstances, there are large economic, social and environmental dividends from good policy. This is the challenge for the country's leadership in the second Jokowi presidency and beyond.

References

Basri, Chatib and Hal Hill. 2020. 'Making economic policy in a democratic Indonesia: The first two decades'. *Asian Economic Policy Review* 15(2): 214–34. doi.org/10.1111/aepr.12299

Basri, Chatib, Rema N. Hanna and Benjamin A. Olken. 2020. 'Insight: Don't forget the middle class in social protection programs'. *Jakarta Post*, 16 April. www.thejakartapost.com/academia/2020/04/16/insight-dont-forget-the-middle-class-in-social-protection-programs.html

Fealy, Greg. 2020. 'Jokowi in the COVID-19 era: Repressive pluralism, dynasticism and the overbearing state'. *Bulletin of Indonesian Economic Studies* 56(3): 301–23. doi.org/10.1080/00074918.2020.1846482

Grenville, Stephen and Roland Rajah. 2020. 'COVID-19 and Indonesian monetary policy'. *The Interpreter,* 17 September. Lowy Institute. /www.lowyinstitute.org/the-interpreter/COVID-19-and-indonesian-monetary-policy

Kay, John and Mervyn King. 2020. *Radical Uncertainty: Decision-Making for an Unknowable Future.* London: The Bridge Street Press.

Krueger, Anne O. 2020. 'The open secret to reopening the economy'. *Project Syndicate,* 23 July. www.project-syndicate.org/commentary/COVID-1919-virus-will-decide-when-economy-can-reopen-by-anne-krueger-2020-07?barrier=accesspaylog

Olivia, Susan, John Gibson and Rus'an Nasrudin. 2020. 'Indonesia in the time of COVID-19'. *Bulletin of Indonesian Economic Studies* 56(2): 143–74. doi.org/10.1080/00074918.2020.1798581

Sparrow, Robert, Teguh Dartanto and Renate Hartwig. 2020. 'Indonesia under the new normal: Challenges and the way ahead'. *Bulletin of Indonesian Economic Studies* 56(3): 269–99. doi.org/10.1080/00074918.2020.1854079

Suryahadi, Asep, Ridho Al Izzati and Daniel Suryadarma. 2020. 'Estimating the impact of COVID-19 on poverty in Indonesia'. *Bulletin of Indonesian Economic Studies* 56(2): 175–92. doi.org/10.1080/00074918.2020.1779390

3 COVID-19 and monetary policy[1]

Stephen Grenville and Roland Rajah

Abstract

Monetary policy has a limited role in the COVID-19 crisis, with the main macro challenge falling to fiscal policy. That said, Bank Indonesia has two important tasks. The first is to ensure the continuity of short-term portfolio inflows. So far so good: the outflows that occurred early in the crisis have largely stabilised, though vulnerability remains. We make several suggestions on currency and bond market intervention policy. The second, more challenging and unaccustomed task is to help fund the expanded budget deficit. An important element in Indonesian macropolicy has been fiscal discipline—with recent deficits funded largely by raising funds in the rupiah bond market. Faced with the COVID-19 crisis, Bank Indonesia is now directly purchasing government bonds, including some 'burden sharing' of the interest cost. This funding mode, often dubbed 'money printing', has become routine in many developed economies but is less common in emerging economies. It presents risks to macrostability and Bank Indonesia independence, particularly if the crisis persists, but is justified by the vital need for budget funding and the lack of alternatives. However, Bank Indonesia needs an exit strategy to limit this resort to unconventional funding. In the longer term, the emphasis needs to be on mobilising domestic savings as a more stable way to fund the budget.

---

1 With thanks to James Yetman for his help.

Introduction

COVID-19 represents a twofold global challenge—how to handle the health aspects while softening the economic recession caused by the combined effect of imposed restrictions and the public's behavioural changes. The main economic task is to support the incomes of those put out of work and the viability of businesses in temporary forced hiatus. Thus the main macropolicy response is fiscal expansion.

Nevertheless, Bank Indonesia is playing several important roles. It is playing a traditional central banking function by cutting interest rates, ensuring adequate system liquidity and providing support for on-lending by banks. It has also intervened heavily in the currency and bond markets to stabilise these in the face of very large capital outflows, mostly in March and April. Finally, it is providing significant direct financing to the government—a process often (if incorrectly) called 'money printing'.

Section 1 sets out Bank Indonesia's formal response to COVID-19. Section 2 briefly describes the routine actions that Bank Indonesia has taken to support bank credit and financial markets. Section 3 then looks at the successive episodes of volatile capital flows, especially the most recent, arguing that these have proven a major policy distraction despite an underlying pattern of strong mean reversion. Section 4 discusses the vexed issues involved in Bank Indonesia's funding of the budget deficit and argues that the present strategy creates unwelcome risks to Bank Indonesia's hard-won independence, even if the usual concerns about an imminent surge in inflation are unfounded. Section 5 explores intervention strategies and the need to develop less volatile sources of budget funding through deepening domestic financial markets. We conclude by noting that the great unresolved puzzle is why an economy with a reasonably high savings rate remains so reliant on volatile foreign portfolio flows to fund the government budget.

1. Monetary/financial policy response

Bank Indonesia's policy initiatives so far are:

- The policy interest rate (the reverse repo rate) was reduced marginally by 100 basis points to 4 per cent, and the deposit facility (for banks' surplus reserve holdings at Bank Indonesia) to 3.25 per cent.

- Adequate liquidity is being provided for banks to support lending. By early May, Bank Indonesia had added Rp 500 trillion of liquidity via quantitative easing operations involving market purchase of government bonds, repos and foreign exchange (FX) swaps and a reduction in reserve requirements by 300 basis points to 3.5 per cent.

- Bank Indonesia obtained a US$60 billion repo facility from the US Fed (the central bank of the United States), which would allow it quick access to Indonesia's US dollar FX reserves if needed.
- Bank Indonesia stands ready to act as purchaser of last resort—operating in the secondary market, the primary market (i.e. participating in the bond tender) and private placements—to ensure that the budget deficit can be funded.
- The Financial Services Authority (Otoritas Jasa Keuangan, OJK) will lighten microprudential regulation, and encourage banks to maintain existing loans and make new loans.
- The Ministry of Finance is ready to make loans to banks to fund onward lending to business.

2. Supporting the financial sector and its borrowers

The policy objective is to ensure that the financial sector remains viable and that it supports borrowers through debt forbearance and low interest rates.

The reduction in the interest rate is small and will not do much to encourage more credit or lighten the interest burden of borrowers. The binding constraint on credit expansion will be the uncertainty that inhibits both borrowers and lenders. The main task will be to encourage banks to maintain existing loans even if borrowers have temporary repayment difficulties. In this, OJK's role will be more important than Bank Indonesia's, as OJK can offer regulatory forbearance.

Bank Indonesia's injection of substantial additional liquidity will ensure that no bank is liquidity-constrained. As well, Bank Indonesia is ready to repo government bonds (*surat berharga negara*, SBNs) held by banks at the policy rate (i.e. provide short-term loans to banks based on the collateral of the bank's SBN holdings). The banking system has large SBN holdings, so available bank liquidity is, to say the least, ample. Providing repos seems mostly about limiting the risk of a sell-off of SBNs. Perhaps similarly unnecessary is the Ministry of Finance's readiness to make loans to banks.

3. Flighty capital flows

Foreign capital surges and reversals have been at the heart of Indonesia's macropolicy challenges, most notably during the 1997 Asian financial crisis. 'Sudden stop' outflows have occurred with regularity—in 2008, 2013, 2015, 2018 and now in the 2020 COVID-19 episode (Figure 3.1).

Figure 3.1 Flighty foreign equity and bond holdings, January 2010 –
September 2020 (rolling 3-month basis, rupiah trillion)

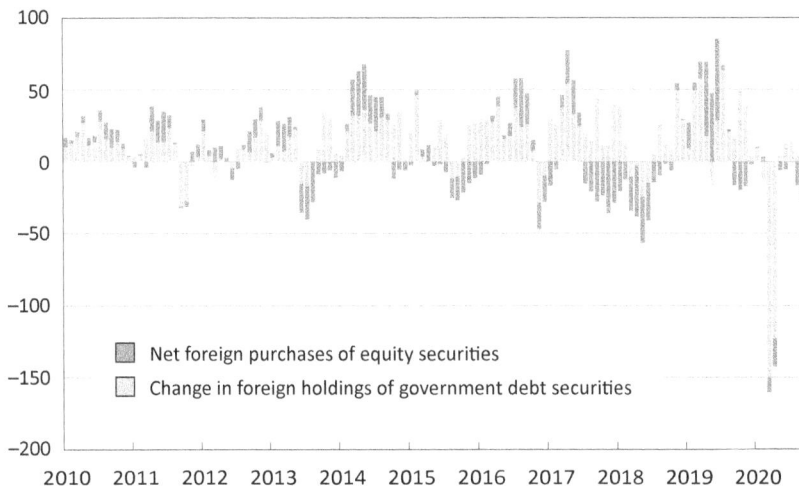

Source: CEIC; Ministry of Finance; Indonesia Stock Exchange.

Why are capital flows so flighty?

After the 2008 global financial crisis, foreign bank lending to Asia was curtailed, but was replaced by a surge in portfolio flows (Figure 3.2). This altered composition made the inflows more flighty: bank loans are relatively stable, but portfolio flows reflect day-by-day decisions by individual investors and fund managers with a high degree of flexibility to shift funds.

These bond holdings are of special interest here. Not only does foreign bond-holding provide well over half of portfolio inflows (and a quarter of total capital inflows), but it is the most volatile component. In recent years before the pandemic, foreigners typically held around 40 per cent of SBNs, with their behaviour dominating the market (Figure 3.3).

Now, with the urgent need for additional funding sources for the prospective larger budget deficit, this funding source cannot be expanded easily, or safely. Even maintaining existing foreign holdings presents a challenge.

Let's look more closely at the characteristics of these 'sudden stop' episodes (Figure 3.4).

The inflow surges and capital-flow reversals are triggered largely by external factors rather than domestic events, reflecting 'risk-on/risk-off' reassessments in global capital markets (Rey 2013).

Figure 3.2 Portfolio inflows by main components, December 2010 – June 2020 (rolling 4 quarters, US$ billion)

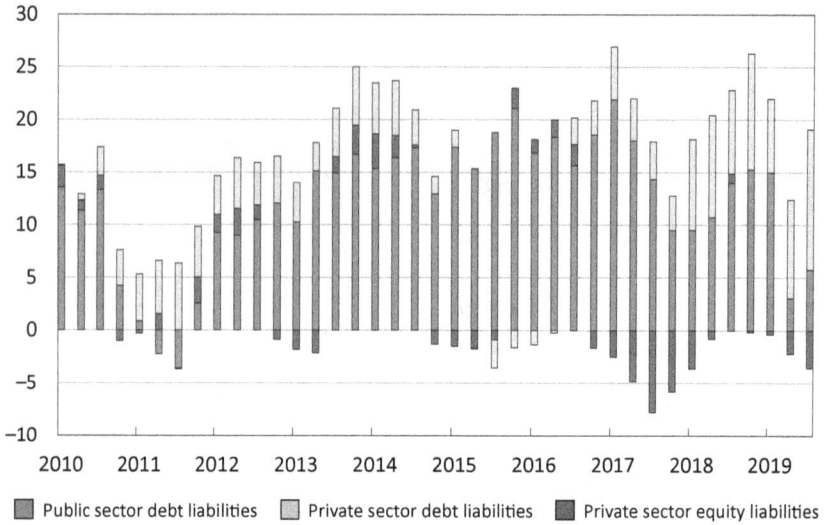

Public sector debt liabilities   Private sector debt liabilities   Private sector equity liabilities

Source: CEIC; Bank Indonesia.

Figure 3.3 Tradeable government rupiah debt securities (rupiah trillion)

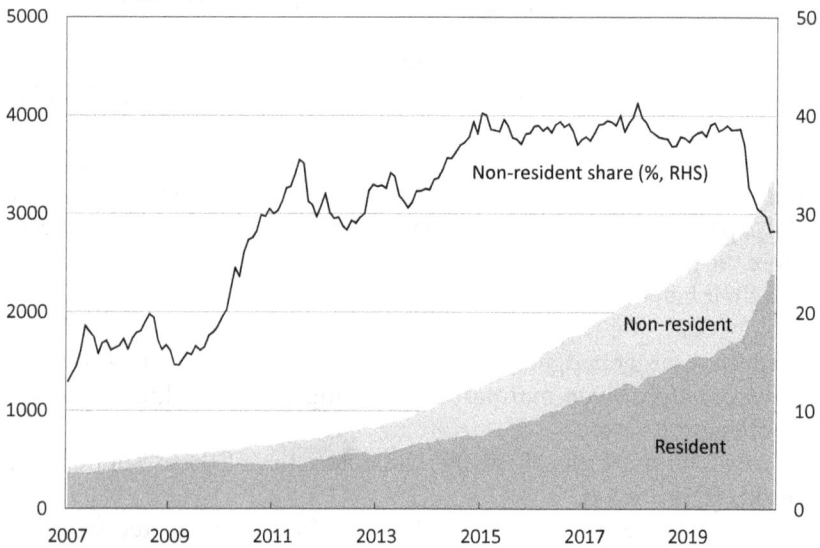

Source: CEIC; Ministry of Finance.

Figure 3.4 International reserves and the rupiah during recent outflow episodes

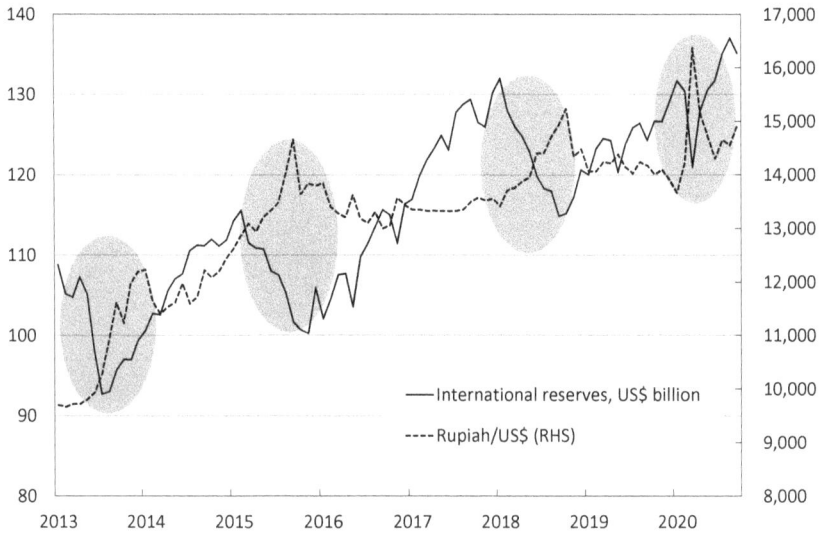

Source: CEIC; Bank Indonesia.

Each episode has its own characteristics, but common factors are present, with the 2013 'taper tantrum' and its policy response setting the pattern (Basri 2017). In each episode, bond sales by foreigners were an important (sometimes dominant) element of the capital reversal. Typically, foreigners reduced their SBN holdings by around 10 per cent and the exchange rate fell by 15–20 per cent, despite Bank Indonesia's FX intervention, which often roughly matched the dollar value of the portfolio outflow. In the shallow bond market, bond yields generally rose sharply (100–300 basis points) in response to the outflow. In addition to FX intervention, Bank Indonesia usually responded by tightening monetary policy.

This pattern of relatively short-term surges and reversals was superimposed on strong 'reversion-to-mean' equilibrating forces—the changes to exchange rates and bond yields were transient shocks, not shifts to new equilibria. If we compare the real effective exchange rate (REER), bond yields, the trend in foreign holdings of SBNs and FX reserve levels over the decade 2010–2019, the stability is more striking than any structural shift, with the 'sudden stop' episodes showing up as minor transient departures from trends (Figure 3.5).

Figure 3.5 Real effective exchange rate and bond yields

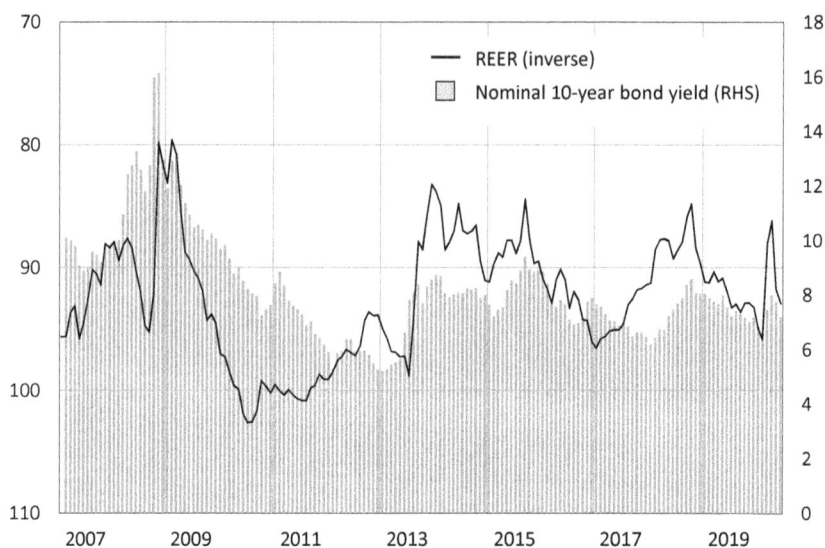

Source: CEIC; Bank Indonesia; Bank for International Settlements.

So far, the March 2020 episode has followed the usual pattern, although the outflows from the bond market were much larger—around US$10 billion, compared with a typical outflow in earlier episodes of US$2 billion (Figure 3.6).

One important innovation in the policy response was that Bank Indonesia purchased Rp 168 trillion of SBNs—undoubtably larger (and more public!) than earlier bond-market interventions.

The COVID-19 context required some modification to the usual policy response mix. Raising interest rates would be inappropriate for an economy operating well below capacity. And rather than tighten the budget (as occurred in 2013), the central element of the COVID-19 policy response is a substantial expansion of the budget deficit.

While Bank Indonesia has come through this latest episode with apparent ease so far, four elements raise concerns:

- First, the greater size of the outflow.

- Second, the size of Bank Indonesia's direct purchase of SBNs from departing foreigners. More importantly, it might establish some unhelpful precedents and expectations (see Section 4).

Figure 3.6 Recent portfolio inflows by main components, March 2019 – June 2020 (quarterly, US$ billion)

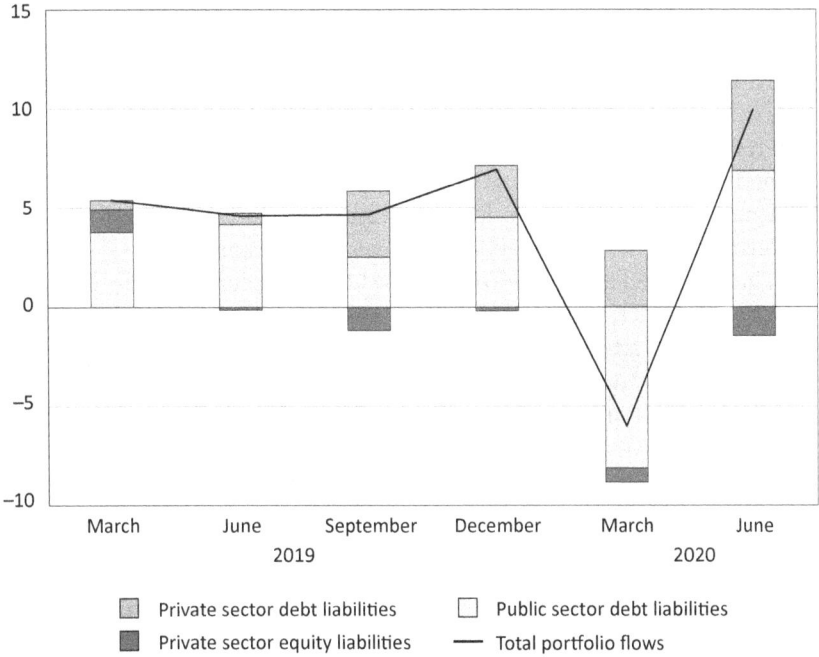

Source: CEIC; Bank Indonesia.

- Third, the budgetary expansion has not yet been fully implemented (see Section 4). Market reaction to these developments could present new pressures on outflows, although the most flighty foreign investors may have already left.

- Fourth, despite strong 'mean reversion' characteristics, these episodes have been a major distraction in the policy process. The tail has wagged the dog, in terms of relatively modest and transient falls in portfolio investment requiring a substantial macropolicy response. These concerns have probably also caused cautious policymakers to trim underlying growth ambitions.

The growing heft and volatility of the bond flows raises important policy issues. We will return to these issues in Section 5.

4. Funding the deficit

Money-financing of the deficit is the most significant policy initiative to date. This challenges the existing separation between government and Bank Indonesia and has arguably gone beyond even deep policy coordination into a fair degree of policy integration ('burden sharing').

This is a significant departure from longstanding Indonesian practice and reflects the powerful historical legacy of the Sukarno economic chaos of the 1960s. In that historical experience, the neat division between fiscal and monetary policy was lost. The most obvious manifestation was hyperinflation, which exceeded 1000 per cent in 1966.

That changed in 1967, with the New Order implementing a 'balanced-budget' policy. The budget was not quite balanced in an accounting sense, but the balanced-budget commitment was outstandingly effective in barring money-funding.

Until 1999, Bank Indonesia was part of the government (with the governor attending cabinet meetings and monetary policy decided by a committee chaired by the Minister of Finance). This changed following the 1997 Asian financial crisis, when Bank Indonesia's independence was legislated. Separately, legislation set specific limits on budget funding—3 per cent of gross domestic product (GDP) until recently.

Alternative sources of funding are limited. The Ministry of Finance has succeeded in issuing nearly US$10 billion of foreign currency debt. Modest amounts are available from the Asian Development Bank and the World Bank. While the International Monetary Fund (IMF) has widened access to its programs, there remains a powerful stigma preventing recourse to the IMF, more than two decades after the 1997 Asian financial crisis.

Regulation in Lieu of Law No. 1/2020 allows Bank Indonesia to buy government bonds at the time of initial tender (previously prohibited in the 1999 legislation). Technically, this is a relatively minor change compared with buying bonds in the secondary market but in practice it signals a readiness to remove the in-principle sanction on Bank Indonesia funding the budget deficit. It is not clear how reluctant Bank Indonesia might have been to agree to budget funding; the burden sharing would surely have been unwelcome. That said, Bank Indonesia stands ready to buy bonds at the primary tender, in the secondary market and, if necessary, in ad hoc additional arrangements, as 'funder-of-last-resort'.

Just how novel and tradition-breaking Bank Indonesia bond purchases turn out to be will depend on the scale, how this works in practice, and whether the practice definitively reverts after the crisis.

All central banks hold government bonds and routinely deal in bonds for open-market operations. Central banks also have a strong tradition of supporting financial markets in times of market turbulence. The US Fed illustrated this with its QE1 operations in 2008. The Fed also used its bond market operations (QE2 and QE3) to lower the benchmark bond yield curve to stimulate lending and economic activity in 2009–2014. Other central banks (notably the Bank of Japan and the Reserve Bank of Australia) have set a specific target level for interest rates at a certain maturity—yield curve control. Lastly, and more controversially, central banks have sometimes provided governments with assured budget funding through a commitment to purchase bonds, which will also lower the cost of budget funding.

These variations overlap to some degree, and useful analysis requires an attempt to identify the main motivation, scale and operational limits.

Since the mid-1980s, Bank Indonesia has used bonds in its monetary operations. For the past decade, Bank Indonesia's bond buying has gone beyond this, purchasing bonds when yields were spiking in the shallow bond market, especially during the 'sudden stop' episodes discussed above.

COVID-19 has brought two changes in bond operations.

First, Bank Indonesia's purchase of Rp 168 trillion of bonds from foreign holders in March shows scale and intent not demonstrated in earlier bond market interventions. This was clearly intended to lower the yield spike and restore confidence to the bond market. Bank Indonesia seems ready to repeat this intervention as needed. This purchase also helped to fund the budget, but this was not its primary purpose: if Bank Indonesia had done nothing, yields would have risen until a buyer came forward for these already-issued bonds, with the budget funding continuing to be met in the market. The amount approximately matched the foreigners' outflow.

The second component is explicitly money-financing of the deficit.

Current plans are for a budget deficit of 6.3 per cent of GDP this budget year and 5.5 per cent next year. Of this 2020 deficit of Rp 904 trillion, Bank Indonesia has agreed to finance Rp 574 trillion (US$40 billion) by a direct purchase of bonds. Bank Indonesia has had to accept this will embody some burden sharing, with the budget paying no interest servicing cost on some of the bonds and a reduced interest rate on others. The Bank Indonesia governor has made a general commitment to continue deficit-funding for the 2021 budget.

Burden sharing presents unnecessary risks. First, it blurs the institutional separation of Bank Indonesia from government. Bank Indonesia has had to agree to take on costs in order to explicitly subsidise the government budget, both through below-market interest rates and having to return any interest on the same day it is received. Second, it is a false saving anyway, since the government owns Bank Indonesia.

It reduces transparency around the true cost of borrowing. It could thus encourage politicians to look to the central bank as a source of easy financing even beyond crisis times. Finally, while there has been no direct challenge to Bank Indonesia's ability to set interest rates, burden sharing could be a sign that Bank Indonesia will prove sensitive to the government interest burden when making future interest rate decisions.

Burden sharing also seems to create one more non-standard government security,[2] while the objective should be to create a deep market for the standard SBN. Issuing Bank Indonesia with a standard SBN, say of three years maturity, would give Bank Indonesia the flexibility to use this in its repo monetary operations and, if the crisis is over in less than three years, to sell the bond into the normal market. The bond's maturity in three years would set an informal target for ending the money-financed deficit.

Money-financed deficits present three concerns:

- Does the 'money printing' cause inflation?
- Does it encourage budget profligacy, excessive official debt and undermine Bank Indonesia independence?
- Does it distort the financial sector?

Money creation and inflation

The view that inflation is 'too much money chasing too few goods' and that 'inflation is always and everywhere a monetary phenomenon' is associated with Milton Friedman. But these aphorisms related to a financial system where bank credit was determined by the credit multiplier and additional base money led to credit expansion. In a deregulated banking system, credit growth is constrained by the level of interest rates interacting with the demand for credit. Policy operates by influencing lending rates via changes in the short-term rate. If necessary, excessive credit growth can be restrained by macroprudential measures (as has become routine in Indonesia). In short, excess reserves do not trigger credit creation.

Inflation has steadily come down over the past decade. Headline inflation is clearly greatly affected by administered price changes (notably petroleum), but core inflation in the medium term reflects the output gap and the constraining impact of inflation targeting on inflation expectations. If the economy starts to grow quickly (not a likely

---

2   The fraught experience of the Surat Utang Pemerintah (SUP), the special-purpose debt instrument created to accommodate Bank Indonesia's 1997 funder-of-last-resort actions, is a salutary reminder of the long-lasting damage of these special-purpose IOUs. These SUPs are still on the Bank Indonesia balance sheet, paying virtually zero interest.

prospect), Bank Indonesia can tighten monetary policy and impose stricter macroprudential measures.

Fiscal profligacy and Bank Indonesia independence

Money-financed deficits have significant attraction for governments. This avoids the often-challenging task of selling bonds to the public. For Indonesia it raises these funds at 4 per cent or less, which is significantly below the yield on a ten-year bond. It is assured finance: the banking system as a whole has no choice but to fund the expenditure.

Even if this is not 'free money' (as is sometimes claimed), it removes the usual budget constraint—that expenditure has to be paid for by taxation or selling bonds. It gives governments a strong incentive to keep interest rates low, which may be a threat to inflation in the longer term.

And it weakens Bank Indonesia's hard-won independence. The dangers are illustrated by current parliamentary discussions on revisions to the 1999 Bank Indonesia law which would allow for deficit monetisation beyond the current crisis. Combined with the proposal for Bank Indonesia to be overseen by a monetary board led by the finance minister, such changes would cast the independence of the central bank and its ability to resist unwarranted pressures to fund the budget deficit in serious doubt. Ironically, if these changes were passed, the erosion of Bank Indonesia's credibility with financial markets would likely make it harder, not easier, for the central bank to support the government budget through the current crisis without triggering destabilising capital outflows. The changes being discussed therefore seem largely counterproductive and would reduce the policy space available to Indonesia at a time when this needs to be maximised.

Thus, the established tradition of quarantining central banks from government pressures to fund budget deficits is sensible. Hence Bank Indonesia funding should be a last resort after all other sources have been fully exploited.

A 'repressed' financial sector?

Money-financed deficits are funded by forcing the banking system to hold the residual base money created by this method of funding. This is a form of what McKinnon (1973) called 'financial repression'.

Will this funding dominate the balance sheets of either Bank Indonesia or the banks? The prospective size of the money-financed component of the deficit this year is Rp 574 trillion. This might be compared with the Rp 200 trillion of bonds[3] often held by Bank Indonesia in the past. If Bank Indonesia's bond holdings caused banks' reserve holdings to rise by around Rp 600 trillion, this is only around 10 per cent of banks' total balance sheets.

Banks are, in fact, already holding substantial reserves, with 'repressive' effect. For scaling, banks currently hold around Rp 1000 trillion in various forms of assets at Bank Indonesia, which is around 20 per cent of their total balance sheet.[4] Nevertheless, the more bank balance sheets are weighed down with budget funding, the less credit they will provide for private borrowing.

On balance …

Given the exigency of the crisis, some money-financing of the deficit seems a sensible last resort. The main risk is the 'slippery slope'—that this will become the funding norm. Although the government and Bank Indonesia have said the financing package is a one-off, the economic downturn, capital-flow problems, and the need for a large fiscal deficit will likely persist—next year's deficit is already put at 5.5 per cent, and other sources of funding remain uncertain. Bank Indonesia needs an exit strategy and some serious discussion about the risks of overloading the banking system with budget funding.

In the short term, managing expectations is key. In particular, many market participants will have the usual monetarist concerns about inflation. Others will recall the Bank Indonesia Liquidity Assistance (Bantuan Likuiditas Bank Indonesia, BLBI) experience of 1997, although today's circumstances are quite different, with system-wide bank failure unlikely. On the positive side, the market reaction has been muted so far and the ratings agencies do not seem to have raised major concerns for now. But if money-financing continues in a similar fashion and scale to this year, the risks will quickly mount.

Why is Bank Indonesia resorting to unconventional monetary operations when the policy interest rate, at 4 per cent, has plenty of room for further reductions? (Unlike the developed economies, where the zero lower bound has already largely been reached.) Indonesia must go on

---

3 Plus Rp 160 billion of SUPs.
4 If banks use their excess reserves to buy SBN at tender, the outcome is much the same—the banking system funds the deficit, probably reducing its private-sector lending (i.e. still 'repressed'). This would be closer to a market outcome, but would be more expensive funding (the market SBN yield rather than the Bank Indonesia policy rate).

providing incentive for foreign capital to remain, implying the policy rate is already close to the effective lower bound.

5. More stable financial markets

As noted in Section 3, Bank Indonesia's dual intervention strategy has handled the post-2010 surges and reversals, but the cost has been high. These modest flows (not much more than 1 per cent of GDP) are forcing Indonesia to slow the economy whenever these flows reverse. In addition, these surges and reversals require Indonesia to hold well over US$100 billion in FX reserves—funds that could be invested elsewhere with substantially higher returns.

The core problem is that the budget is funded by flighty foreign portfolio investment. The policy suggestions made here have two objectives: (1) to discourage those portfolio flows which are so flighty as to make their cost greater than their benefit, and (2) to enhance the behavioural characteristics of the two markets—FX and bonds—so they are more effective in doing the job of price discovery and maintenance of an equilibrium price.

The two key markets involved here are both shallow, with some participants ever-ready to exit ahead of other investors. There are no stabilising speculators, ready and able to take a position in these markets (buying rupiah when the currency is weak and bonds when the yields are abnormally high). The outcome is a price that can depart significantly from the underlying equilibrium. The problem is not short-term volatility. These departures last for some time, usually because they are driven by a change of foreign market sentiment. The other key characteristic is that price movements in these two markets are linked. When foreign investors sell bonds, they also sell the rupiah.

Bank Indonesia's intervention strategy of 'leaning into the wind' (Figure 3.7) is understandable given the history, but is a poor fit with the source of the disturbance: flighty portfolio flows. Active portfolio managers have an incentive to sell early, ahead of the market, with the aim of buying back in at the trough.[5] Bank Indonesia's strategy of

---

5   For investors in open-ended mutual funds and their managers, SBNs offer a modest return, but one that can be dramatically increased by active management. A foreign investor who was a stable holder of SBNs during the decade to end-2019 would have earned around 3 per cent per annum on average, in US dollar terms. This modest return (especially when risk is considered, with large losses in the 2013–2015 period) could be made worthwhile by well-timed exiting and repurchase in each of the three episodes, adding perhaps an additional 4 per cent annually to the return.

Figure 3.7 Real exchange rate movements and foreign exchange intervention

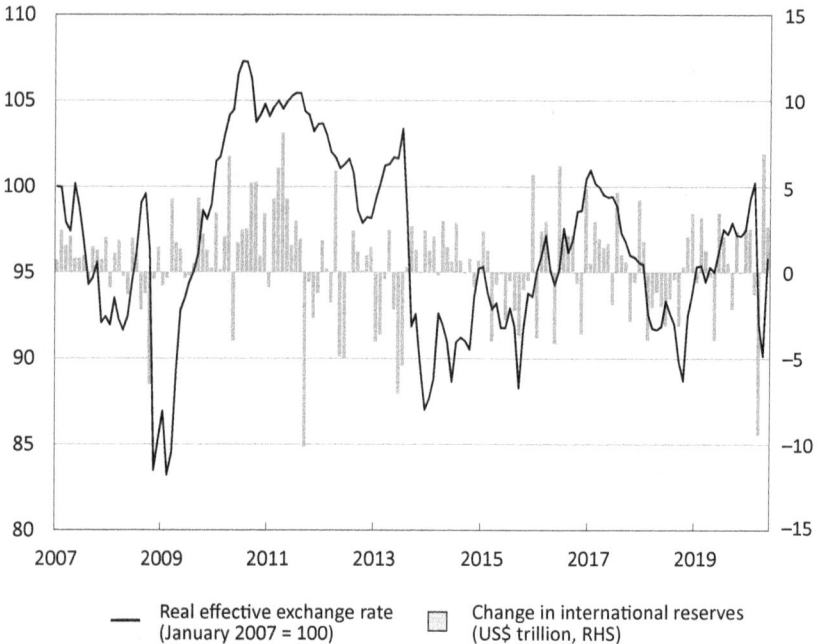

Real effective exchange rate (January 2007 = 100)

Change in international reserves (US$ trillion, RHS)

Source: CEIC; Bank Indonesia; Bank for International Settlements.

incremental early intervention plays into their hands, allowing them to exit the Indonesian bond market early in the outflow phase and buy back in again profitably during the reversion phase of the episode.

Moreover the inherent volatility in this form of funding may well increase over time. The latest episode had by far the largest outflows.

What might be done?

Our suggestions here are for action now to tweak the method of intervention in the bond market, and a longer-term post-crisis proposal, to modify Bank Indonesia's FX intervention strategy.

Further Bank Indonesia money-financing of the deficit should follow the buyer-of-last-resort function as currently structured, linking the yield to prevailing market interest rates through a non-competitive tender at the regular bond auctions. This would minimise the issues raised above about burden sharing and the creation of non-standard SBNs.

If there is another episode of capital reversal, our suggestion is to modify the current Bank Indonesia intervention strategy to target the yield curve. With a 'yield curve stabilisation' policy, Bank Indonesia would not aim to push down yields (as the Reserve Bank of Australia has done). Rather, it would act to stabilise yields to prevent them from deviating too far from equilibrium.

Specifically, Bank Indonesia would buy bonds in the secondary market with the aim of capping bond yields at say 100 basis points above what Bank Indonesia judged to be the equilibrium rate. This notion of 'equilibrium' might be based on a moving average over, say, the past three years. The three-year bond yield could be targeted, as this will be easier to unwind and involves fewer judgements about the equilibrium price. The effects should flow on to longer maturity bonds.

The 100 basis points upper band would leave enough space for the market to still set the price while countering spikes driven by short-term investor behaviour. It would also reduce perceptions that Bank Indonesia was providing cheap financing to government.

Targeting the yield curve would send a strong signal to markets, likely reducing the amount of bonds Bank Indonesia would need to purchase. Because Bank Indonesia cannot run out of rupiah, the commitment would have strong credibility. This would also reduce capital outflows, as it would remove Bank Indonesia as a ready counterparty for short-term speculation. In turn, more effective stabilisation in the secondary market would reduce the need for Bank Indonesia to participate directly in the primary market.

Putting this together, the yield curve stabilisation approach would: (1) reduce the costs of bond market intervention for Bank Indonesia through a more credible policy commitment, (2) limit the need to monetise the deficit via either primary or secondary market purchases, (3) ensure any further deficit financing is linked to the government's equilibrium borrowing costs and (4) support Bank Indonesia independence by being fully under the control of Bank Indonesia based on its assessment of economic conditions (including fiscal policy settings) and could be adjusted or ended accordingly. Bank Indonesia could articulate a set of conditions that would see it exit the policy.

Beyond the COVID-19 crisis, Bank Indonesia might look to retain the yield curve stabilisation policy. That would involve an informal strategy of intervening only when bond yields move, say, 100 basis points from the assessed equilibrium value.

Looking ahead to the post-crisis period, a similar approach could be applied to the exchange rate. Rather than targeting volatility (implemented by 'leaning into the wind'), Bank Indonesia should refrain from intervention until the exchange rate reaches a predetermined margin away from what was judged to be the normal equilibrium. Intervention could then be substantial, with the objective of stabilising the rate at around this level.

This is, in essence, the 'basket, band and crawl' intervention strategy suggested by John Williamson (2001), with an intervention band either side around a slow-moving notional equilibrium rate, largely based on a moving average of past rates.

This strategy addresses the nature of the surges and sudden stops, which are sustained departures from equilibrium but with strong reversion-to-mean characteristics. It provides no convenient counterparty for profit-making by active foreign investors.

There are, of course, risks in this strategy. Bank Indonesia's current eagerness to undertake early FX intervention reflects the history of extrapolative momentum-driven exchange rate movements. The fear is that a rapid initial fall in the exchange rate might develop its own momentum and set off a 1997-style crisis. Well-judged setting of the bandwidth, carefully explained introduction and a phased transition to the new system (perhaps with soft bands without rigid commitment) could address these concerns.

Figure 3.8 illustrates what a 'basket, band and crawl' strategy might look like. The moving average is three years and the band is set at 10 per cent either side. In practice these parameters would be set after substantial research and might include other factors such as the terms-of-trade and interest differentials, but even this simple example suggests that intervention to defend a 10 per cent departure from equilibrium seems feasible.

The principal benefit should be to discourage the flighty components of the capital inflow, while encouraging those investors who value stability.

There are other measures that might usefully discourage the most volatile of the flows without affecting the stable flows. Measures which reduce the degree of liquidity (minimum holding periods), a small transaction tax (a 'Tobin Tax' (Basri 2017)) or a Chilean-style *encaja* tax aimed at discouraging short-term inflows might enhance stability without loss to the structural flows. There is still a perception of opprobrium associated with capital controls, which the International Monetary Fund's half-hearted endorsement of 'capital-flow management' has reinforced. Thus, once again, careful public explanation of the benefits would be needed.

The net effect of these various possible policy initiatives is uncertain, but, in any case, Indonesia needs to look elsewhere for budget funding. We turn now to alternatives.

Figure 3.8 'Basket, band and crawl' illustration

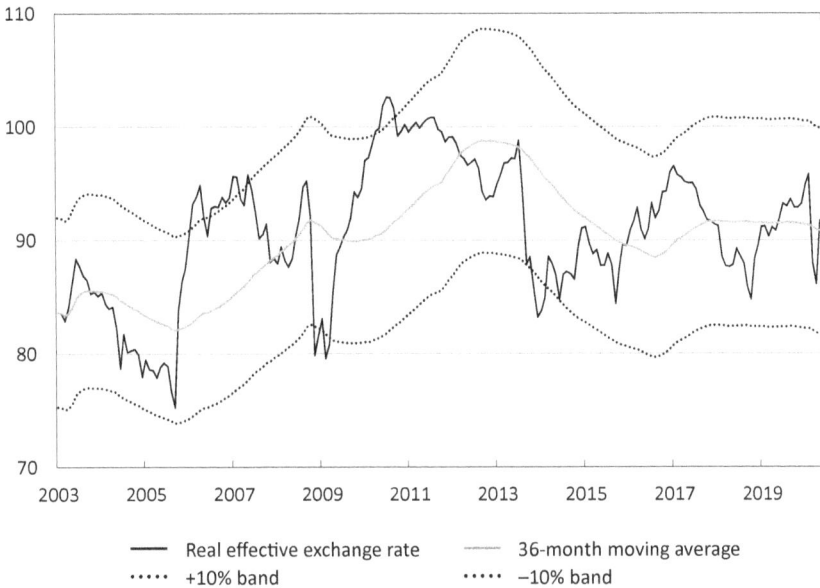

Source: CEIC; Bank Indonesia; Bank for International Settlements.

Deepening Indonesia's financial markets has been a perennial policy topic (see, for example, Bank Indonesia 2018: Chapter 6). Nevertheless, Indonesia's comparative position remains far behind its regional peers (Figure 3.9).

Many reasons are offered, often related to Indonesia's poor legal and financial infrastructure. This is no doubt true for more complex financial instruments that require dependable legal and arbitration infrastructure and reliable bankruptcy processes.

But the priorities here have been misdirected. Financial market development (futures/forwards markets, repos) has facilitated short-term flows and provided liquidity for investors, which are the very elements that facilitate active management by flighty investors.

The mindset on development of the longer-term market has also misread the priorities. It was fashionable, two decades ago, to see the problem of 'original sin' (Eichengreen and Hausmann 1999) as the central concern, to be solved by developing domestic-currency instruments. This just shifted the FX rate risk from domestic to foreign parties, without

Figure 3.9 Financial depth across emerging Asia (% of GDP)

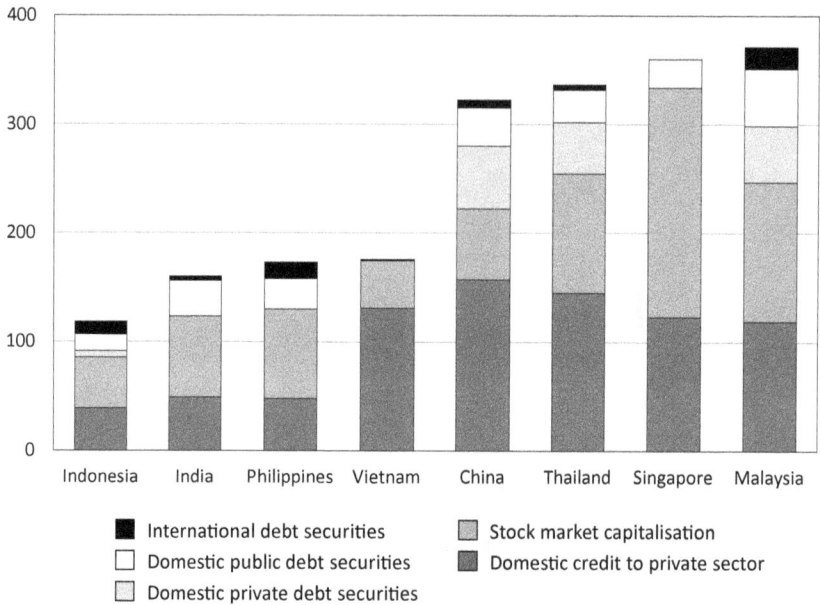

Legend:
- International debt securities
- Domestic public debt securities
- Domestic private debt securities
- Stock market capitalisation
- Domestic credit to private sector

Source: World Bank Global Financial Development Database.

changing the essential problem of unavoidable currency mismatch arising from a current account deficit. This has been belatedly recognised in Hofmann and colleagues' (2020) discussion of 'original sin redux'.

Conclusion

Here is the unresolved puzzle. Indonesia saves nearly 35 per cent of its GDP in a normal year, yet very little of this domestic saving is invested in the safe, marketable, high-return SBN. Instead, this funding task is given to flighty foreign portfolio flows.

The COVID-19 crisis seems likely to require substantial budget deficits for some years to come. While justified as a short-term exigency, continuation of large money-funded deficits risks financial sector distortion through financial repression and feeding forces towards future fiscal imprudence. Instead, if other funding is available from the market at broadly reasonable cost—whether in rupiah or hard currency bonds—this should be taken up to the extent possible, with less concern about the government's rising interest bill and greater focus on protecting the credibility of Bank Indonesia and its ability to intervene as a true last resort.

Beyond the COVID-19 crisis, continuing to rely on budget funding through foreign purchase of government bonds is not the answer. Financial markets impose a de facto current account limit on Indonesia that, if exceeded, threatens to precipitate another 'sudden stop'. These problems would be lessened if a greater part of the current account deficit was to be financed by foreign direct investment rather than by portfolio flows, and a greater share of the funding of budget deficits relied on domestic savings rather than foreign.

References

Bank Indonesia. 2018. *Economic Report on Indonesia*. www.bi.go.id/en/publikasi/laporan-tahunan/perekonomian/Pages/LPI_2018.aspx

Basri, M. Chatib. 2017. 'India and Indonesia: Lessons learned from the 2013 taper tantrum'. *Bulletin of Indonesian Economic Studies* 53(2): 137–60. doi.org/10.1080/00074918.2017.1392922

Eichengreen, Barry and Ricardo Hausmann. 1999. 'Exchange rates and financial fragility'. *NBER Working Paper* No. 7418. doi.org/10.3386/w7418

Hofmann, Boris, Ilhyock Shim and Hyun Song Shin. 2020. 'Emerging market economy exchange rates and local currency bond markets amid the COVID-19 pandemic'. *BIS Bulletin* No. 5. www.bis.org/publ/bisbull05.htm

McKinnon, Ronald I. 1973. *Money and Capital in Economic Development*. Washington, DC: Brookings Institution.

Rey, Hélène. 2013. 'Dilemma not trilemma: The global financial cycle and monetary policy independence'. Paper presented at Global Dimensions of Unconventional Monetary Policy symposium, 21–23 August 2013. Sponsored by the Federal Reserve Bank of Kansas City, Jackson Hole, Wyoming.

Williamson, John. 2001. 'The case for a basket, band and crawl (BBC) regime for East Asia'. Paper presented at Future Directions for Monetary Policies in East Asia conference, 24 July 2001. Sydney: Reserve Bank of Australia. www.rba.gov.au/publications/confs/2001/williamson.html

4 Fiscal policy in managing the economic recovery[1]

Masyita Crystallin and Abdurohman

Abstract

The COVID-19 pandemic has afflicted the Indonesian economy significantly. The first half of 2020 saw a sizeable GDP contraction on the back of disrupted economic activities exacerbated by strict social distancing measures domestically and overseas. Prolonged weaker real sector activities will eventually lead to further distress in the financial sector. Unlike in other episodes of economic downturn that focus on stimulating demand, this unprecedented crisis requires the government to boost resources for pandemic containment measures, health care, and an emergency lifeline for poor and vulnerable families as well as businesses. As a result, the government has to confront unprecedented fiscal pressures from both spending and revenue sides. The fiscal deficit is likely to widen to a historical record in five decades. In this chapter we highlight Indonesia's fiscal policy in responding to the pandemic crisis and managing the economic recovery. More specifically, we underscore three main issues: (1) heightening fiscal pressures on the back of underperformed revenue collection and rising fiscal needs to contain and mitigate the pandemic crisis, (2) government strategies to finance the cost of the pandemic crisis and (3) lessons learned for future reform.

---

1 Opinions expressed here are those of the authors and do not reflect the opinions or views of the authors' employers.

Introduction

Indonesia's economic fundamentals were in relatively good shape at the end of 2019. Higher volatility emerged in the global financial market as the United States – China trade war put pressure on the global economy. At the same time, escalating geopolitical tension created uncertainty over oil prices. Yet global economic conditions stabilised towards the end of 2019, trade tensions eased somewhat, and capital flows started to return to emerging markets, including Indonesia.

Pressures to the financial market eased significantly in the last quarter of 2019. The rupiah appreciated by 5 per cent between 31 May 2019 and 31 January 2020 and the ten-year yield decreased by 138 basis points during the same period. A calmer global financial environment is an important factor for countries such as Indonesia that are highly dependent on foreign flows to push economic growth above its potential.

Several reforms were underway, aimed at higher economic growth to escape the middle income trap by 2045, the anniversary of Indonesia's 100 years of independence. To achieve this, Indonesia must grow above its potential level of around 5–5.5 per cent, according to the Finance Ministry's calculation in 2019 (*Jakarta Globe* 2019), and was trending down after the commodity boom period ended in 2013 (World Bank 2015). In 2019, macroeconomic indicators were sound: stable economic growth, manageable inflation, a manageable current account deficit and an improved primary balance deficit, which has reached almost zero after persisting in deficit territory since 2012. The broad-based reforms ranged from education reforms to address the human capital gap, fiscal reforms to increase revenue and spending quality, reforms in infrastructure delivery, and logistics reforms to improve competitiveness.

In less than three months, Indonesia's good economic momentum was reversed due to the coronavirus disease (COVID-19) pandemic. The virus has gone globally viral since the first case of infection—a pneumonia-like disease—emerged in late December 2019 in Wuhan, China (WHO 2020). By mid-February 2020 nearly 50,000 cases had spread to 27 countries. The first case in Indonesia was recorded on 2 March 2020. The World Health Organization announced a pandemic status for COVID-19 on 11 March 2020, at which time the global financial market was not yet affected.

The global financial market finally priced in and crashed on 20 March 2020, with deeper capital outflows than the last two outflows: the taper tantrum of 2013 and the global financial crisis of 2008. For Indonesia, foreign net capital outflows reached Rp 158.3 trillion, while during the taper tantrum and the global financial crisis, foreign investors still recorded positive net flows of Rp 36 trillion and Rp 7.3 trillion, respectively (Bloomberg Terminal). The Volatility Index, which indicates volatility in the equity market, touched the highest level since the index commenced in 2004, at 85.47. All other indicators overshot as well, showing a significant decline in economic activity and business confidence: consumer confidence index, Purchasing Managers' Index, and measures of mobility and luminosity. Emerging market currencies plunged, the rupiah depreciated from Rp 14,318 per US dollar in February 2020 to its lowest level since the Asian financial crisis at Rp 16,575 per US dollar on 23 March 2020.

The impact of the pandemic is much deeper than the global crisis in 2008 because strict physical limitations hit directly on economic activities such as consumption, trade and investment. In response, the government announced a fiscal package amounting to 6.3 per cent of gross domestic product (GDP)[2] (Presidential Regulation (Peraturan Presiden, Perpres) No. 72/2020 on the State Budget Revision) that focuses on three major areas: health; social safety nets; and support for real sectors, especially for small and medium enterprises (SMEs). Although the recovery path could be more challenging with the absence of a vaccine, these stimulus packages might cushion the Indonesian economy from a deep contraction that could put an extra 5.5 million Indonesians under the poverty line, reversing years of improvement in poverty alleviation which has been at the lowest level in history (9.8 per cent).

In this chapter we discuss the pressure faced by the fiscal authority in designing and financing economic recovery programs during heightened fiscal pressure. We also discuss the economic recovery program design as well as the financing strategy. For the first time since 1998, an unconventional monetary policy is set to allow Bank Indonesia to buy government bonds in the primary market. A new burden-sharing scheme between the central bank and the government is also introduced to help calm the storm without interfering with the central bank's independence and monetary policy's effectiveness. Last, for every crisis there is an opportunity to advance reforms, and, to build better, we outline several areas that could be a priority during the economic recovery.

Fiscal pressures heighten significantly

The outbreak of COVID-19 is resulting in a health crisis and a drop in economic activities. The global economy is projected to slow down sharply,

---

2 The fiscal deficit under the original budget was 1.76 per cent, revised to 5.07 per cent under Perpres No. 54/2020 and to 6.34 per cent under Perpres No. 72/2020 as conditions became more severe than originally expected.

at a rate and magnitude much worse than the 2008–2009 global financial crisis. Unlike in other episodes of economic downturn in which the key goal of fiscal policy is to stimulate demand, this crisis is different. Since its early stages, the main objective has been to increase healthcare resources and provide emergency lifelines for poor and vulnerable families and businesses. As a result, the government has to confront unprecedented fiscal pressures from both spending and revenue sides.

On the revenue side, total government revenue is projected to drop from 12.3 per cent of GDP in the previous year to 10.4 per cent this year to correspond with external shocks (that is, sharp economic slowdown and falling commodity prices) and fiscal measures undertaken by the government (for example, tax relief) (Table 4.1). Lower corporate profit, declining consumption, contracting imports and rising unemployment will lead to a drop in revenue from corporate and personal income taxes, consumption-based taxes and international taxes. Total tax revenue is expected to hit a record low in two decades at 8.6 per cent of GDP or shrink by 1.0 per cent compared to 2019. This revenue shrinkage is mainly driven by a sizeable fall in income taxes. Falling commodity prices are largely reflected in the decline of non-tax revenue, which has been contributed mainly by natural-resources revenue. Tax relief measures undertaken by the government to help maintain businesses' cash flow during the pandemic have further eroded national revenue. This includes an earlier-than-expected adoption of a cut to the corporate income tax rate, from 25 per cent to 22 per cent, initially planned to be effective in 2021.

On the expenditure side, the urgent need to boost resources for health care and a social safety net has escalated government spending. The 2020 state budget was revised largely to incorporate a fiscal package of Rp 695.2 trillion, equivalent to 4.2 per cent of GDP. The fiscal package focuses on three priorities: strengthening health care, expanding the social safety net program, and providing emergency support for businesses to prevent them from failing as well as to prevent widespread layoffs. The package will be implemented through a combination of revenue, expenditure and 'below the line' measures.[3] However, the largest part of it will be delivered through expenditure, amounting to around Rp 387.6 trillion or 2.4 per cent of GDP.

---

3 These measures are not part of revenue and expenditure, but classified under the financing side, namely investment financing. For example, direct capital placement to state-owned enterprises and capital placement to state-owned banks to support credit restructuring programs for the real sector during the current COVID-19 pandemic crisis.

Table 4.1 Fiscal position, 2018–2020

Items	2018	2019	2020B	2020RB
		Rupiah trillion		
Total revenue and grants	1,942.3	1,953.4	2,233.2	1,699.9
Total revenue	1,928.5	1,950.2	2,232.7	1,698.6
Tax	1,521.4	1,527.0	1,865.7	1,404.5
Income tax	751.5	765.8	929.9	670.4
Consumption tax	697.9	691.6	866.4	679.7
Trade tax	45.8	40.9	42.6	33.5
Non-tax	407.1	423.2	367.0	294.1
Total expenditure	2,202.2	2,268.3	2,540.4	2,739.2
Central government	1,444.4	1,457.2	1,683.5	1,975.2
Transfer to region & Village Funds	757.8	811.1	856.9	763.9
Primary balance	−87.3	−20.1	−12.0	−700.4
Overall balance	−325.9	−296.0	−307.2	−1,039.2
		% of GDP		
Total revenue and grants	13.1	12.3	12.8	10.4
Tax	10.3	9.6	10.7	8.6
Income tax	5.1	4.8	5.3	4.1
Consumption tax	4.7	4.4	5.0	4.1
Non-tax	2.7	2.7	2.1	1.8
Total expenditure	14.8	14.3	14.5	16.7
Central government	9.7	9.2	9.6	12.1
Transfer to region & Village Funds	5.1	5.1	4.9	4.7
Primary balance	−0.6	−0.1	−0.1	−4.3
Overall balance	−2.2	−1.9	−1.8	−6.3
Memorandum				
Government debt	29.8	30.2	26.9	37.6
Health care & PEN Program*				4.2
Revenue				0.8
Spending				2.4
Below the line				1.1

Note: 2020B refers to the initial budget and 2020RB refers to the revised budget based on Perpres No. 72/2020. The government debt level for 2020 is the authors' estimate.

* National Economic Recovery Program (Program Pemulihan Ekonomi Nasional, PEN).

Total government expenditure for 2020 is expected to surge significantly to 16.7 per cent of GDP from 14.5 per cent in the initial budget. This extra expenditure is planned to be financed through additional debt issuance as well as budget reallocation at both central government and regional transfers.

Shrinking revenue and escalating expenditure will weaken Indonesia's fiscal position. The fiscal deficit is expected to widen to a record high in the past five decades to 6.3 per cent of GDP from 1.8 per cent in the initial budget. Inevitably, the government issued an 'emergency' law, Regulation in Lieu of Law (Peraturan Pemerintah Pengganti Undang-Undang, Perppu) No. 1/2020, to relax the existing rule to maintain the fiscal deficit below 3 per cent of GDP.[4] The wider fiscal deficit will be funded largely via bond issuance and upsized borrowing from multilateral creditors. As a consequence, government debt is likely to elevate sharply from 30.2 per cent of GDP in 2019 to 37.6 per cent in 2020.

While in the short run the economy is facing risk of contraction, in the medium term the government is likely to face tougher fiscal challenges. In the next three years the fiscal deficit is projected to be above 3 per cent of GDP. The wider deficit over this medium term will be financed largely through borrowing, resulting in increasing government debt to an alarming level of around 40 per cent of GDP. Subsequently, the interest payment will go up sizeably, crowding out more development spending over the medium term.

Financing the recovery and concerns over debt dynamics

As revenues decrease significantly, due both to weakening economic activities and the various tax incentives given to stimulate the economy, countries are facing significant challenges in the financing front. At the height of global volatility—from the end of February through March—the stream of outflows towards safe-haven assets hit many emerging economies' exchange rates.

This is not new. The procyclicality of net capital inflows, which means that external borrowing increases in good times and falls in bad times, is well documented for both advanced and emerging economies (Kaminsky et al. 2004). In fact, for emerging economies, capital inflows are associated with expansionary macroeconomic policies. This procyclicality could be exacerbated when countries are faced with higher liquidity constraints, as were evidenced in most emerging markets. However, Frankel et al.

---

4   As stipulated in Law No. 17/2003 on State Finances.

(2011) found that several emerging markets were more able to escape from procyclical fiscal policies with improvement in institutional quality.

This time, capital flows do not show procyclical behaviour. As global financial markets started pricing in the impact of the pandemic, investors fled towards safe-haven assets. This reversal period coincides with expansionary monetary and fiscal policy in an attempt to fight the economic fallout of the pandemic. In fact, for the first time, several emerging economies have embarked into new territory of quantitative easing by allowing central banks to buy government bonds.

The increase in volatility and cost of financing has raised concerns over debt sustainability for countries, with or without market access. In March this year, the G20 launched a debt payment forbearance for low-income countries to help overcome unsustainable levels of debt. Discussions were raised at the global level on the need for private investors to follow bilateral donors in giving debt payment forbearance. This is important so that additional financial resources from these debt payment forbearances will be diverted towards these investors rather than for dealing with the pandemic. Emerging economies with market access, such as Indonesia, are in much better standing; however, with the spike in financing costs and uncertainty of how long this economic 'freeze' will last, emerging market countries must bear much higher debt payment costs.

For Indonesia, the net outflows during this period reached Rp 158.3 trillion by April, much larger than during the height of the global financial crisis in 2009 and taper tantrum in 2013, during which times Indonesia recorded a positive net inflow (Table 4.2). On 23 March 2020 the rupiah fell to Rp 16,575 per US dollar, its lowest level since the Asian financial crisis. Yield soared, reflecting tighter liquidity globally, and the ten-year yield increased by 175 basis points on 24 March, its strongest level since 19 February 2020. This was quite a turnaround, as the global

Table 4.2 Capital flow in Indonesia's financial market (stocks, government bonds and central bank certificates) (rupiah trillion)

2009	2013	2016	2018	2019	Jan – 17 April 2020
Global financial crisis	Taper tantrum		Monetary normalisation in the US		COVID-19
69.9	36.0	124.9	7.3	22.1	−158.3

Source: Bloomberg; CEIC; Finance Ministry, 2020.

financial market was still bullish towards emerging market assets until February 2020.

Higher financing needs during periods of high uncertainty have raised concerns over debt dynamics. In the decade prior to the COVID-19 pandemic, emerging market and developing economies have accumulated large debt growth, from a total of 60 per cent of GDP in 2010 to 170 per cent of GDP in 2019 (Kose et al. 2020). The current low interest rate environment, which is likely to continue well into the future, could relieve the burden on debt repayment. However, because the global financial market is segmented, advanced economies enjoy lower interest rates than emerging economies, creating an uneven playing field.

In addition to segmentation in the global financial market, several other factors could increase the cost of financing for emerging economies. First, emerging economies must bear a higher cost of external financing to compensate for higher risk and tighter liquidity. Second, weakening exchange rates increase the cost of foreign currency–denominated debt. Third, as growth contracts and external balance worsens, countries might face credit ratings downgrades, which increase their financing costs further.

Moreover, Indonesia's local currency yields are relatively high compared to emerging country peers such as the Philippines and Mexico. Several factors are affecting yield premiums, including inflation, policy rate, twin deficits (fiscal and current account), risk perception, exchange rate volatility and relatively shallow financial markets. The most important determinants for Indonesia are the current account balance and exchange rate volatility (Figure 4.1).

Yet, since fiscal policies are at the forefront of the COVID-19 pandemic response, and to prevent a long-lasting economic recession, debt expansions are inevitable. Priorities of fiscal spending in many countries, including Indonesia, are focused on health, targeted social safety nets for affected workers, and support to help businesses stay afloat until economic activity resumes. Even though debt expansion is inevitable, countries must be cautious to spend it for GDP-enhancing purposes in order to maintain a sustainable debt dynamic (Kose et al. 2020).

As Indonesia revised its budget, from the original budget prior to the COVID-19 pandemic at Rp 307.2 trillion or 1.8 per cent (Law No. 20/2019 on the 2020 State Budget) to the latest figure of Rp 1039.2 trillion or 6.3 per cent (Perpres No. 72/2020), financing needs increased to Rp 1220.5 trillion from Rp 359.3 trillion last year. The debt-to-GDP ratio increased from 30.2 per cent in 2019 to 36.6 per cent (estimated) in 2020 and could increase further to around 40 per cent (estimated) in 2021. Despite significant changes, Indonesia's debt-to-GDP ratio is still far from its peers (Figure 4.2) and

Figure 4.1 Yield and external vulnerabilities, 2014–2019

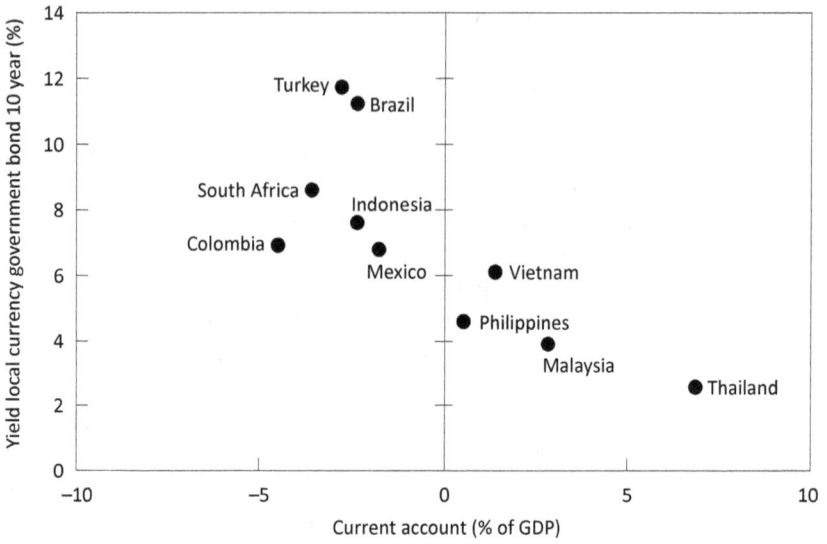

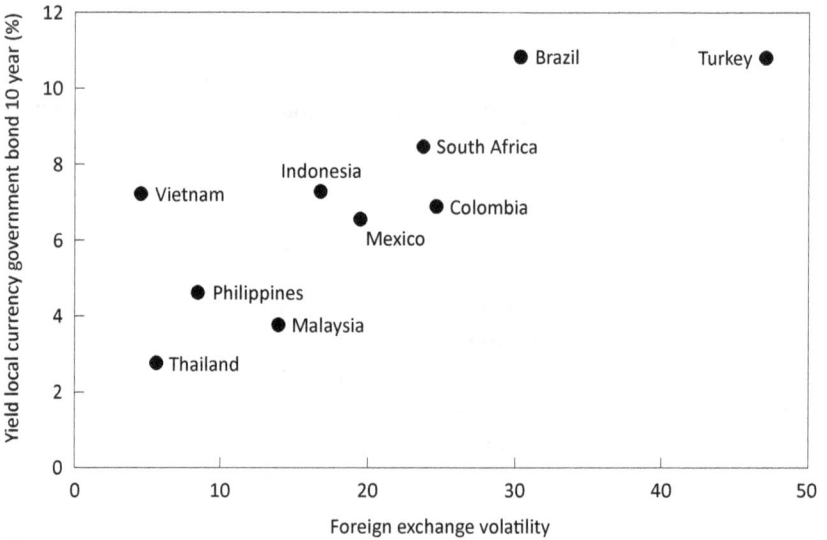

Source: Directorate General of Budget Financing and Risk Management, and World Bank, 2020, unpublished.

Figure 4.2 Indonesia's debt-to-GDP ratio compared to other countries (%)

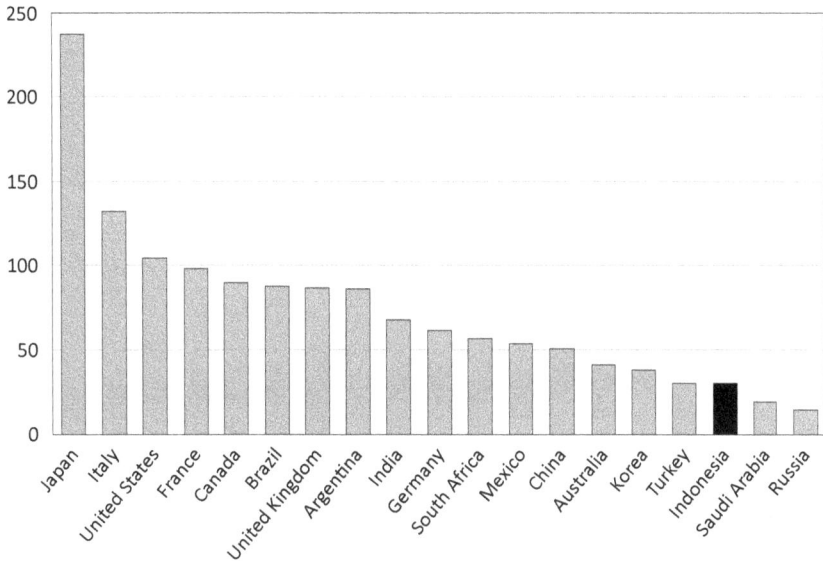

Source: IMF (2020a); Finance Ministry.

from the upper limit of 60 per cent under Law No. 17/2003 on State Finances (article 12(3)).[5] The debt-to-GDP trend has increased slightly since the end of the commodity period during which weaker growth coincided with fiscal expansion for priority spending such as infrastructure.

Higher financing needs and debt repayment will lower the fiscal space. In the current medium-term fiscal framework, the debt-to-GDP ratio is estimated to peak in 2022, while interest payments expenditure is estimated to peak in 2023 (Figure 4.3). As the fiscal deficit will start to narrow and be back within 3 per cent in 2023, the debt-to-GDP ratio and interest payment in terms of revenue or expenditure will start to normalise as well (Figure 4.3).

The increase in debt payment means at least two things: debt payment might crowd out important spending for several years to come, and revenue must catch up with the increase in debt payment to maintain debt sustainability.

---

5 Nevertheless, the optimal benchmark of the debt-to-GDP ratio suggested by the IMF (2002) is 40 per cent for developing countries.

Figure 4.3 Debt-to-GDP ratio, debt interest payment and fiscal deficit

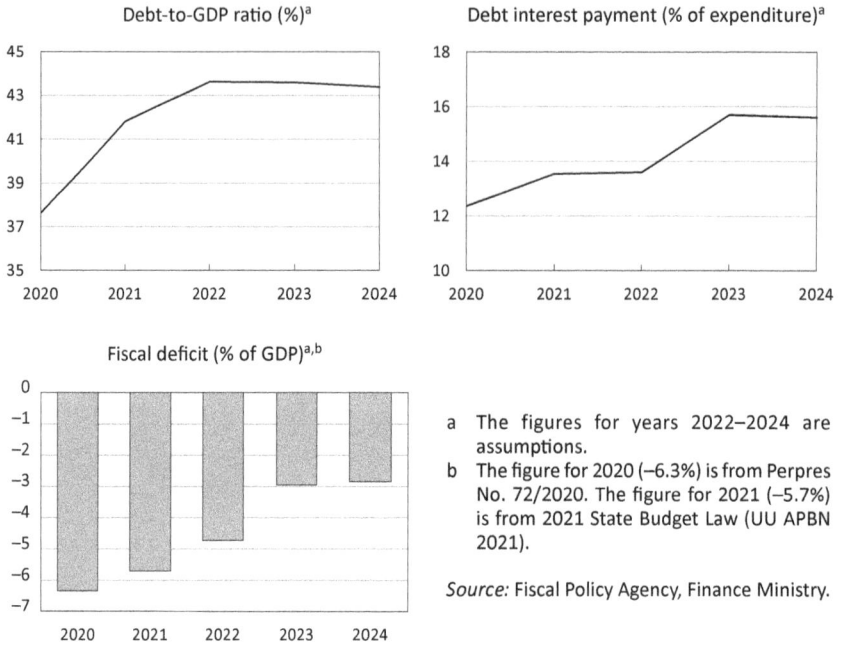

Debt-to-GDP ratio (%)[a]

Debt interest payment (% of expenditure)[a]

Fiscal deficit (% of GDP)[a,b]

a   The figures for years 2022–2024 are
    assumptions.
b   The figure for 2020 (–6.3%) is from Perpres
    No. 72/2020. The figure for 2021 (–5.7%)
    is from 2021 State Budget Law (UU APBN
    2021).

Source: Fiscal Policy Agency, Finance Ministry.

Financing strategy and burden sharing

Following other emerging economies that have adopted a quantitative
easing similar to what has been done in the United States, Europe and
Japan, the Finance Ministry and Bank Indonesia created a one-off debt
monetisation scheme called 'burden sharing', under which Bank Indonesia
can buy government bonds in the primary market. This scheme began in
early March. In addition, Indonesia is starting a new mechanism in which
Bank Indonesia bears part of the interest rate payment as forgone revenue.

Market integrity is at the forefront of the burden-sharing scheme. The
government bonds bought by Bank Indonesia are long term, tradeable and
marketable. The tenure is also chosen to maintain balanced debt maturity
profiles, and issuance will be staged depending on financing needs and
cash management strategy. The debt monetisation scheme is a one-off
policy, which is important in keeping an independent monetary policy
and sustainable debt dynamics as well as keeping investor sentiment
positive towards Indonesia. After the burden-sharing scheme was
announced on 7 July 2020, and the market was assured that this is a

one-off policy, government bonds rallied (Moss 2020). As of 21 July 2020, Bank Indonesia had absorbed Rp 40.9 trillion from the primary market.

The scheme has three different burden-sharing scenarios: public goods (with zero interest cost to the government), non-public goods (with seven-day repo rate minus 1 per cent) and other spending (market rates) (Table 4.3).

- Public goods have been allocated Rp 397.6 trillion. Bank Indonesia will carry the full amount through the purchase of government bonds in a private placement mechanism and return the coupon payment made by the government. The interest rate cost to the government is zero, but the bonds bought are marketable. This is a new initiative and has been received positively by the market (Moss 2020).

- Non-public goods have been allocated Rp 177.0 trillion. The government will offer government securities (*surat berharga negara*, SBNs) to the market. Bank Indonesia will carry the difference between the market rate and the three-month reverse repo Bank Indonesia rate minus 1 per cent. The cost to the government is equal to the three-month reverse repo Bank Indonesia rate minus 1 per cent.

- Expenditure needs for other non-public goods in the amount of Rp 328.9 trillion will be borne entirely by the government through the issuance of SBNs with coupons based on market rates.

- For all non-public goods financing (amounting to Rp 505.9 trillion), which is related to economic recovery and support for the business sector, market mechanisms will be used, and Bank Indonesia will continue to play the role of last resort, following the 1st joint decree between the Finance Ministry and Bank of Indonesia (Surat Keputasan Bersama 1) of 16 April 2020.

The National Economic Recovery Program

The pandemic has turned 2020 from a more optimistic year into a global recession. The International Monetary Fund announced that the world entered a recession from March 2020. The chance of a V-shaped recovery has dimmed as many countries are struggling to flatten the COVID-19 curve. Global growth predictions have been downgraded significantly by almost all institutions (Figure 4.4). By June 2020, the Organisation for Economic Co-operation and Development (OECD) estimated global growth to contract by 6 per cent under a single-hit scenario and by 7.6 per cent under a double-hit scenario. The International Monetary Fund and the World Bank estimated a global contraction of 4.9 per cent and 5.2 per

Table 4.3 Burden-sharing scheme to finance Indonesia's economic recovery

Type of spending	Burden sharing	Mechanism	Budget (Perpres No. 72/2020)
Public goods (Rp 397.6 tn)	Borne fully by Bank Indonesia (7DDR)	Private placement mechanism	Health (Rp 87.6 tn) Social safety net (Rp 203.9 tn) Line ministries and local government (Rp 106.1 tn)
Non-public goods (Rp 177.0 tn)	Borne partly by government (3-month 7DDR minus 1%)	Market mechanism (Bank Indonesia as non-competitive bidder in auction, green-shoe option or private placement)	Micro, small and medium enterprises (MSMEs) (Rp 123.5 tn) Corporations (Rp 53.6 tn)
Other non-public goods (Rp 328.9 tn)	Borne fully by government (market rate)	Market mechanism (Bank Indonesia as non-competitive bidder in auction, green-shoe option or private placement)	Other non-public goods (Rp 328.9 tn)

Source: Finance Ministry.

Figure 4.4 Global economic growth predictions, 2020–2021

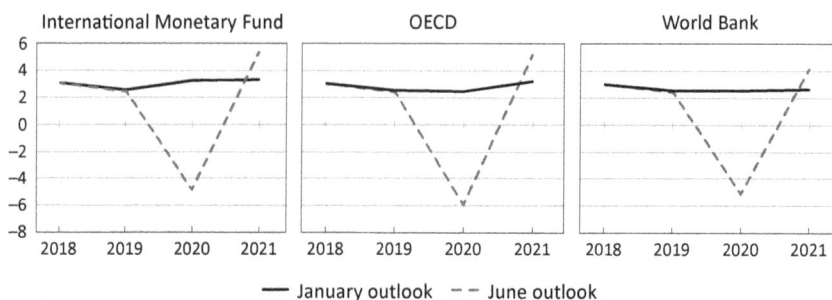

Note: Under a double-hit scenario in which there is possibility of a second wave of COVID-19, the OECD projects a deeper contraction in global growth of 7.6 per cent.

Source: IMF (2020b); OECD (2020); World Bank (2020b).

cent, respectively, in June. All three institutions estimated positive global growth in their January to March forecasts.

The lockdown and physical distancing measures implemented by most governments are unavoidably needed to flatten the epidemiology curve of COVID-19. However, these measures have dire economic consequences as they freeze business activities in many sectors, hit business and consumer confidence, and lower commodity prices as demand slumps. Combined with the risk of a second wave—in the absence of a vaccine—these factors weigh on the confidence for a V-shaped global recovery. To overcome this situation, many countries are embarking on significant fiscal and monetary easing (Figure 4.5).

Various fiscal stimulus programs have been effected by the Indonesian government since early February 2020, followed by the National Economic Recovery Program (Pemulihan Ekonomi Nasional, PEN) on 31 March 2020. A legal breakthrough, Perppu No. 1/2020, the so-called emergency law, has been a historical milestone by the government. The law is an immediate response that aims to overcome the adverse impact of the pandemic through three major areas: health, expanding social safety nets, and supporting the business sector, particularly SMEs.

A benign inflation environment had provided space for Bank Indonesia to loosen the policy rate four times (to a total of 100 basis points) by July

Figure 4.5 Stimulus amid the COVID-19 pandemic

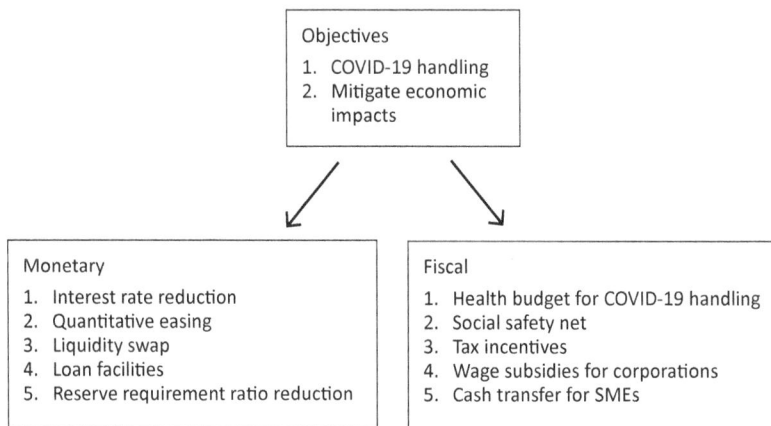

Source: IMF Policy Tracker (www.imf.org/en/Topics/imf-and-covid19/Policy-Responses-to-COVID-19); Finance Ministry.

2020, lower the rupiah reserve requirement, and expand the monetary operation by providing banks and corporations a term-repo line using government bonds, to support the economic recovery during the pandemic. On top of buying government bonds in the primary market in which Bank Indonesia entered as a non-competitive bidder, there are also green-shoe options (Bank Indonesia enters the next day using the price from the last auction) and private placement. Bank Indonesia strengthened the triple intervention to maintain rupiah stability in both the spot and domestic non-deliverable forward markets, as well as purchasing government bonds in the secondary market. Additionally, Bank Indonesia increased the frequency of foreign exchange market swap auctions from three times per week to daily auctions, effective from 19 March 2020, to support onshore foreign exchange market liquidity.

For emerging markets, besides inflation, the policy rate is also constrained by possible outflows from global investors who tend to flee emerging markets when economic indicators or sentiments worsen. Benign inflation during weak growth may provide more room for monetary policy, yet the concern is more towards capital outflows. Historically, emerging economies had to tighten policy rates during a sudden reversal in times of crisis, which exacerbates the contraction of aggregate demand (see Gupta (2016) for India's case and Forbes and Warnock (2012) for a sudden stop of capital flows). Regardless of the muted inflation, room for central banks to adjust policy rates further is limited by the fickle global sentiment.

As the pandemic requires large-scale social restriction in many regions, many economic activities enter a 'freeze' state. Both supply and demand sides are hibernated, not to mention turmoil in the health and social side. From the health side, for example, a crisis can occur due to a shortage of medical supplies, medical devices, medical and nursing staff, and hospital capacity. From the social side, a halt in economic activities heavily impacts labour absorption, specifically in the non-formal sector.

For Indonesia, disruption in the flow of capital goods and raw material from China has thwarted production since February 2020. Also, there was a significant downturn in real sector performance due to the implementation of large-scale social restrictions. From the demand side, public consumption deteriorated significantly, investment was disadvantaged by the postponement of several infrastructure projects, and ongoing projects slowed. GDP exports and imports have weakened, although the trade balance has somewhat improved due to the slowdown of imports. But contraction of raw materials and capital goods imports— accounting for around 90 per cent of total imports—also means lower investment in the quarters ahead.

The first half of 2020 GDP data confirmed that adverse impacts of the pandemic have started to materialise. After a sharp slowdown in the first quarter of 2020, GDP growth in the second quarter began to enter negative territory, contracting by 5.3 per cent compared to 5.1 per cent in the same quarter in 2019, dampened by a drop in investment and private consumption growth (Figure 4.6). Private consumption, which contributes around 56 per cent of GDP, hit a record low in a decade as stricter social distancing measures started. Meanwhile, fear about the disease and weakening demand disrupted investment, which plunged to −8.6 per cent in the second quarter of 2020, the lowest since the Asian financial crisis. Growth on the production side also confirmed expectations: that the pandemic will hit most on tourism-related sectors and manufacturing as transportation, both domestic and international travel, is restricted and imports are disrupted (Figure 4.7).

In the financial sector, investor confidence was disrupted due to sudden capital flight. A slowdown in economic activity has increased the likelihood of non-performing loans or loans at risk. The Financial Services Authority (Otoritas Jasa Keuangan, OJK) has eased credit restructuring for debtors affected by the pandemic. It has also granted a more lenient approach for determining asset quality for SMEs via OJK Decree No. 11/2020 on National Economic Stimulus as a Countercyclical Policy on the Effect of the Coronavirus Disease 2019 Outbreak, aimed to lower non-performing loan surges. Companies' revenue and profitability has dropped, and many employees have been furloughed to lower labour and overhead costs.

Given the overarching impact of the COVID-19 pandemic, it will be crucial to address all issues in tandem. Health issues remain a priority (other chapters in this volume will address health). From the socioeconomic point of view, it is critical to address both demand side and supply side.

Law No. 2/2020 has allowed the fiscal deficit to exceed its normal upper limit of 3 per cent of GDP. The deficit currently widens at 6.3 per cent for the fiscal year 2020—according to Perpres No. 72/2020—given the additional Rp 695.2 trillion spending that aims to limit the COVID-19 spread and recover the economy. Priorities are given for health, demand-side support (e.g. social protection expansion), sectoral and regional government support, supply-side support for SMEs, and corporate financing including tax incentives and facilities (Table 4.4).

Figure 4.6 GDP growth: Demand side (%, year on year)

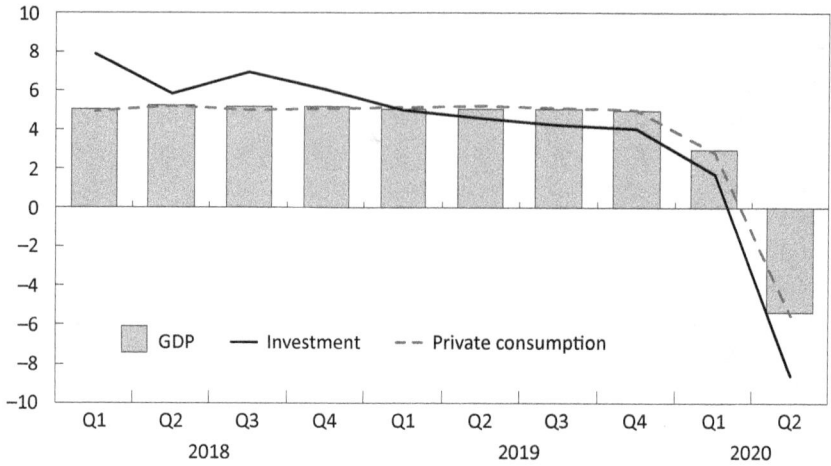

Source: CEIC database.

Figure 4.7 GDP growth: Production side (%, year on year)

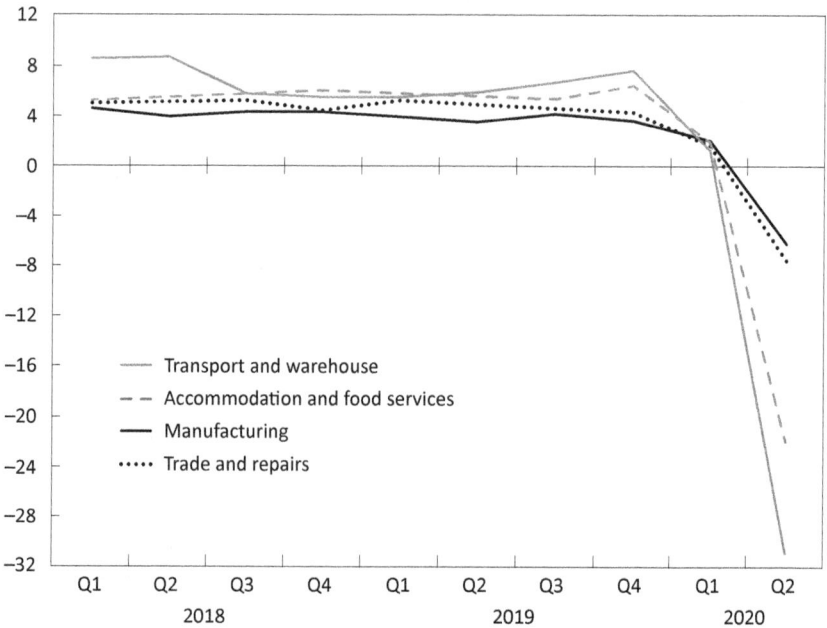

Source: CEIC database.

Table 4.4 Fiscal policy package, 2020

Program	Subprogram	Objectives
1. Health measures (Rp 87.6 trillion)	(1) incentives for health officials (2) death benefits for medical workers (3) COVID-19 mitigation and prevention (4) subsidy for National Health Insurance System (Badan Penyelenggara Jaminan Sosial Kesehatan, BPJS) premium (5) COVID-19 task force expenses (6) tax incentives on medical supplies and medicines	To control the spread of the disease and to strengthen the healthcare system in dealing with the pandemic.
2. Support for micro, small and medium enterprises (MSMEs) (Rp 123.5 trillion)	(1) interest rate subsidies (2) working capital guarantee (3) return guarantee (4) investment financing for cooperatives (5) fund placement for credit restructuring (6) final income tax break facility	To soften the impact of the COVID-19 pandemic by reducing the financial stress faced by MSMEs, which is hoped to prepare them to jump start their businesses when the pandemic is under control.
3. Social safety net (Rp 203.9 trillion)	(1) Family Hope Program (Program Keluarga Harapan, PKH) (2) Staple Food Card (Kartu Sembako) (3) staple food package assistance for Jabodetabek (Greater Jakarta) area (4) cash transfers for non-Jabodetabek area (5) Pre-employment Card (Kartu Prakerja) (6) Village Funds cash transfers (BLT Dana Desa) (7) electricity bill discounts (8) reserved fund for food security	To expand and complement existing social assistance programs in order to soften the impact of the COVID-19 pandemic on poor and vulnerable families. The key target is to keep the poverty rate at a one-digit level.

Table 4.4 (continued)

Program	Subprogram	Objectives
4. Tax relief for corporations (Rp 120.6 trillion)	(1) income tax relief for employees in selected sectors (2) income tax exemptions for import of goods (3) reductions in income tax instalments (4) accelerated refunds for value-added tax (5) income tax reductions for corporations (6) other incentives	To reduce the tax burden of corporations in order to ease their cash flow problems during the pandemic.
5. Support for sectoral and regional government (Rp 106.1 trillion)	(1) labour-intensive programs in the Ministry of Public Works and Public Housing, Ministry of Agriculture, and Ministry of Marine Affairs and Fisheries (2) extension of housing credits (3) tourism sector support (4) regional economic recovery program (5) additional specific fund for housing and agriculture (6) regional financing facility (7) reserve fund for other regional activities	To keep labour-intensive public works moving in order to create jobs while at the same time developing basic infrastructure in the region.
6. Corporate financing (Rp 53.6 trillion)	(1) capital injection to state-owned enterprises (2) bailout investment for working capital (3) credit restructuring for labour-intensive corporations	To help state-owned enterprises keep running their businesses, prevent worker layoffs and allow enterprises to contribute in softening the impact of the crisis.

Source: Finance Ministry.

Supporting the demand side

Expanding social safety nets

Domestic economic growth slowed significantly to 3.0 per cent in the first quarter of 2020 and is estimated to contract in the second quarter. Domestic consumption grew at 2.8 per cent from 5.0 per cent in the previous quarter and investment at 1.1 per cent from 5.0 per cent. The Finance Ministry estimates there will be at least 5.2 million newly unemployed and 5.7 million new poor if economic growth falls to −0.4 per cent in 2020. This estimate could be bigger if growth plunges further. In fact, what is equally important is the underemployment issue as companies cut working hours and salaries to stay afloat. As the number of poor and vulnerable people will increase due to the pandemic, social safety net beneficiaries and coverage need to be expanded beyond what has been covered previously.

Social safety net beneficiaries expanded to the bottom 50–60 per cent of the population as more people fell below the poverty line due to loss of income (Table 4.5). Existing beneficiaries of the Family Hope Program (Program Keluarga Harapan, PKH) and Staple Food Card (Kartu Sembako) are being given additional benefits to sustain their lives. Moreover, the government provides electricity subsidies for 450 VA and 900 VA users,[6] which account for around 24 million and 7.2 million families, respectively, or the bottom 50 per cent of the population.

Meanwhile, expansion of direct transfers to people eligible for, but not currently receiving, Family Hope Program or Staple Food Card benefits is undertaken through regional government. Data availability due to the exclusion error[7] has been a serious challenge in expanding the social safety net beyond the bottom 40 per cent of the population. Better, wider and updated datasets will be pivotal for the future development of this program (see Alatas, this volume).

Sectoral and regional government support

Local governments are at the forefront of pandemic countermeasures and need additional support to ensure sufficient resource mobilisation for labour-intensive projects, for instance, the Regional Incentive Fund

---

6 Perusahaan Listrik Negara (PLN, the state-owned energy company) classifies household consumers into several classes. Those with 450 VA (volt ampere) and 900 VA are the smallest household consumers and are the target beneficiaries of an electricity subsidy.

7 The exclusion error refers to a situation in which eligible people are not included in the program due to database (social registry) weaknesses.

Table 4.5 Social protection expansion

Income decile	Family Hope Program (PKH)	Staple Food Card (Kartu Sembako)	Electricity subsidy	Cash transfers (non-Jabodetabek)	Basic food package (Jabodetabek)	Village Funds cash transfers (BLT Dana Desa)	Pre-employment Card (Kartu Prakerja)
6							
5			Free bill for 24 million households (450 VA)		Excluding PKH and food voucher recipients		5.6 million households Training Rp 1 million/mth
4			50% discount for 7.2 million households (900 VA)	Excluding PKH and food voucher recipients			Allowance Rp 600,000/mth
3				9 million households	1.3 million households 600,000 households	11 million households, excluding PKH and food voucher recipients	Survey (3x) Rp 50,000/mth
2		20 million households benefits increased by 33.3% to Rp 200 million/mth		Apr–Jun: Rp 600,000/mth	Apr–Jun: Rp 600,000/mth	Apr–Jun: Rp 600,000/mth	
1	10 million households benefits increased by 25%			Jul–Sep: Rp 300,000/mth	Jul–Sep: Rp 300,000/mth	Jul–Sep: Rp 300,000/mth	
Time frame	Monthly, for 12 months	Monthly, for 12 months	6 months (Apr–Sep)	9 months (Apr–Dec)	9 months (Apr–Dec)	6 months (Apr–Sep)	Apr–Oct/Nov Allowance for 4 months
Additional budget (rupiah trillion)	8.3	15.5	6.9	32.4	6.8	31.8	10.0
Total budget (rupiah trillion)	37.4	43.6	6.9	32.4	6.8	31.8	20.0

Source: Integrated Database for Social Welfare (Data Terpadu Kesejahteraan Sosial, DTKS), Ministry of Finance.

(Dana Insentif Daerah, DID), the Special Allocation Fund for Capital Spending (Dana Alokasi Khusus Fisik, DAK Fisik) and regional loan facilities. Local governments are also facing revenue pressure as locally owned revenue sources have diminished from external and internal shocks. Liquidity provision in the form of cheap loans could potentially help local governments stay afloat in overcoming the adverse effects of the pandemic.

Supporting the supply side

Supporting small and medium enterprises

Adverse effects of the pandemic on the real sectors began in February 2020. China's lockdown has affected tourism and supplies of raw material; the latter has mostly affected the textile and electronics sectors. In previous crises, the informal sector and SMEs were relatively resilient. But now, SMEs and informal economies are likely to suffer disproportionately from the impacts of the pandemic, especially those in low-value-added services. The economic fallout on SMEs has had a significant impact on GDP, GDP per capita and livelihoods because SMEs account for 60 per cent of GDP and 97 per cent of employment (2017 figures) (116.7 million people, 60 per cent women). Therefore, support for SMEs includes interest rate subsidies, loan restructuring and additional working capital. The government also provides tax relief for SMEs.

Supporting labour-intensive sectors

Indonesia still has a high proportion of informal workers—57 per cent of total employment. The top three GDP contributors—agriculture, manufacturing and trading services—employ significant numbers of informal workers (Figure 4.8). Yet it is not easy to precisely estimate the impacts of the pandemic on underemployment, due to the high proportion of informal workers and the lack of frequent surveys on unemployment and underemployment. Meanwhile, direct targeting in the delivery of social safety nets is considered more desirable for effectiveness in a narrowed fiscal space.

As mentioned, the three largest GDP contributors are agriculture (13 per cent), manufacturing (21.6 per cent) and trading services (13.7 per cent). These three major sectors are also the top three contributors to employment: agriculture (29.5 per cent), trading services (19 per cent) and manufacturing (14 per cent). Due to the different nature of these sectors, the type of support they require also differs. In the agriculture sector, for example, 90 per cent of employees are informal workers. Manufacturing

Figure 4.8 Formal and informal workers by sector, 2019

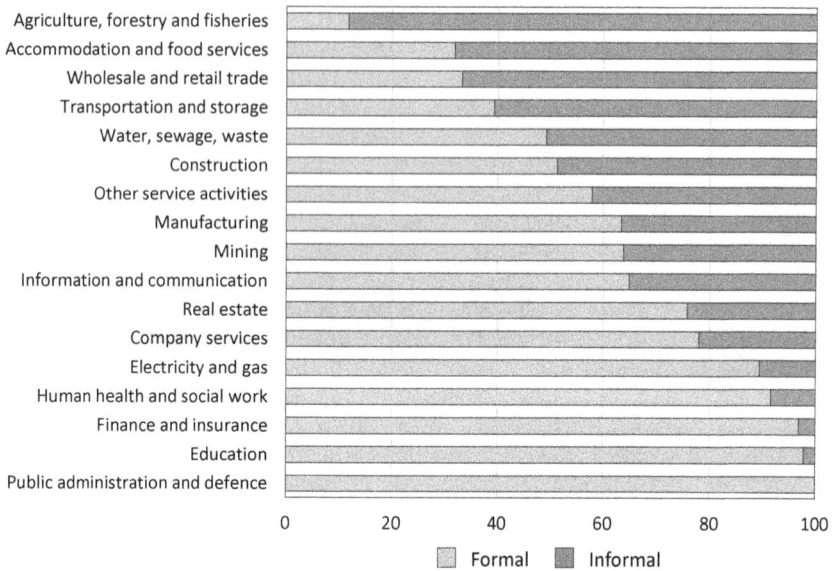

Source: CEIC; National Labour Force Survey (Survey Angkatan Kerja Nasional); Finance Ministry, 2020.

has only 37 per cent informal workers. So, support for agriculture workers is directed towards social safety net expansion while manufacturing could be supported through tax incentives, credit restructuring and working capital loans through companies.

Supporting other corporate sectors

Support for other corporate sectors is in the form of tax incentives, loan restructuring and a state guarantee provision for working capital loan expansion. The government has provided tax relief amounting to Rp 123 trillion through various measures: temporary waivers for personal income tax and corporate income tax, accelerated value-added tax (VAT) refunds and a permanent cut of the corporate income tax rate from 25 to 22 per cent. Moreover, to speed up the process in supporting banks to provide cheap loans, the Finance Ministry has placed state funds previously deposited at Bank Indonesia with other banks. These funds are to be used only to extend liquidity to the real sectors and must not be used to buy government bonds or for exchange rate trading.

Lessons learned for future reforms

Fiscal headroom and leverage have worsened in all countries as revenue has weakened and debt-to-GDP ratio and financing costs have increased. This unprecedented situation is a good opportunity to call for deeper reforms in many areas of the United Nations Sustainable Development Goals, including education, health, social safety nets, financial inclusiveness, environment, inclusivity, institution building and even gender equality. Measures needed to contain the spread of COVID-19 have impacted the poor the hardest and could widen the inequality gap.

Indonesia still aspires to move up the income ladder and become a high-income country by 2045. In order to achieve that, potential growth must be maintained above the current level of 5 per cent (prior to the COVID-19 pandemic). Reforms that are underway include fiscal reforms in the area of revenue and spending, social safety nets, education, health, data for better policymaking, and reforms to address productivity and improve competitiveness.

The current pandemic has underlined the need to fast forward reform in certain areas. We would like to highlight three important areas that are relevant for fiscal policy.

First, building a modern and strong social protection program is crucial. The government has responded strongly to mitigate adverse impacts of the COVID-19 pandemic on poor and vulnerable families by expanding existing social assistance programs as well as initiating new ones. The execution, however, exposes some weaknesses as highlighted by the World Bank (2020a). The existing database to identify households in need, the Integrated Database for Social Welfare (Data Terpadu Kesejahteraan Sosial, DTKS), cannot capture households that fall into poverty as a result of a sudden shock, such as the pandemic or a natural disaster. In addition, the coverage of existing social assistance programs has been concentrated among poor households, while parts of the aspiring middle class are left uncovered. A well-designed social assistance program that can deliver a more inclusive and effective system is needed. To protect the economy and population during economic shocks, crises, natural disasters or epidemic outbreaks, a social protection system should be responsive to shocks and could act as an automatic stabiliser.

For this reason, the need for integrated beneficiaries and social registries is critically important. The DTKS is a good place to start as it covers the bottom 40 per cent of the population. Updating data frequently to reflect dynamic socioeconomic conditions is crucial. The use of technology to support dynamic inclusion needs to be developed. Usually on-demand registration methods lend themselves to more dynamic inclusion. In the short run, new data collected to expand beneficiaries during the pandemic can be added to the DTKS. In addition, the social and beneficiary registry should integrate poor households' data in local governments from other line ministries (for example, the Ministry of Marine Affairs and Fisheries has data on fisherman and the Ministry of Agriculture has data on farmers). All data should be matched with the Population Identification Number (Nomor Identifikasi Kependudukan, NIK).

Second, the current environment of lower commodity prices provides an opportunity for the government to reform energy subsidies. Despite its targeting as typical of a commodity-based subsidy, energy compensation has been a source of financial stress for the state-owned energy enterprises, which are often repaid in arrears by the government, complicating cash management. In terms of targeting, according to an estimate based on the latest National Socioeconomic Survey (Survei Sosio-Ekonomi Nasional, Susenas) data, of the bottom 10 per cent of households, around 50 per cent are excluded from the liquid petroleum gas (LPG) subsidy and 25 per cent are excluded from the electricity subsidy (Figure 4.9). In contrast, more than 60 per cent of the richest decile benefit from the subsidy.

The reform could be carried out by gradually integrating the LPG and electricity subsidies into an expanded social assistance program, particularly the Staple Food Card program. The government could expand the program in both its benefit and coverage to compensate those not receiving an energy subsidy. With a smaller targeting error, the expanded Staple Food Card program would be a more effective tool to alleviate poverty and reduce income inequality while at the same time detaching the oil price setting from the politics.

Third, tax reform is crucial to provide adequate revenue streams to support higher economic growth and sustainable development. Indonesia's tax ratio, at 9.8 per cent in 2019 (Figure 4.10), is relatively low compared to its peers and needs to catch up to the lower middle income countries average at 12.5 per cent.[8] The tax base has continued to narrow, reflecting low tax buoyancy (still below 1). A structural shift from the tradeable sector (agriculture, mining and manufacturing), which typically offers a broader tax base, towards the non-tradeable sector (services) could be part of tax reform. Another factor could be related to the rapid increase of the digital economy, which is difficult to capture in the system.

---

8   The World Bank reports that the tax ratio for middle income countries is 11.9 and for upper middle income countries is 11.8 (World Bank World Development Indicators, 2017. https://databank.worldbank.org/source/world-development-indicators).

Figure 4.9 Distribution of subsidy and social assistance beneficiaries
by decile (%)

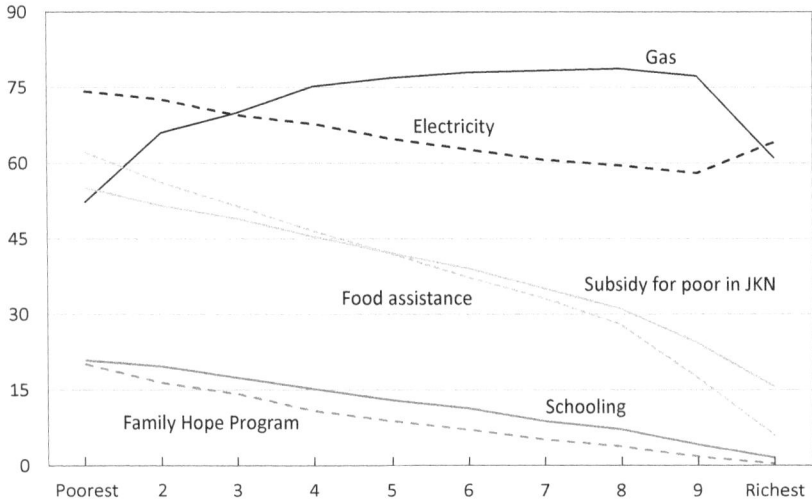

Source: Fiscal Policy Agency, Ministry of Finance.

Figure 4.10 Indonesia's tax ratio, 2015–2019 (% of GDP)

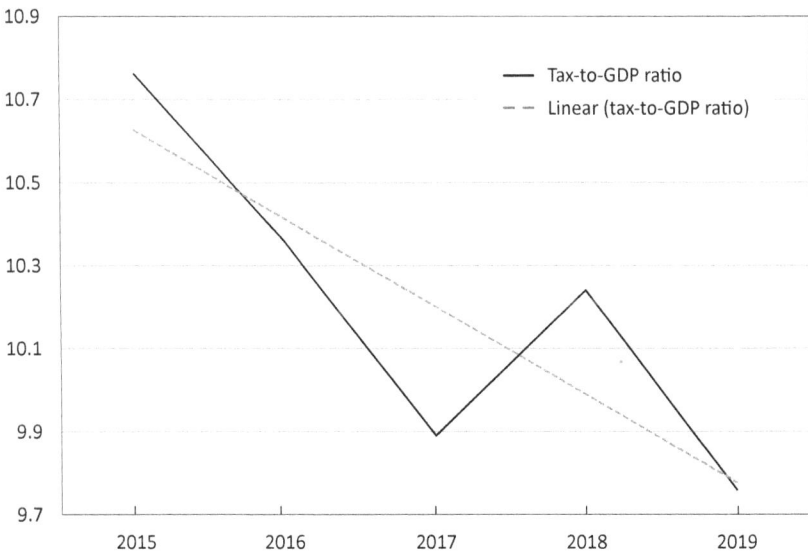

Source: Fiscal Policy Agency, Ministry of Finance.

The government has begun to address the low revenue challenges, aiming at both tax administration and policy. Major tax-law changes have been in preparation for some time. In an effort to enhance tax administration and boost compliance, the government has continued to modernise the Directorate General of Taxation through several ways: (1) improvement in the information technology (IT) system to simplify tax services and procedures as well as to enhance compliance and reduce tax evasion, (2) organisational restructuring in response to the fast changes of digital transactions and (3) staff upskilling, especially related to IT development. On the policy front, the government has sought to introduce an excise tax on plastic bags and to bring sales on digital platforms under the VAT. Another option worth considering is increasing progressivity of personal income tax. The personal income tax regime could be made fairer by adjusting tax brackets as well as raising the top income tax rate.

References

Forbes, Kristin J. and Francis E. Warnock. 2012. 'Capital flow waves: Surges, stops, flight, and retrenchment'. *Journal of International Economics* 88(2): 235–51. doi.org/10.1016/j.jinteco.2012.03.006

Frankel, Jeffrey A., Carlos A. Végh and Guillermo Vuletin. 2011. 'On graduation from fiscal procyclicality'. *NBER Working Paper* No. 17619. doi.org/10.3386/w17619

Gupta, Poonam. 2016. 'Capital flows and central banking: The Indian experience'. *World Bank Policy Research Working Paper* No. 7569. doi.org/10.1596/1813-9450-7569

IMF (International Monetary Fund). 2002. 'Assessing sustainability'. 28 May. www.imf.org/external/np/pdr/sus/2002/eng/052802.pdf

IMF (International Monetary Fund). 2020a. 'Policies to support people during the COVID-19 pandemic'. *Fiscal Monitor,* April. www.imf.org/en/Publications/FM/Issues/2020/04/06/fiscal-monitor-april-2020

IMF (International Monetary Fund). 2020b. 'A crisis like no other, an uncertain recovery'. *World Economic Outlook Update,* June. www.imf.org/en/Publications/WEO/Issues/2020/06/24/WEOUpdateJune2020

Jakarta Globe. 2019. 'Indonesia's short-term growth potential maxed out at 5.5%; reform needed: Finance minister'. *Jakarta Globe,* 16 July. https://jakartaglobe.id/context/indonesias-shortterm-growth-potential-maxed-out-at-55-reform-needed-finance-minister/

Kaminsky, Graciela L., Carmen M. Reinhart and Carlos A. Végh. 2004. 'When it rains, it pours: Procyclical capital flows and macroeconomic policies'. *NBER Working Paper* No. 10780. doi.org/10.3386/w10780

Kose, M. Ayhan, Peter Nagle, Franziska Ohnsorge and Naotaka Sugawara. 2020. 'Policies: Turning mistakes into experience'. In *Global Waves of Debt: Causes and Consequences.* Washington, DC: World Bank.

Moss, Daniel. 2020. 'Can an emerging market become a policy pioneer?' *Bloomberg*, 10 July. www.bloomberg.com/opinion/articles/2020-07-09/indonesia-s-debt-monetization-sets-a-model-for-emerging-markets?sref=q7L9NzMQ

OECD (Organisation for Economic Co-operation and Development). 2020. *OECD Economic Outlook*, June. www.oecd.org/economic-outlook/june-2020/

WHO (World Health Organization). 2020. 'Coronavirus disease 2019 (COVID-19) situation report – 94'. 23 April. https://apps.who.int/iris/handle/10665/331865

World Bank. 2015. 'High expectations'. *Indonesia Economic Quarterly*, March. Jakarta: World Bank.

World Bank. 2020a. 'The long road to recovery'. *Indonesia Economic Prospects*, July. Jakarta: World Bank.

World Bank. 2020b. *Global Economic Prospects, June 2020*. Washington, DC: World Bank. www.worldbank.org/en/publication/global-economic-prospects

5 COVID-19: Impact on the finance and delivery of local public services in Indonesia

Blane D. Lewis and Ruth Nikijuluw

Abstract

We examine the potential effects of COVID-19 on district government revenues, district and household spending, and ultimately local public service access. We find that the government forecasted decrease in economic growth and knock-on effects on central government budget revenues might lead to a 5.5 per cent decline in district intergovernmental transfer revenue, a 6.0 per cent decrease in district spending and a 7.5 per cent decrease in household spending. We estimate that the combined downturn in district and household expenditure would result in a 2 percentage point reduction in household access to local services from the projected baseline, a modest impact. We conclude that while COVID-19 may have a significant negative impact on local public services it will likely not derive from districts' reduced access to funding or lower household spending. Central government has already organised a program of conditional cash transfers to needy households and this may help dilute any negative service effects related to declining household expenditure. Some observers have argued for a large increase in intergovernmental grants to combat the adverse effects of falling district spending. We do not advocate this approach, given the longstanding ineffectiveness of districts in using their considerable fiscal resources to enhance local service delivery.

Introduction

COVID-19 continues to have severe negative health and economic impacts across the vast majority of countries in the world. Indonesia has not escaped these destructive effects. As of this writing, Indonesia has experienced 320,000 cases of COVID-19 and 11,500 related deaths. Many observers believe these figures significantly underestimate the reality. Indonesia has not yet managed to 'flatten the curve' and COVID-19 cases and associated deaths are increasing at a rapid rate. COVID-19 is expected to have a large negative effect on economic growth in 2020 and possibly beyond into 2021. The Ministry of Finance estimates that the economic growth rate in 2020 may drop to between 2.3 per cent and −0.4 per cent from about 5.0 per cent in 2019.

COVID-19 will also likely have a substantial negative impact on local public service delivery, especially in the education, health, and water and sanitation sectors. Hard data are difficult to come by at this stage, of course, but anecdotal evidence confirms the expected adverse effects. With primary and secondary schools forcibly shut down across much of the country, educators have shifted to online learning. However, according to a recent World Bank survey (Purnamasari and Sjahrir 2020), only around 40 per cent of students have access to online schooling resources. The same survey suggests that 25 per cent of households seeking care from local health centres (*puskesmas* and *posyandu*) were unable to access some commonly needed services, such as immunisations. Experience shows that as more people have become confined to their homes, household and community demand for improved water—via a local water company (*perusahaan daerah air minum*, PDAM)—rises significantly, constraining overall supply and leaving some families without their usual level of access (Palaniappan 2011). A recent study demonstrates that as many as 50 per cent of households in some parts of Indonesia are unable to wash their hands properly due to problems accessing water (Staddon et al. 2020). Finally, a new assessment by UNICEF (2020) suggests that 40 per cent of households across eighteen provinces have experienced reduced access to sanitation facilities.

What drives the apparent decrease in access to local public services? Two possible explanations immediately present themselves. First, reduced intergovernmental funding to districts has led to declining expenditures, which in turn has caused disruption to the supply of key services. Second, lower personal incomes has limited households' ability to pay for such services.

This chapter examines the effects of COVID-19 on the finance and delivery of local public services in Indonesia. We investigate both public and private financial impacts, where these relate to intergovernmental transfers and household spending, respectively. Service delivery effects focus on household access to education, health and infrastructure services.

The chapter proceeds as follows. First, we provide some background information on the geography of COVID-19 in Indonesia and the role of subnational governments in responding to the health and economic crises. Second, we review the conceptual model that provides the framework within which we conduct our empirical analysis. Third, we estimate the major impacts of COVID-19 on the model's components that ultimately drive service access effects—economic growth, central government revenues, intergovernmental transfers, and district and household spending. Fourth, we investigate the impact of these inputs on local service outputs. Fifth, we make several caveats to our analysis and indicate potential avenues for future work. Sixth, we examine several policy initiatives that government might consider with a view to mitigating the negative impact of COVID-19 on local public services. A final section concludes.

The geography of COVID-19 and the role of subnational governments

By early October 2020, COVID-19 had spread to all 34 provinces in Indonesia, with 482 out of 514 districts having recorded active cases. DKI Jakarta has the highest number of cases, accounting for more than 25 per cent of the total number nationally, followed by East Java with almost 15 per cent. Bangka Belitung Islands has the fewest cases, with less than 500. Central government, through its Task Force for Rapid Response, officially classifies regions into four different zones, from green for regions that do not have any recorded cases to red for those regions with high virus transmission. The classification also incorporates various health indicators such as surveillance and response services. The classification is updated once a week and serves as a basis for making decisions about lifting social distancing restrictions in the regions. As of this writing, there are 57, 307 and 121 districts categorised as high, moderate and low risk, respectively. About 70 per cent of districts have moderate to high risk of exposure to COVID-19.

Figure 5.1 shows the distribution of cases across districts in Indonesia as of 6 October 2020. Overall, districts in Java have recorded more cases than districts outside Java, while districts with no recorded cases are mostly concentrated in eastern Indonesia. Within island groups, there is significant variation in caseload across districts. For instance, within Papua, Mimika and Jayapura have a relatively high number of cases, while

Figure 5.1 Cumulative confirmed COVID-19 cases by district, 6 October 2020

0.0

2051.9

Source: KawalCOVID19, https://datawrapper.dwcdn.net/MwHOx/226/

Figure 5.2 Cumulative confirmed COVID-19 cases per million population by province, 8 October 2020

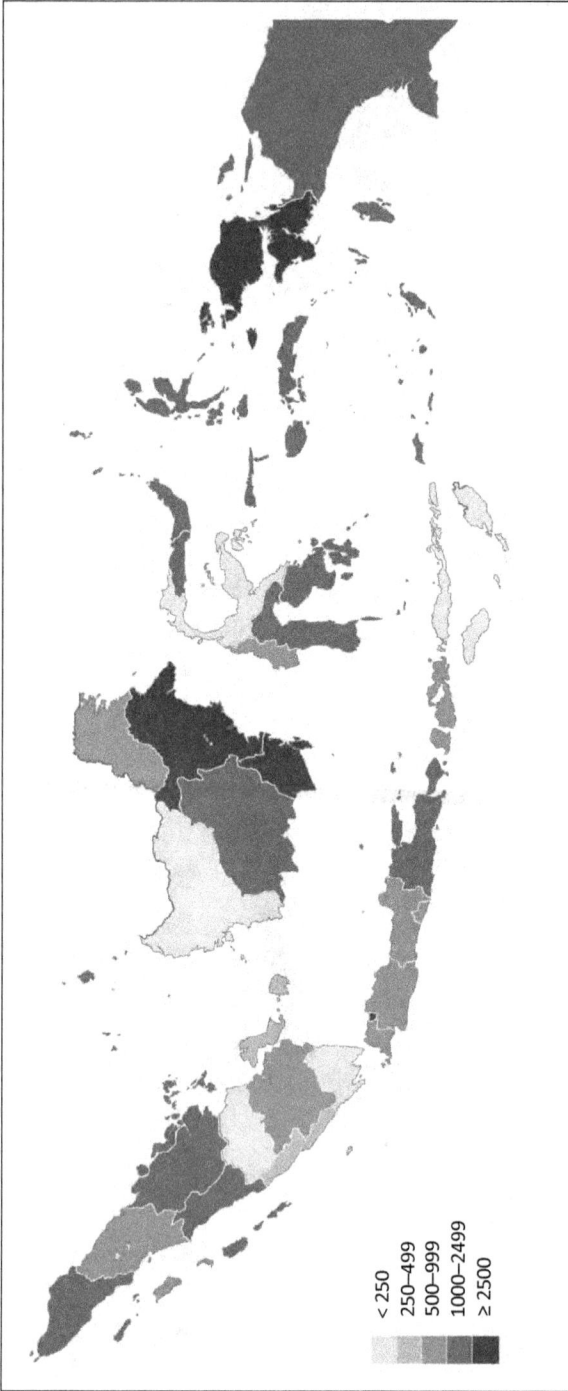

< 250
250–499
500–999
1000–2499
≥ 2500

Source: KawalCOVID19, https://commons.wikimedia.org/w/index.php?curid=90617451

some neighbouring districts recorded zero cases. Besides DKI Jakarta, Surabaya and Makassar have recorded the highest number of cases among municipalities, followed by Sidoarjo in East Java and Semarang in Central Java.

Figure 5.2 shows the distribution of confirmed cases per million persons by province as of 8 October 2020. While DKI Jakarta still has the highest number of confirmed cases per capita, provinces outside Java such as West Papua and South Kalimantan have also recorded relatively high caseloads per capita. The readiness of districts off Java to handle the crisis has been questioned. Dzakwan (2020) assesses the readiness of regions based on the number of potential COVID-19 cases and access to health services designed to mitigate the negative effects of the crisis. He finds sixteen provinces outside Java that do not have COVID-19–ready hospitals and have limited budgetary resources to deal with rising caseloads.

Subnational governments have a potentially crucial role to play in responding to the pandemic. However, the involvement of districts and provinces seems to have been discouraged to a certain extent so far by the central government (Dzakwan 2020). Subnationals may lead COVID-19 mitigation efforts, but they still need to adhere to strict national guidelines in doing so. Districts are responsible for implementing large-scale social restrictions but only after receiving approval from the Ministry of Health, for example.

Nevertheless, districts are actively involved. They have their own task forces, comprising officials from various local offices (*dinas*). These task forces monitor the implementation of health protocols and guide the overall local response to COVID-19. Community health centres (*puskesmas*) are responsible for initial screening, contact tracing and monitoring suspected cases.[1] Together with public hospitals, health centres administer rapid tests for people under tracing surveillance (*orang dalam pemantauan*, ODP). Health centre workers are also expected to educate communities about the disease and how to implement hygiene practices.

Although many of government's COVID-19 responses are initiated and managed at the centre, some programs are implemented locally. The Ministry of Finance has instructed that local fiscal policy must be reoriented to respond to the crisis (Djalante et al. 2020). In this context, villages are now reallocating some of their funds (Dana Desa) as unconditional cash transfers to households.[2]

---

1 Based on technical guidance from the Ministry of Health, http://kesmas-id.com/download/juknis-pelayanan-puskesmas-pada-masa-pandemi-covid-19/
2 The Dana Desa cash transfer will operate for six months from April 2020.

Conceptual model

Our conceptual model is illustrated in Figure 5.3. The emerging literature on the economic effects of COVID-19 frames the impact in terms of both supply and demand shocks (del Rio-Chanona et al. 2020; Guerrieri et al. 2020). Businesses are constrained by government social distancing measures or shuttered completely and output declines. This supply shock is shown in our figure by the vertical line from COVID-19 to Business. The supply shock in turn creates a demand shock. Put simply, the loss of income as a function of declining private sector activity alters household spending. This demand shock is illustrated by the horizontal line running from Business to HHEXP in the figure. Note that there is a secondary demand shock as well, whereby household expenditure is affected by loss of income due to illness or death from COVID-19 (McKibbin and Fernando 2020). Overall, household spending is expected to decline. But the structure of demand may also shift towards health services and away from all others. The supply and demand shocks lead to declining economic growth. These effects on economic growth are shown in the figure by the lines running from Business and HHEXP to gGDP. Note that the arrows on these two lines appear on both ends. This indicates that the causal relations between business activity and household income and economic growth run in both directions.

In this chapter we focus on the impact of declining GDP growth on household access to local public services. In this context, the main relations of interest are highlighted by the grey arrows in Figure 5.3. As the figure shows, there are two main transmission mechanisms for the impact of economic growth on service access. The first runs from growth through

Figure 5.3 Impact of COVID-19: Conceptual framework

gGDP	Growth of GDP	
CREV	Central government revenue	
Transfers	Intergovernmental transfers per capita	

DEXP	District expenditure per capita
HHEXP	Household expenditure per capita
Services	Household access to services

central government revenues, intergovernmental transfers, and district spending to household service access. The second mechanism operates from economic growth through household spending to service access. As before, double-ended arrows illustrate possibly simultaneous causal relations among the variables of concern. We now turn to estimating the main effects illustrated in the figure.

Estimating model inputs

Economic growth

As noted above, the Ministry of Finance estimates that the effects of COVID-19 will reduce annual economic growth in 2020 to between 2.3 per cent and −0.4 per cent, down from 5.0 per cent in 2019. This suggests that the change in economic growth rates between 2019 and 2020 may be somewhere between −2.7 and −5.4 percentage points. There are many other independent estimates of the impact of COVID-19 on growth in Indonesia. The most pessimistic estimate of economic growth in 2020 comes from the World Bank (2020), which suggests that growth may decline to −3.5 per cent. See Suryahadi et al. (2020) for a review of recent growth estimates. In the analysis below we take the Ministry of Finance's most severe case as our baseline estimate of changes to economic growth.

Central government revenues

A decline in the economic growth rate would be expected to negatively affect central government revenues. Reduced growth automatically leads to a downturn in both tax and non-tax public revenues. To gauge the effects of COVID-19 on national public revenues we examine the relevant effects for past crises in Indonesia (Table 5.1).

Table 5.1 Economic growth and central government revenue, AFC and GFC

	Asian financial crisis			Global financial crisis		
	1997	1998	Δ	2008	2009	Δ
Economic growth rate (% year on year)	4.6	−14.1	−18.7	5.8	4.5	−1.3
Government revenue (rupiah trillion)	813.8	641.8	−21.1	1,222.1	976.3	−20.1

Note: Figures are in constant 2010 terms. Δ for economic growth is the difference in growth rates. Δ for government revenue is the per cent change.

During the Asian financial crisis, economic growth declined from 4.6 per cent in 1997 to −14.1 per cent in 1998, representing a change in growth rate of −18.7 percentage points. As Table 5.1 shows, government revenues declined 21 per cent between 1997 and 1998. The global financial crisis resulted in a decline in economic growth from 5.8 per cent in 2008 to 4.5 per cent in 2009, indicating a change in growth rate of only −1.3 per cent. Nevertheless, government revenues declined by 20 per cent—nearly as much as during the Asian financial crisis.

The Ministry of Finance estimates that government revenues in 2020 will drop by about 21.5 per cent. Note that this decline in revenues is mostly a result of so-called automatic stabilisers, that is, public revenue shortfalls that derive from reduced economic activity. Some of the decline, however, is a function of government policy—income tax, import duty and VAT incentive schemes.

Intergovernmental transfers

Declining central government revenues would also be expected to lead to a reduction in intergovernmental transfers. This is because some transfers to provinces and districts are derived directly from those public revenues. Tax and non-tax transfers to regions are based on national personal income tax and natural resource revenues, respectively. The General Allocation Fund (Dana Alokasi Umum, DAU) is fixed at a minimum of 26 per cent of domestic revenues (net of those revenues already shared with regions). Currently, the government sets the DAU at 27.5 per cent of net domestic revenues. Special Autonomy Funds for Aceh, Papua and West Papua are also tied to national public revenues. Special Allocation Funds (Dana Alokasi Khusus, DAK) are the only major transfers that are not directly tied to central government revenues.

Table 5.2 shows the impact of declining revenues on transfers during the global financial crisis. As already noted, total central government revenues declined by about 20 per cent from 2008 to 2009. As shown in Table 5.2, intergovernmental transfers to provinces and districts declined 3.5 per cent between those two years. The Ministry of Finance estimates that intergovernmental transfers in total (not including village transfers—Dana Desa) will decline by 8.5 per cent in 2020 from 2019 levels. Under the assumption that transfers to districts make up slightly more than 75 per cent of the total (which is historically the case), this suggests that total transfers to districts will decline by about 6.5 per cent. In per capita terms this represents a reduction in district transfers of about 5.5 per cent (since population growth is currently estimated as around 1 per cent per annum).

Table 5.2 Government revenue and intergovernmental transfers, global financial crisis (rupiah trillion)

	2008	2009	Change (%)
Government revenue	1,222.1	976.3	−20.1
Intergovernmental transfers	345.4	333.4	−3.5

Note: Figures are in constant 2010 terms.

District spending

District revenues are dominated by intergovernmental transfers, which comprise about 90 per cent of the total on average. Not surprisingly, district spending is determined to a large extent by the transfers districts receive from central government. To determine the effect of intergovernmental transfers on district spending more precisely, we estimate the following model:

$$S_{it} = \alpha + \beta_1 T_{it} + \beta_2 X_{it} + \eta_i + \gamma_t + \varepsilon_{it} \qquad (1)$$

In equation (1) i and t represent the district and year, respectively; S is log district spending per capita; T is log district transfer revenue per capita; X is a set of exogenous covariates (log population, log population squared, poverty rate and log gross regional domestic product (GRDP) per capita); η are fixed district effects; γ are fixed time effects; ε is the usual error term; and α, β_1 and β_2 are the parameters to be estimated. β_1 represents the impact of transfers on spending, our main coefficient of interest.

On the face of it, equation (1) is a standard fixed effects model. A particular complication in the current instance is that intergovernmental transfers per capita, T, may be endogenous in the determination of district spending per capita, S, due to 'reverse causality'. Final Special Allocation Funds for Capital Spending (Dana Alokasi Khusus Fisik, DAK Fisik), which are made in three tranches over the course of the fiscal year, are a function of the extent to which various tranches are spent, for example. In order to accommodate the endogeneity of T, we estimate equation (1) by difference-generalised method of moments (diff-GMM) techniques. Diff-GMM proceeds by taking first differences of equation (1), which eliminates the fixed district effects. Moment conditions imply that second lags and beyond of T_{it} may serve as instruments for ΔT_{it}. We employ the second, third and fourth lags of T as instruments and 'collapse' them to reduce their overall number. Estimated as such, the model may be seen as a static version of the more typical dynamic panel data (DPD) model. See Roodman (2009) for a detailed discussion of estimation procedures used here.

Estimation output is provided in Table 5.3. We show estimation results from three versions of the model: ordinary least squares (OLS), fixed effects and diff-GMM. We supply the first two sets of results for reference only. Our main estimates of interest are those related to the diff-GMM model. Most importantly, the output shows that a 1 per cent increase in district transfer revenue per capita leads to a 1.1 per cent increase in district spending per capita. This estimate implies that a 5.5 per cent change in district transfers would lead to about a 6.0 per cent change in district per capita spending. The diagnostics found at the bottom of the table suggest that the null hypothesis of no second-degree autocorrelation cannot be

Table 5.3 Explaining district spending per capita, 2010–2018

Independent variable	OLS	Fixed effects	Diff-GMM
Log district transfers per capita	0.756***	0.615***	1.097***
	(0.037)	(0.044)	(0.166)
Exogenous controls	yes	yes	yes
District fixed effects	no	yes	yes
Time fixed effects	yes	yes	yes
Number of observations	4,271	4,271	4,271
Number of cross section units	–	508	508
Number of instruments	–	–	17
Diagnostics			Stat (*p* value)
Arellano-Bond test for AR(2)	–	–	–0.25 (0.803)
Hansen test of overriding restrictions	–	–	1.23 (0.540)

Note: Dependent variable is log district spending per capita. Exogenous controls include log population, log population squared, poverty rate and log GRDP per capita. OLS and fixed effects models assume all explanatory variables are exogenous. Diff-GMM model assumes that district transfers are endogenous. Instruments are constructed using three lags of endogenous variables (in levels). All fiscal and economic variables are measured in constant 2010 terms. Dashes mean 'not applicable'.

Standard errors (in parentheses) are robust. * $p < 0.1$; ** $p < 0.05$; *** $p < 0.01$.

rejected and that the null hypothesis that instruments are exogenous cannot be rejected. We also test for instrument strength and find that the instruments are sufficiently strong. We do not show these results in the table in order to save space.

Household spending

As previously mentioned, it is expected that declining economic growth would be associated with reduced household spending. To more precisely account for the relationship between changes in growth and spending by households, we use growth elasticity estimates derived by Suryahadi et al. (2020). They estimate a simple regression model for Indonesia that suggests that a 1 percentage point change in the economic growth rate is associated with a 1.4 per cent change in household spending per capita. As such, a change in the economic growth rate of −5.4 will be associated with a change in household per capita spending of approximately −7.5 per cent. We employ this estimate in our simulations of the impact of COVID-19 on service access below.

Estimating model outputs: Service delivery

Main results

We begin our examination of the impact of COVID-19 on household access to services by estimating the relationship between district and household spending and changes to service access. We define service access as the simple average of junior and senior secondary school enrolment rates, per cent of births attended by a health professional, and household access to improved water and sanitation. Underlying data are taken from the National Socioeconomic Survey (Survei Sosio-Ekonomi Nasional, Susenas).

$$\Delta O_{it} = \alpha + \beta_1 O_{it-1} + \beta_2 S_{it} + \beta_3 H_{it} + \beta_4 X_{it} + \eta_i + \gamma_t + \varepsilon_{it} \quad (2)$$

We posit the following specification:
In equation (2), i and t are district and year, as before; O is the level of service output and ΔO is the annual change in output; S is log district spending per capita; H is log household spending per capita; X are the exogenous covariates (which are the same as those used above); η are fixed district effects; γ are fixed time effects; ε is the error term; and α, β_1, β_2, β_3 and β_4 are the parameters to be estimated. β_2 and β_3 represent the impact of district and household spending on changes in service access, respectively, and these are our main coefficients of interest in this case.

A noteworthy aspect of the above model is that changes in service access are assumed to be a function of the lagged level of service access. It is expected that higher levels of lagged service access will lead to smaller current changes in access. The specification also implies that lagged service access is endogenous. District spending and household spending are also assumed to be endogenous in the determination of changes to service access as a function of reverse causality. To accommodate the endogeneity, we estimate equation (2) by diff-GMM procedures, as before. In this instance we use the first, second and third lags of lagged service access and the second, third and fourth lags of district spending and household spending as instruments.

Table 5.4 presents the results. As above we provide OLS, fixed effects and diff-GMM estimation output, where the latter represents our preferred results. The table shows that as lagged service output increases by 1 percentage point the change in service access is reduced by 0.4 percentage points. More importantly, the output implies that a 1 per cent change in district spending per capita leads to a 0.21 percentage point change in service access, and a 1 per cent change in household spending per capita results in a 0.12 percentage point change in access to services. As before, the diagnostic statistics suggest that the model is well behaved.

We now use estimated equation (1) to simulate the impact of changes to both district spending and household spending on changes to service access. But first we summarise the results so far in Table 5.5, which shows the estimated effects of COVID-19 on economic growth, central government revenues, intergovernmental transfers, district spending and household spending.

We simulate (i.e. predict) the impact of a simultaneous 6.0 per cent decrease in district spending per capita and a 7.5 per cent decline in household spending per capita on the change in annual service access based on estimated equation (2). Skeels and Taylor (2014) demonstrate that the predictor based on the use of actual values of endogenous variables in a specification of the kind we have in equation (2) is inconsistent. They suggest using predicted values of endogenous variables instead of the actual values, and that is the procedure we adopt here. More precisely, we use the estimated coefficients from equation (2); the relevant simulated values of (log) district spending per capita and (log) household spending per capita; the predicted value of endogenous lagged service access; and the actual values of all exogenous variables to predict average changes in service access. The predicted values of endogenous lagged service access are estimated from an OLS regression of the variable against all internal instruments (i.e. the various lagged variables of the endogenous

Table 5.4 Explaining changes in service access, 2010–2018

Independent variable	OLS	Fixed effects	Diff-GMM
Lagged change in service access	–	–	–0.403*** (0.078)
Log of district spending per capita	0.082 (0.219)	0.068 (0.373)	21.013** (10.693)
Log of household spending per capita	–0.570** (0.234)	2.466*** (0.891)	11.722** (4.821)
Exogenous controls	yes	yes	yes
District fixed effects	yes	yes	yes
Time fixed effects	yes	yes	yes
Number of observations	3,801	3,801	3,801
Number of cross section units	–	508	508
Number of instruments	–	–	19
Diagnostics			Stat (*p* value)
Arellano-Bond test for AR(2)	–	–	1.65 (0.098)
Hansen test of overriding restrictions	–	–	5.41 (0.493)

Note: Dependent variable is annual change in service access index. Exogenous controls include log population, log population squared, poverty rate and log GRDP per capita. OLS and fixed effects models assume all explanatory variables are exogenous. Diff-GMM model assumes that lagged service access, district spending and household spending are endogenous. Instruments are constructed using three lags of endogenous variables (in levels). All fiscal and economic variables are measured in constant 2010 terms. Dashes mean 'not applicable'.

Standard errors (in parentheses) are robust. * $p < 0.1$; ** $p < 0.05$; *** $p < 0.01$.

variables, as described above) and the exogenous variables. The results of the simulation are presented in Table 5.6.

In the table, the baseline is the actual average annual change in household access to services drawn from the data over the 2010–2018 period. The estimated baseline is the predicted value of average changes in service access based on the simulation model, where predicted values of all endogenous variables are used instead of actual values and actual values are employed for all exogenous covariates. As Table 5.6 shows, these estimates of percentage point changes in service access are close— 1.83 and 1.84 for the former and latter, respectively. We present these

Table 5.5 COVID-19 effects, 2020

Variable	Effect
Economic growth rate	−5.4
Central government revenues	−21.5
Transfers per capita	−5.5
District spending per capita	−6.0
Household spending per capita	−7.5

Note: Effect for economic growth rate is the percentage point change in the rate of growth. Effects for all other variables represent per cent changes.

Table 5.6 Impact of COVID-19 on household service access, annual change

Baseline	Baseline, estimated	Impact, estimated	Difference
1.83	1.84	−0.37	−2.21
(0.059)	(0.165)	(0.165)	−

Note: Numbers are percentage point changes in service access. Figures in parentheses are standard errors.

results only to inspire confidence in model simulations that follow. The simulated impact of a simultaneous 6.0 per cent decrease in district spending per capita and a 7.5 per cent decline in household spending per capita, using the procedure outlined in the previous paragraph, is −0.37, indicating a slight percentage point reduction in household service access. The difference between the estimated baseline and the simulated impact is −2.2 percentage points.

Heterogeneity

It is worth emphasising the fact that the above analysis provides an estimate of the average impact of COVID-19 on household service access across all districts. However, there is likely to be some nontrivial heterogeneity of those effects across regions of the country. Differential impacts across districts on and off Java may be substantial, for example. Such heterogeneity is difficult to estimate with any precision. In order to rigorously examine the heterogeneity we would need to have separate estimates of the impact of COVID-19 on economic growth on Java and off

Java and some indication of the subsequent effects on transfers, district spending and household spending on Java and off Java districts as well. We do not have such estimates.

The best we can do is to estimate the differential impact of COVID-19 on service access on and off Java under the assumption that the initial effects of the crisis on economic growth, intergovernmental transfers, and district and household spending are consistent across regions. Given these assumptions we can then estimate equation (2) separately for districts on and off Java and simulate the differential impacts on service access. Table 5.7 provides the results.

For districts on Java the estimated baseline annual change in service access is 1.5 percentage points. The estimated annual change in access under COVID-19 is −0.4 percentage points, implying a differential effect of 1.9 percentage points. For districts off Java the estimated baseline change is 1.9 percentage points and the estimated change under COVID-19 is 0.2 percentage points, indicating a differential impact of 1.7 percentage points. These estimates suggest that the impact of COVID-19 may be greater for districts on Java compared to districts off Java but that the magnitude of difference in effects across the two regions is insubstantial.

Table 5.7 Impact of COVID-19 on annual household service access, Java and off Java

	Java	Off Java
Baseline	1.52 (0.083)	1.94 (0.073)
Baseline, estimated	1.53 (0.188)	1.93 (0.160)
Impact, estimated	−0.36 (0.188)	0.21 (0.160)
Difference	−1.89	−1.72

Note: Numbers are percentage point changes in service access. Figures in parentheses are standard errors.

Caveats

In carrying out our analysis we have adopted several simplifying assumptions. Such assumptions may call into question the validity of our results. We now review three of the most important simplifying assumptions and indicate how they may have affected our results.

Provinces

We have focused our analysis of the impact of COVID-19 on service access among districts. This is appropriate for the most part since the locus of public service delivery is found at the district level. Nevertheless, provinces do, in fact, have some responsibility for key public services. Provinces are now responsible for senior secondary school. Provinces have authority over regional hospitals. And provinces are responsible for the development of cross-district infrastructure, as well. Although we cannot specifically quantify the impact of declining provincial government and household spending on provincial service delivery, it is safe to assume that the impact will add to the negative effects felt at the district level.

Own-source revenues

In our examination of district spending we focused specifically on the influence of intergovernmental transfers. We did not examine own-source revenues as a potential determinant of spending. In some preliminary regression analyses we found that the impact of own-source revenues on district spending was not statistically significant and so we dropped the variable from the investigation. That own-source revenues do not seem to assist in the determination of district spending may be a function of the relative unimportance of such revenues in district budgets. Own sources make up only 10 per cent of total revenues on average.

However, the importance of own-source revenues varies significantly across districts. The share of own-source taxes and charges in local revenue budgets ranges from around only 4 per cent to over 75 per cent. Table 5.8 lists the top twenty districts ranked according to their own-source revenue shares. It might be the case that own-source revenues are important determinants of spending for those districts in which own sources are relatively significant in budgets.

The table highlights two main points. First, districts with high shares of own-source revenues are predominately urban. Thirteen of the twenty places are *kota* (cities) and most of the others are heavily urbanised *kabupaten* (districts). Property tax revenues and hotel and restaurant sales taxes are especially important for these urbanised places. Badung is a possible exception in terms of the degree of urbanisation but it has substantial own-source revenues from tourism.

Second, high share own-source revenue districts are for the most part located on Java. Eighteen of the districts listed are on Java. The two exceptions are Batam (Riau Islands) and Medan (North Sumatra). Own-source revenues in these places are likely to decrease significantly given COVID-19. People are not paying their property taxes. Hotel and restaurant sales are down significantly. Tourism has declined precipitously. To the extent that own-source revenues are important determinants of spending for these districts we would expect spending to decline as well and this would have negative effects for public service delivery in those districts. This offers some additional support for the argument made above that the negative impact of the ongoing crisis on local service delivery may be especially strong for districts on Java.

Table 5.8 Share of own-source revenues in total budgets

Rank	OSR share	District	Province
1	77.2	Kab. Badung	Bali
2	57.8	Kota Surabaya	East Java
3	45.6	Kota Tangerang Selatan	Banten
4	44.3	Kota Denpasar	Bali
5	43.1	Kab. Tangerang	Banten
6	41.4	Kota Tangerang	Banten
7	40.0	Kab. Sidoarjo	East Java
8	39.1	Kab. Gresik	East Java
9	38.3	Kab. Bekasi	West Java
10	37.9	Kota Batam	Riau Islands
11	36.5	Kota Bandung	West Java
12	35.4	Kota Medan	North Sumatra
13	35.1	Kota Semarang	Central Java
14	34.0	Kota Cilegon	Banten
15	33.7	Kota Bekasi	West Java
16	33.2	Kab. Bogor	West Java
17	32.8	Kota Yogyakarta	Yogyakarta
18	31.6	Kota Depok	West Java
19	31.3	Kab. Gianyar	Bali
20	31.0	Kota Sukabumi	West Java

Note: OSR share is own-source revenues as a per cent of total revenues. Kab. means Kabupaten.

Public service quality

Our investigation in this paper has focused on the impact of COVID-19 on service access. Due to a lack of data we have not been able to examine the effects of the crisis on service quality. The potential impact of COVID-19 on local service quality is not immediately clear. Most research on Indonesia suggests that district and household spending is less strongly tied to service quality than it is to service access. As such, we might anticipate that any crisis-driven decline in district or household spending might not have a profoundly negative effect on service quality.

Other channels may be quite important in this context, however. The quality of education, already suspect in Indonesia, may further suffer as schools shift to online learning. And as the attention of healthcare workers in local health centres and hospitals turns to COVID-19 patients, the quality of care related to other health issues may deteriorate. These examples suggest that nonpecuniary effects of the crisis are likely to be more important in determining service quality. While the impacts cannot be quantified, they are likely to be negative and substantial.

Government policy responses

How might central government mitigate the negative impact of COVID-19 on local service delivery? Government already has plans to expand on its program of conditional cash transfers and this may help ease adverse service delivery effects related to the potential downturn in household spending. Apart from conditional cash transfers, several options present themselves.

Government could decide, for example, to increase intergovernmental transfers, either to all regions or to those places that are particularly hard hit by the crisis. We would argue that this is probably not a good idea for four reasons. First, expanding transfers over current levels would require government to run a higher deficit. The deficit is already expected to be 6.3 per cent of GDP and raising it would probably not be fiscally prudent. Second, it is not obvious that government would be able to figure out which districts need additional support and how much. It is one thing to assume that districts on Java are likely to be harder hit by the crisis, it is another to determine exactly which districts need more funds and how much those additional funds should be. A related point is that providing extra grants to only some districts implies a facility with asymmetric approaches to decentralisation that government has not so far demonstrated. Third, many district governments have significant fiscal reserves on which they could draw. If ever there were a 'rainy day'—the purpose to which such funds are meant to be put—it is now. Fourth, district have not in general demonstrated that they are able to use their transfers efficiently. Governance issues abound at the district level and those conditions suggest that any additional funding from central government may well be abused.

Perhaps a better idea would be for central government to offer loans to districts. A crisis loan program has several attractive features. First, lending money, even at possibly subsidised rates, would be significantly cheaper for government than granting additional funds. Second, the approach would place the onus on districts to decide which among them need supplementary funds and how much they would require. Third, a loan program might be expected to instil some fiscal discipline in districts, a capability sorely lacking at present. Finally, a regional loan facility is already in place—the Regional Infrastructure Development Fund. While crisis loans would not be for infrastructure necessarily, loan procedures already in place might be relatively easily adapted. There are many things that would need to be worked out of course—terms and conditions of loans, among others—but the idea would seem to have at least some merit.

It might be useful to note that other, more modern economies have advocated for additional grant funds for subnationals—not loans—to address fiscal problems related to the COVID-19 crisis (McNichol et al. 2020). Our proposal here is not meant to argue with those propositions for those countries. But conditions in Indonesia are significantly different from those found in such places and what is good for the latter may not necessarily be the right approach for Indonesia.

Conclusions

We examine the potential effects of COVID-19 on district revenues, district and household spending, and ultimately access to local public services—education, health and infrastructure. We find that the government forecasted decrease in economic growth and the negative knock-on effects on central government budget revenue might lead to a 5.5 per cent decrease in district intergovernmental transfer revenue per capita, a 6.0 per cent decline in district spending per capita and a 7.5 per cent decline in household spending per capita. We estimate that the combined downturn in district and household spending would subsequently result in an approximate 2 percentage point reduction in access to local public services from the projected baseline. We also find that the negative impact of the crisis on local service delivery may be more acutely felt among districts on Java than places elsewhere, but only slightly so.

The magnitude of the average service delivery impact does not seem particularly sizeable. The muted effects derive for the most part from the relationship between district and household spending on one hand and local public service access on the other. That is, although district and household spending are statistically significant determinants of service access, the causal effects are not substantively large. Ironically perhaps, inefficient district government spending and the rather weak linkage between household spending and public services both help to constrain the negative impact of the crisis on service delivery. This points to the relative importance of more structural factors—initial conditions, population size, poverty rates, the level and structure of economic activity, and a variety of fixed effects (as well as time varying unobservables)—in determining local service delivery outcomes. Put simply: while COVID-19 may have a significant negative impact on local public services it will likely not derive from districts' reduced access to fiscal resources or lower household spending.

Central government has already organised a program of conditional cash transfers to needy households and this may help to further dilute any negative service effects related to declining household expenditure. Although some observers have advocated an increase in intergovernmental grants to regions to combat the adverse impact of falling district spending on service access, we argue that this may not be a good idea. We suggest that all things considered a limited program of district loans might be a more appropriate approach to cover any shortfalls in funding beyond those which districts themselves could cover by drawing down on their reserves.

References

del Rio-Chanona, R. Maria, Penny Mealy, Anton Pichler, François Lafond and J. Doyne Farmer. 2020. 'Supply and demand shocks in the COVID-19 pandemic: An industry and occupation perspective'. *Oxford Review of Economic Policy* 36(Supp. 1): S94–137. doi.org/10.1093/oxrep/graa033

Djalante, Riyanti, Jonatan Lassa, Davin Setiamarga, Aruminingsih Sudjatma, Mochamad Indrawan, Budi Haryanto, Choirul Mahfud, et al. 2020. 'Review and analysis of current responses to COVID-19 in Indonesia: Period of January to March 2020'. *Progress in Disaster Science* 6(100091). doi.org/10.1016/j.pdisas.2020.100091

Dzakwan, Muhammad Habib Abiyan. 2020. 'Memetakan kesiapan pemerintah daerah dalam menangani COVID-19'. *CSIS Commentaries* DMRU-027. Jakarta. https://csis.or.id/publications/memetakan-kesiapan-pemerintah-daerah-dalam-menangani-covid-19

Guerrieri, Veronica, Guido Lorenzoni, Ludwig Straub and Iván Werning. 2020. 'Macroeconomic implications of COVID-19: Can negative supply shocks cause demand shortages?' *NBER Working Paper* No. 26918. doi.org/10.3386/w26918

McKibbin, Warwick J. and Roshen Fernando. 2020. 'The global macroeconomic impacts of COVID-19: Seven scenarios'. *CAMA Working Paper* No. 19/2020. doi.org/10.2139/ssrn.3547729

McNichol, Elizabeth, Michael Leachman and Joshuah Marshall. 2020. 'States need significantly more fiscal relief to slow the emerging deep recession'. Center on Budget and Policy Priorities, 14 April. www.cbpp.org/research/state-budget-and-tax/states-need-significantly-more-fiscal-relief-to-slow-the-emerging-deep

Palaniappan, Meena. 2011. 'Sustainability of supply: The story of community water associations (HIPPAMs) in Malang'. International Water and Communities Initiative, Pacific Institute. www2.pacinst.org/topics/international_water_communities/notes_from_the_field/sustainability_of_supply.htm

Purnamasari, Ririn and Bambang Suharnoko Sjahrir. 2020. 'High-frequency monitoring of socio-economic impact of COVID-19 on households in Indonesia'. World Bank presentation, ANU Indonesia Project Global Seminar Series, 30 September. www.youtube.com/watch?v=4DYck8WOLxk

Roodman, David. 2009. 'How to do xtabond2: An introduction to difference and system GMM in Stata'. *Stata Journal* 9(1): 86–136. doi.org/10.1177/1536867X0900900106

Skeels, Christopher L. and Larry W. Taylor. 2014. 'Prediction after IV estimation'. *Economics Letters* 122(3): 420–22. doi.org/10.1016/j.econlet.2014.01.003

Staddon, C., M. Everard, J. Mytton, T. Octavianti, W. Powell, N. Quinn, S.M.N. Uddin, et al. 2020. 'Water insecurity compounds the global coronavirus crisis'. *Water International* 45(5): 416–22. doi.org/10.1080/02508060.2020.1769345

Suryahadi, Asep, Ridho Al Izzati and Daniel Suryadarma. 2020. 'Estimating the impact of COVID-19 on poverty in Indonesia'. *Bulletin of Indonesian Economic Studies* 56(2): 175–92. doi.org/10.1080/00074918.2020.1779390

UNICEF. 2020. 'Indonesia COVID-19 response situation report'. 13 August – 9 September. www.unicef.org/documents/indonesia-covid-19-situation-report-9-september-2020

World Bank. 2020. *East Asia and Pacific in the Time of COVID-19.* East Asia and Pacific Economic Update, April 2020. Washington, DC: World Bank. doi.org/10.1596/978-1-4648-1565-2

6 The labour market shock and policy responses to the coronavirus pandemic[1]

Chris Manning

Abstract

Like in the Asian financial crisis of 1998, many jobs have been lost during the first year of COVID-19, especially for young people locked out of the labour market. The informal sector seems to have been hit much harder than during the Asian financial crisis, partly because of mobility restrictions and lockdowns. So too have industries heavily dependent on international markets, such as tourism and labour-intensive manufacturing, while non-tradeable transport and construction have also suffered badly. Nonetheless, despite the severity of COVID-19, the Indonesian economy and labour market are doing better than several more globally networked countries in Southeast Asia. Extensive use of the internet has facilitated work from home and skills development, such as through the new Kartu Prakerja (Pre-employment Card). The Unified Database has facilitated government help for the poor, despite delays in disbursals. However, the wide geographic spread of COVID-19 and its effect on labour supply makes support for jobs costly and uneven. Although off to a rocky start in October 2020, reforms seeking to promote investment and employment in the omnibus law Cipta Kerja have the potential to create better jobs during the recovery if managed more wisely.

1 The author appreciates the very helpful comments made by Hal Hill, Sudarno Sumarto and Melissa Wells on an earlier draft of the chapter. The normal disclaimers apply.

Introduction

In the first six months of 2020 the spread of COVID-19 was already a severe setback to labour markets in countries across the globe (IMF 2020a). Indonesia has not been spared, with gross domestic product (GDP) growth declining by a huge 5.3 per cent in the second quarter of 2020. Measures to control the spread of COVID-19—social distancing, lockdowns and restrictions on mobility—that were introduced from April to June 2020, had significant effects on economic activity, which have been reflected in job and labour incomes.

In this chapter I explore Indonesia's labour market adjustments in the first eight months of 2020, covering the six-month period from March to August when COVID-19 spread across the country. It is clear that the impact of COVID-19 on jobs and hours of work—and hence on labour earnings—was already severe in the period of large-scale social restrictions (*pembatasan sosial berskala besar*, PSBB) from March to June 2020, even though the database for evaluating these effects on labour is slim. Analysis of labour market effects depends mainly on forecasts, rapid appraisals and news reports. Rapid appraisal data suggest that at least one-quarter of breadwinners had lost their jobs by May 2020 (Purnamasari and Sjahrir 2020). A larger share, probably around half, were either stood down (*dirumahkan*) or suffered a cut in wages and benefits. The situation was still serious but had improved significantly under the 'new normal' by July–August in most sectors.[2]

Like in many other countries, the Indonesian government has been grappling to control the social and economic effects of the virus, by providing social assistance for the poor and laid-off workers, while at the same time keeping the economy afloat. And like in many other developing countries (Chan 2020), this tension has been especially evident in the capital city, the epicentre of the virus. Compared with previous economic crises, more attention has been given to job and labour incomes in micro, small and medium enterprises (MSMEs) that have been hit hard by the slump in output. I also examine how the central government has responded to the challenge of large-scale job losses, using programs like the Kartu Prakerja (Pre-employment Card) introduced in 2020, one of the few new government programs seeking to intervene directly to support job creation and training.

---

2 For example, World Bank monitoring found that around 70 per cent of those who had lost jobs were back at work in the same job by late July or early August (Purnamasari and Sjahrir 2020).

The next section discusses some of the potential labour market effects of national disasters such as epidemics and pandemics. I then look at various estimates of the impact of the crisis on the labour market in Indonesia through to the last quarter of 2020. Besides reporting on estimates of the impact of COVID-19 on employment, it is also possible to identify which workers are likely to be most affected by both the economic slowdown and government restrictions associated with the health crisis. I next look briefly at government policies and their effectiveness in helping displaced workers and creating more jobs. The chapter closes with some concluding comments on labour market challenges in the near term and post COVID-19.

Economic crises, epidemics and labour market adjustment

What does historical and comparative experience suggest will be the main effects of COVID-19 on the labour market? Three points seem particularly relevant. First, there is no single indicator that one can rely on to evaluate the impact of COVID-19 on labour markets. During recessions, unemployment is more relevant as the main indicator of labour market difficulties in urbanised environments and in more developed countries. But even there it is not the only or maybe even the leading indicator of labour market stress (ILO 2020b; OECD 2009). In many countries, the phenomenon of workers being stood down, forced to work part-time, or even forced to withdraw from the labour market altogether has been found to be equally if not more significant, especially during health crises.[3] Cutting back on hours worked and involuntary part-time work during such recessions is typically most common in the informal sector, which is a large part of the economy (World Bank 2010). The connection between poverty and underemployment may well be stronger than with unemployment, which is mainly associated with the search for formal sector jobs (ILO 2020b).[4]

Second, economy-wide effects from epidemics and their implications for labour markets extend well beyond the direct effects in highly exposed industries like tourism. Lee and McKibbin's (2004) analysis to the international impact of the SARS epidemic in 2003 focuses on three sets

---

3   The necessity to stay at home and look after older family members or children doing teleschooling has a disproportionate effect on females in most societies, especially if they are already secondary earners in the household.

4   See, for example, Frankenberg et al. (1999) and Skoufias and Suryahadi (1999) for discussions of the relationship between real wages and poverty in Indonesia during the economic crisis in 1998.

of influences: the capacity of governments to compensate for a decline in consumer demand in industries directly affected by the crisis; the ability to counter falls in business confidence, measured by movements in risk premiums and inflows of foreign direct investment; and increased costs associated with disease prevention in tourism, transport and related industries. Given increased costs, companies are likely to adjust their labour costs by reducing employment and adopting other labour-saving strategies (see below).

Third, the effects of the virus are likely to differ across industries and population subgroups. Older and secondary earners may not only lose their jobs but also subsequently withdraw from the workforce (Lee and Cho 2016). Similar, more damaging, effects are experienced by younger people who have been laid off, and who also lose a belief in their capacity to move into new jobs (ILO and ADB 2020; OECD 2009). Young people are particularly at risk because they often work part-time in vulnerable industries and jobs and are likely to find it harder to get back into the labour market. Educational pathways are disrupted as well during crises, and the transition from school to work becomes more difficult (ILO and ADB 2020: 7–19; IMF 2020b: 66).

The shake-up in jobs can also have a disproportionate impact across sociodemographic classes. For example, the digital revolution and shift to 'Industry 4.0' will almost certainly accelerate as a result of new patterns of telework and make it more difficult for many older, less-educated persons to return to their former jobs. The multitude of digitised new services can be expected to be taken up by younger and more educated people.

Slower economic growth, shutdowns and employment

Given the breadth of the shock from COVID-19, how might we characterise the Indonesian labour market's capacity to adjust? It is almost certainly less flexible than the less-regulated labour market of the Soeharto years. But it is not as rigid today as some might think. In 1998, during the Asian financial crisis, the gap in earnings and worker characteristics between the formal and informal sector was large, and the informal sector provided around three times more jobs (Manning 1998). Thus it is not surprising that the informal sector absorbed a lot of the labour market pressure (Jellinek and Rustanto 1999). By 2020 the situation was much changed after the passing of the comprehensive labour code in 2003 (Law No. 13/2003 on Manpower). After a period of sluggishness, the formal sector expanded rapidly (Pratomo and Manning 2020). While formal sector jobs have suffered across Indonesia, especially in and around the major cities, the informal sector has also been hit hard by this present crisis.

Estimates of the national effects

While commentators frequently refer to Indonesia's 'employment problem', jobs' growth had in fact been quite rapid in the years leading up to the pandemic. Thus, for example, in February 2020, unemployment was already at record lows for both females and males in the *reformasi* era (5.0 per cent and 6.4 per cent, respectively). While it is true that both unemployment and underemployment had been moderately high in Indonesia by regional standards before COVID-19, both had declined almost continuously over nearly two decades prior to the spread of the virus (Figure 6.1).[5] Typically, as in many other developing countries, underemployment had been higher than unemployment, especially among females and in agriculture. But as the formal sector expanded, underemployment has fallen more quickly, associated with sustained economic growth and structural change (Rosenthal 2020).

That situation changed after February 2020. To assess the overall effect of COVID-19, I fall back on estimates from forecasts and surveys by the government and other research bodies undertaken in the first half of 2020.[6] The chapter looks briefly at the results of four studies which suggest the negative effects for employment have been significant, although probably less severe than that experienced by several neighbouring countries. First, one Asian Development Bank forecast estimates that employment losses were likely to be visible but moderate in most ASEAN countries, including Indonesia during 2020, compared with the non-COVID baseline (Figure 6.2). If the virus was brought under control quickly (i.e. 'short' containment), employment has been estimated to contract by 2.5 per cent in Indonesia in 2020 compared with the non-COVID baseline. This is a similar percentage to the projected decline in Malaysia and Thailand but below the 4.2 per cent fall projected for all of ASEAN; it is below the much higher 10.8 and 7.7 per cent contractions estimated for the more globally exposed Cambodia and Vietnam.

However, the Asian Development Bank also finds that a longer (and more likely) period of containment—a 'U' rather than a 'V' shaped recovery—would mean a 3.9 per cent loss of jobs affecting 4.4 million workers in Indonesia. Based on participation rates recorded in February 2020 in Indonesia, this is equivalent to a well over 50 per cent increase in the number of unemployed to over 11 million or a total national

---

5   Underemployment is measured by the proportion of workers that are engaged less than 35 hours a week and are willing to take on more work.

6   The latest National Labour Force Survey was conducted too early in the year (February 2020) to provide any insights into the effects of the pandemic in Indonesia.

Figure 6.1 Unemployment and underemployment in Indonesia, 2004–2020 (%)

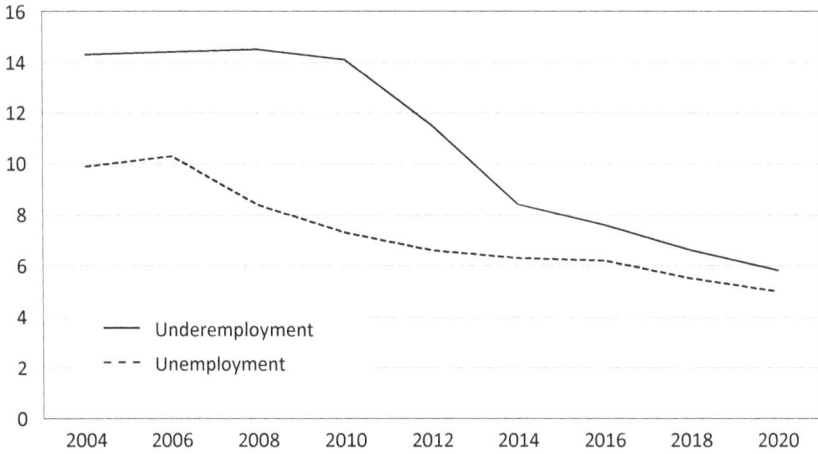

Source: Data are for the August round of the National Labour Force Survey, except for 2020, which are taken from the February round.

Figure 6.2 Projections of employment growth in selected ASEAN countries, May 2020 (% change)*

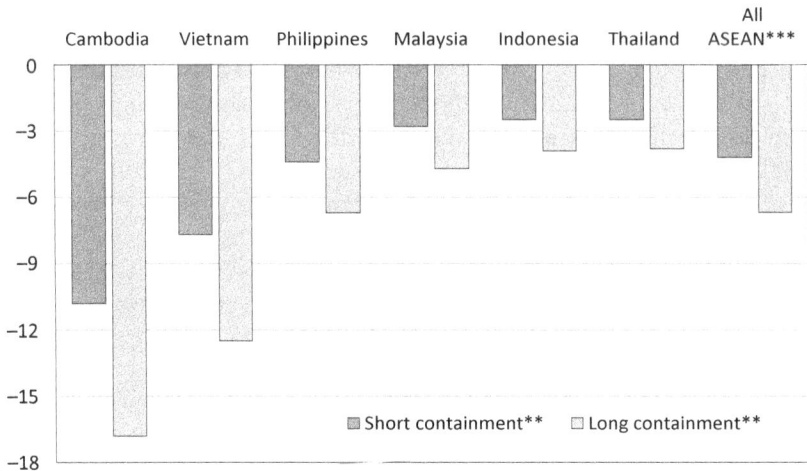

* Outcome under COVID-19 compared with a non-COVID base figure.
** A shorter V-shaped recovery versus a longer U-shaped recovery.
*** Data are for all ten ASEAN countries.

Source: Based on GTAP analysis of the economic effects of COVID-19, see ADB (2020).

unemployment rate of around 8 per cent in 2020. Nationally, Indonesia's unemployment rate would be back to where it was more than a decade earlier (2008), at the end of President Yudhoyono's first term.[7]

The 8 per cent figure may be an upper bound to joblessness this year, given current (mid-2020) trends. Some people who suffer unemployment will move into temporary work in self-employed and family enterprises, as they did during the economic crisis of 1998. This time around, however, the absolute and relative numbers of workers whose incomes will be adversely affected in the short term is likely to be larger. During the first lockdown, social distancing and mobility restrictions directly reduced informal sector activities that, under normal circumstances, are undertaken in a wide variety of physical and social environments. For example, Octavia (2020: 3) identifies street food vendors, tradespeople own-account operators, and online motorcycle and car drivers in Jakarta as experiencing significant (up to 80 per cent) falls in income during the early stages of the pandemic in April 2020. In addition, youth may be particularly vulnerable in Indonesia. Data from the International Labour Organization and Asian Development Bank indicate that the gap in unemployment rates between youth and adults is large compared with neighbouring countries. Young people recorded rates of around 15–20 per cent unemployment compared with 3–4 per cent for adults in Indonesia in the second half of 2019 and early 2020 (ILO and ADB 2020: 10).

The second study is an International Labour Organization survey of just under 600 enterprises in April 2020 that corroborates these findings, especially among small and micro enterprises (ILO 2020a). Two-thirds of enterprises had shut down temporarily or permanently, almost all faced cash flow problems and well over half had stood down or retrenched workers. But, paradoxically, many enterprises also faced difficulties in meeting demand for their products. The lockdown prevented many employees from reporting for work. Thus in the early stages of spread of the virus, informal work in these small enterprises in the cities was unlikely to have acted to the same extent as a 'sponge' for displaced industrial workers as it had during the economic crisis in 1997–1998 (Manning 2000).

A third source on employment effects is from data collected regularly by the World Bank to help guide policy during the crisis. This provides further evidence on the characteristics of those losing jobs or work during

---

7   National unemployment was recorded at 8.5 per cent in August 2008 but has declined continuously since then.

COVID-19.[8] It suggests that workers most affected were concentrated in manufacturing, construction and transport. Job losses were most likely associated with social distancing and the cutback in government projects during the first wave of infections that concentrated in and around the capital city in April–May 2020. Other studies indicate that the effects in labour-intensive sectors in manufacturing have been quite large: for example, garment exports fell by over half in May 2020 and domestic sales fell by 74 per cent in the same month. This occurred in an industry that employs 5.2 million workers or around 3–5 per cent of the total industrial workforce in large and medium enterprises (Pane and Pasaribu 2020).

Regionally, the World Bank data indicate that the effects were greatest in Jakarta and elsewhere in Java and less intensive in most outer island areas in the early lockdown period in May 2020. Given stricter social distancing in Jakarta, labour-intensive industries can be expected to have been hit particularly hard, as has the transport industry (trains, buses and motorcycle taxis), which ferried hundreds of thousands of commuters into the city each normal working day.[9]

Gender effects have also been significant. The Australian Women's Working Futures Project conducted a survey of the impact of COVID-19 on private sector employees (300 men and 300 women) and reports different outcomes by gender in relation to hours worked, incomes, productivity and place of work (Hill et al. 2020: 5–8):

- More women than men reported a reduction in working hours, while twice as many men as women experienced a cut in wages.

- More women than men reported working from home and more men reported working from their regular place of work.

- More women than men reported they were equally or more productive during COVID-19, and more men than women reported being less productive during COVID-19 on account of an increase in domestic work.

In summary, the surveys suggest that employment effects were large both for wage employees and MSMEs during the main lockdown period of March–June 2020, even if they were not especially great in relative terms in the ASEAN context. And working at home had become particularly

---

8   Based on the first round of a World Bank panel phone monitoring survey conducted in May 2020 (World Bank 2020).

9   However, the difference between regions in jobs lost had almost disappeared by July–August 2020 when the World Bank conducted its third wave of high-frequency monitoring of COVID-19 impacts. The longer-term impact on Jakarta may not be as severe as originally anticipated.

important among females, although it impacted more on the productivity of males.

Employment implications of the industry growth rates in 2020

Sectors that have suffered the largest falls in output provide a clue as to which sociodemographic groups are likely to have borne the main brunt of slowdown on jobs, and may also suffer most in the second half of 2020. The following estimates focus on the second quarter, year on year, growth in output and potential impacts on employment across major industries, as COVID-19 began spreading in Indonesia in the first half of 2020.[10]

The details shown in Table 6.1 help us reflect on the potential magnitude and nature of job losses. Declines in output were very large (20–30 per cent) in transport, and hotels and restaurants, and quite big (5–8 per cent) in the sizeable trade and manufacturing sectors over the 12-month period July 2019 to June 2020. It is no surprise that the decline in output was greatest in transport and hospitality. Both were affected directly and indirectly by restrictions on mobility, shutdowns and social distancing that were applied most intensively to the Greater Jakarta region in April and May 2020, and which only began to be relaxed in June 2020.

Subsector effects tell a big part of the story: accommodation (covering hotels, guesthouses and home-stay) and air transport both registered by far the largest decline in output (just under 50 per cent and 80 per cent, respectively) among subsectors. Both were hugely affected by the slump in tourism, as numbers of foreign and domestic visitors plummeted in the first half of 2020.[11] The effects were likely to be especially large in urban areas, and not only among employees in transport companies like Garuda but also among informal sector workers serving the tourist industry—for example, drivers, travel agents, guides and souvenir sellers.

Second, although the decline in output was not so marked in trade and manufacturing, the employment effects were likely to be substantial since these industries are two of the largest employers in Indonesia. Meanwhile four industries, including the large catch-all 'other' services industries (including many government employees) were less affected. Not surprisingly, the relatively small information and communications

---

10 The distribution of employment across sociodemographic groups in August 2019 acts as a benchmark for calculating the potential impact on jobs.

11 The number of foreign tourists nearly halved over the first six months of 2020 after Indonesia closed its borders to foreign visitors in early April. By July the flow had virtually stopped. Bali and Yogyakarta, the two major tourist destinations, were two of the three provinces recording negative economic growth rates in the first quarter of 2020 (Aditya 2020).

Table 6.1 GDP growth by industry and the potential impact on urban and informal jobs, Indonesia, 2017–2020

Industry	Share of GDP (%)	Share of jobs (%)	Growth of output (% p.a.)*			% jobs urban**	% of jobs in the IFS**
			2017–18	2018–19	**2019–20**		
Transport	3	4	9	6	**−31**	73	59
Accommodation and restaurants	2	7	6	6	**−22**	74	68
Trade and repairs	13	**19**	5	5	**−8**	67	66
Manufacturing	20	**15**	4	4	**−6**	66	35
Electricity and gas	1	1	8	2	**−5**	74	35
Construction	10	7	6	6	**−5**	57	49
Mining	7	1	3	−1	**−3**	41	36
Other services***	19	**19**	6	7	**−2**	69	16
Agriculture	14	**27**	5	5	**2**	20	87
Information and communications	6	1	5	10	**11**	85	30
All industries	100	100	5.3	5.1	**−5.3**	55	56
	Rp 2590 trillion	Rp 126.6 million					

* Year on year growth, June quarter.

** August 2019. Formal sector workers consist of employers and employees with regular wage jobs; all other workers are defined as informal (all self employed, casual workers and family workers).

*** Government, business, community and personal services.

Source: GDP data from national accounts (CEIC); jobs data from Sakernas, August 2019.

sector recorded significant increases in sales, most likely due to the spread of online businesses in education, health and other service delivery, as COVID-19 intensified.

The data in Table 6.1 suggest that industries employing a high proportion of informal workers were just as vulnerable to COVID-19 as industries with a more formalised employment structure. Informal-sector workers are more heavily represented in three of the four industries mentioned above, where growth rates have been most affected. The trade and repair sector stands out with two-thirds of workers employed informally (see last column, Table 6.1). Hotels and restaurants are also conspicuous as major employers of informal workers.

Several other sets of worker characteristics—gender, age and education—were also examined across industries (Figure 6.3). The data suggest that females could be particularly hard hit if the current rates of decline in output continue and if job losses are distributed reasonably evenly according to the current balance by gender in each industry. Females accounted for close to 60 per cent of all employees in accommodation and restaurants (Figure 6.3), compared with the average share of female employees across all industries of just under 40 per cent.[12]

The likely impact by education seems more mixed. Less-educated people were over-represented in the more heavily affected hospitality industry, whereas the tertiary educated were under-represented in this industry. At the other extreme, a high proportion of employees in industries that have not been heavily affected by COVID-19—information and communications and other services—employed a significant proportion (around 40–45 per cent) of younger and tertiary graduates. Thus, the employment impacts in services seem to have been less damaging to upper-income groups. And the future demand for jobs in new digitally based activities and industries will most likely be attractive to young graduates who have already experienced several months' exposure to distance learning during COVID-19.

International experience reminds us of the need for a focus on the job prospects of young people in particular during major setbacks such the COVID-19 pandemic. From rich country data, we know that current and future job prospects of young workers can be affected particularly

---

12 Males were also likely to be heavily impacted in transport and construction, where they dominate total employment. The International Monetary Fund finds that school closures in particular contributed to lower mobility among women under COVID-19 in European countries; similar sharp falls in mobility were found for the youngest cohort (18–24 years), who were more likely to work in casual jobs (IMF 2020b: 66, 72–73).

Figure 6.3 Characteristics of workers in COVID-sensitive industries, 2019

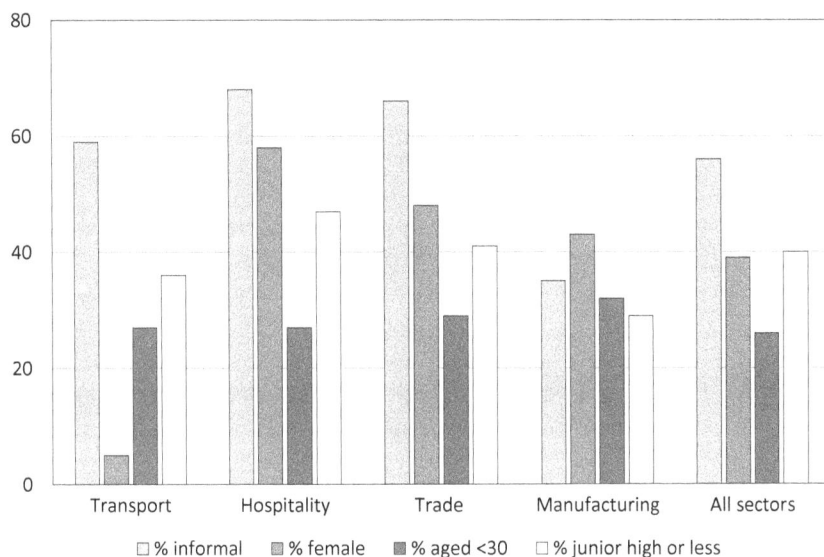

Source: GDP data from national accounts (CEIC); jobs data from Sakernas, August 2019.

harshly by economic shocks (OECD 2009). In Indonesia, young people aged less than thirty make up close to 30 per cent of all workers in four of the five industries that the ILO and ADB (2020) report identifies as being particularly hard hit by the pandemic—transport, hospitality, trade and manufacturing (Figure 6.3).[13]

The policy response to job losses

The government's response to the pandemic has focused mainly on poor and disadvantaged households. It has also targeted business and workers, in several programs designed to stimulate investment, raise consumption and assist displaced or struggling workers directly.[14] Programs seeking to

---

13 Across Asia and the Pacific, youth made up close to one-third of all workers in manufacturing and trade that were hardest hit by the pandemic.

14 See Olivia et al. (2020) for a detailed description of the government programs. These activities fall under the National Economic Recovery Program (Program Pemulihan Ekonomi Nasional, PEN) signed off as Law No. 2/2020. The PEN allocates money to different sectors including social protection, MSMEs and corporate financing.

support workers directly have been less prominent, such as public works and the Kartu Prakerja scheme.

Four points are relevant to the discussion of jobs. First, when COVID-19 broke out, the government was in a good position to create jobs indirectly by beefing up the now well-established welfare programs such as the Family Hope Program (Program Keluarga Harapan, PKH), cash transfers and the Staple Food Card (Kartu Sembako), using a unified household database and targeting the bottom two to three deciles by expenditure.[15] These programs can be expected to help stimulate jobs in rural areas especially, where most of the poor still reside. This assistance will have been less useful to low-income wage earners who live in and around the major cities but who are above the poverty line. The latter will be better helped by bolstering consumption through new programs—electricity subsidies, further cash and groceries assistance—with a focus on Jakarta where social distancing and home study and work has been implemented most consistently.

Second, two programs in particular have focused on creating jobs: the Kartu Prakerja (see next section) and the Village Funds (Dana Desa). Village Funds monies are mostly distributed in rural areas that have not been affected by the pandemic as much as the cities. Insofar as the funds are allocated for public works programs, they are well suited to dealing with emergency conditions like the pandemic because they promote spending and jobs at a community level.

Third, an important aspect of social assistance during this crisis has been the rapid mobilisation of support for MSMEs, the most important employer in the economy. Compared with the crisis in 1998, the government is fiscally in a better position to help small-scale businesses with a variety of programs that will support employment. Early on it allocated a large amount of funds (Rp 123 trillion or US$8.5 million) for subsidised credit interest and working capital, extension of tax payment deadlines and tax refunds for investments in training as well as offers to restructure loans. At the same time, the government has made cash transfers available to micro firms who depend heavily on working capital. Regrettably, as with other programs, a major complaint has been the slow rate of disbursements of assistance.

One new initiative to fill the gap in the assistance packages has been direct support for wage workers who have been laid off, stood down or now employed on a part-time or a rotational basis but are not registered among the poor in the Unified Database (Pratama 2020). In August 2020,

---

15 Payments were boosted one-third overall (Rp 24 trillion) in early 2020.

the government announced a support program of 13.8 million private sector employees with a monthly wage below Rp 5 million (US$350), partly in response to criticism of this gap in social assistance. Initially the funds were to be channelled to lower-wage employees through the government social security body for employees (BPJS-TK).[16] Recipients could also be identified from the list of jobseekers registered with the Ministry of Manpower, although many casual and informal workers would still be excluded. Thus, a major concern voiced by union leaders such as Said Iqbal was that the money would not go to the people most in need (Basri et al. 2020). Also, like many of the other social support programs, implementation has been hindered by administrative problems, such as failure to keep records of workers' bank accounts up to date.

Kartu Prakerja

Probably most controversial among the social assistance programs has been the Pre-employment Card. This is Indonesia's first serious venture into the area of government assistance for the unemployed and was strongly promoted by President Joko Widodo during the 2019 election campaign. From the start there was widespread scepticism regarding the funding and execution of the scheme, and whether it was appropriate for Indonesia. The original goal of Prakerja was to help young jobseekers gain skills to help them transition into more productive jobs—an objective high on the president's reform agenda during his first term (Manning and Pratomo 2018).[17] Besides charges of pork barrelling in the offer of Prakerja support during the election campaign, many critics pointed out that the potentially infinitely elastic demand for government assistance for the unemployed threatened to make Prakerja financially unsustainable.

Initially, the program was to consist of government-funded training and financial support for cost-of-living expenses for jobseekers over a period of 6–12 months. With COVID-19, the program was revised totally. First and foremost, it now sought to provide short-term social support for displaced workers rather than new jobseekers, while at the same time

---

16 Officially the Badan Penyelenggara Jaminan Sosial Ketenagakerjaan (the Administering Body of Social Security for Manpower).

17 President Widodo promoted the Kartu Prakerja intensively during the election campaign as one solution to youth unemployment and low productivity. He was roundly criticised by the Prabowo camp for making reckless promises and unnecessarily funding the unemployed (e.g. Idris 2019).

funding their training (or retraining) and improving their labour market prospects through access to online courses.[18]

There was huge interest among young people in the scheme when it was launched in April 2020. However, major teething problems threatened to undermine the entire project, leading to a report by the Corruption Eradication Commission (Komisi Pemberantasan Korupsi, KPK) to the government.[19] After a suspension for more than two months and a range of amendments to operating procedures, new rounds of the Kartu Prakerja were advertised and set in motion from early August 2020 (Fauzia 2020). Similar strong interest was shown in the program—800,000 applicants signing up for several batches advertised in August and early September—many of whom were already registered with the Ministry of Manpower for traditional, 'offline' courses.

It is too early to evaluate the impact of Kartu Prakerja on the job prospects for displaced workers and young jobseekers. It is clear, however, that it has been one channel for getting social support money out to displaced workers based on self-registration, given that the infrastructure for the project was in train when the pandemic struck Indonesia in March 2020. Innovative aspects of the project, including government cooperation with well-established digital commerce companies such as Bukalapak, Tokopaedia and Ruangguru, suggest that online engagement of jobseekers in training courses funded by the government could become an important element of a recovery program for the labour market; these would be in addition to offline courses managed by the Ministry of Manpower or funded through the established vocational training centres and vocational high schools.

Concluding thoughts

In conclusion, I have argued that employment in Indonesia has been severely impacted by COVID-19, like several other labour markets within the ASEAN region. Given the failure to control the spread of the virus and its impact on the economy during July and August 2020, the situation may worsen in the last quarter of 2020 if further shutdowns are needed.

---

18   The initial budget committed before COVID-19 was doubled to Rp 20 billion (US$1.4 million) to be allocated to 5.6 million jobseekers (around 4 per cent of the workforce) with Rp 2.4 million allocated to cost of living and a further Rp 1 million to training providers for each jobseeker.

19   See especially Idris (2020), who details seven problems with the early design and implementation of Prakerja, including a statement by the Minister of Finance that these and other funding commitments made by the Jokowi team were giving her a 'stomach ache' (*sakit perut*)!

Government support, mainly in the form of social protection, has been and can be important for jobs, although its impact has been hindered by the slow rollout of promised support. At the same time, by early December 2020 it had become clear that the government was unlikely to get on top of the virus by conventional means, and the far-reaching health respite needed to revive the economy and jobs depends very much on the widespread administration of a safe vaccine in Indonesia—a major challenge for much of 2021 and maybe also 2022.

As of September 2020, the continuing steady spread of COVID-19 in Indonesia suggests there is likely to be continuing pressure on jobs and the need for programs of support for workers terminated from formal and informal sector jobs, running well into 2021.[20] It is quite likely that unemployment will rise from around 5 per cent to at least 6–7 per cent, which is not high by middle income standards. But the broader labour market effect will also include a potential rise in underemployment, reduced incomes and a fall in participation in the workforce, as well as likely worsening conditions of work, especially among more vulnerable new job entrants and females. Taking a regional perspective, the employment shock in the medium term may well be closer to that in the Philippines—where COVID-19 cases continued to rise in the second half of 2020—than in Malaysia, Thailand or Vietnam.

It has been argued that the crisis response package does not deal adequately with potential long-term poverty through the impact on employment (Sparrow et al. 2020). One initiative in this space has been a comprehensive 'omnibus' reform bill, Cipta Kerja, aimed at creating more jobs by stimulating investment, output and jobs. The bill, covering some 75 laws and regulations in many fields and sectors of the economy including labour, was passed by the House of Representatives (Dewan Perwakilan Rakyat, DPR) on 5 October 2020. But it appears to have been poorly prepared and rushed through parliament. The final, controversial clauses were not all signed off by key labour leaders, who together with students led angry demonstrations across the country in the first week of October calling for withdrawal of the bill (BBC Asia 2020). This is unfortunate because several of the clauses—such as reform of the controversial severance pay regulations of 2003—offered important and not unrealistic compromises, including new government support for unemployed workers. But socialisation of this quite sweeping reform

---

20 For example, in response to a sustained rise in COVID-19 cases over the previous fortnight, the Governor of Jakarta announced a return to strict lockdown in the capital beginning 14 September 2020.

process for Indonesia has clearly needed more time than the government has been prepared to give to it.

Experience with the Asian financial crisis in 1998 suggests that two potential developments need to be watched closely: unemployment rates among educated youth and proliferation of informal work arrangements. High rates of unemployment among educated youth had long been a feature of the labour market until it was somewhat brought under control. This problem seems likely to re-emerge after some important gains over the past decade. Special efforts are likely be needed to help young people to get back into work, including targeted wage subsidies, continuing efforts to support skills, job information and apprenticeship programs in industries with good job prospects, as well as special support for the engagement of young people in MSMEs.

Second, the capacity of formal sector workers to move into informal and part-time jobs during economic slowdowns is well known and has been occurring under COVID-19 (Octavia 2020). While such shifts can provide displaced workers with temporary respite, they are also likely to lead to lower wages and less favourable working conditions than in many formal sector jobs. Many households in which former employees have taken up new jobs are likely to need some continuing income support and social assistance.

There are some potentially mitigating factors for Indonesia amid this pressure on the labour market that mirror some of the challenges Indonesia faced after the Asian financial crisis in the early 2000s. First, the economy is embedded in East Asia, the most dynamic region in the world with respect to economic growth, trade and investment. Provided the spread of the virus is brought under control in the region and the Indonesian economy remains open, renewed economic growth could turn the labour market situation around for most people quite quickly in 2021. Reversal of current economic and closely related labour market developments depends very much on a sustained recovery of the Chinese economy, which dominates trade and plays an increasingly significant role in foreign investment in Indonesia. Second, Indonesia has a history of prudent economic management that bodes well for investment and jobs in uncertain times. And finally, Indonesia has a large and youthful population. A large population means that it is not as exposed to the same extent to global shocks as some neighbouring countries, such as Cambodia and Vietnam. And the youthful population means that new job entrants are well placed to take advantage of new jobs in the digital and gig economies of the future, many of which have emerged during COVID-19.

References

ADB (Asian Development Bank). 2020. 'An updated assessment of the economic impact of COVID-19'. *ADB Brief* No. 133. http://dx.doi.org/10.22617/BRF200144-2

Aditya, Nicholas Ryan. 2020. 'Kunjungan wisman pada Januari-Juni 2020 anjlok 59 persen'. *Kompas*, 3 August. https://travel.kompas.com/read/2020/08/03/143000727/kunjungan-wisman-pada-januari-juni-2020-anjlok-59-persen

Basri, M. Chatib, Rema N. Hanna and Benjamin A. Olken. 2020. 'Insight: Don't forget the middle class in social protection programs'. *Jakarta Post*, 16 April. www.thejakartapost.com/academia/2020/04/16/insight-dont-forget-the-middle-class-in-social-protection-programs.html

BBC Asia. 2020. 'Thousands protest against "omnibus law" on jobs'. BBC Asia, 8 October. www.bbc.com/news/world-asia-54460090

Chan, Benjamin Tak-Yuen. 2020. 'Cities are crucial to fighting the coronavirus pandemic'. *Jakarta Post*, 17 April. https://www.thejakartapost.com/academia/2020/04/17/cities-are-crucial-to-fighting-the-coronavirus-pandemic.html

Fauzia, Mutia. 2020. 'Sisa kuota 2,6 juta, pendaftaran Kartu Prakerja dibuka 4 gelombang lagi'. *Kompas*, 31 August. https://money.kompas.com/read/2020/08/31/162359926/sisa-kuota-26-juta-pendaftaran-kartu-prakerja-dibuka-4-gelombang-lagi

Frankenberg, Elizabeth, Duncan Thomas and Kathleen Beegle. 1999. 'The real costs of Indonesia's economic crisis: Preliminary findings from the Indonesia Family Life Surveys'. *Labor and Population Program Working Paper* No. 99-04. New York: Rand Corporation.

Hill, Elizabeth, Marian Baird and Suneha Seetahul. 2020. *Indonesia and COVID-19: Impact on the Private Sector*. Sydney: University of Sydney. https://investinginwomen.asia/knowledge/indonesia-covid-19-impact-on-private-sector/

Idris, Muhammad. 2019. 'Kartu Pra Kerja Jokowi, sudah kontroversi sejak kampanye'. *Kompas*, 30 December. https://money.kompas.com/read/2019/12/30/163600926/kartu-pra-kerja-jokowi-sudah-kontroversi-sejak-kampanye?page=all

Idris, Muhammad. 2020. '7 kontroversi pelatihan online Kartu Prakerja Jokowi'. *Kompas*, 22 April. https://money.kompas.com/read/2020/04/22/104134326/7-kontroversi-pelatihan-online-kartu-prakerja-jokowi?page=all

ILO (International Labour Organization). 2020a. 'The clock is ticking for survival of Indonesian enterprises, jobs at risk: Key findings of the ILO SCORE Indonesia COVID-19 enterprise survey'. Jakarta: ILO.

ILO (International Labour Organization). 2020b. 'A policy framework for tackling the economic and social impact of the COVID-19 crisis'. *Policy Brief*, May 2020. Geneva: ILO.

ILO and ADB (International Labour Organization and Asian Development Bank). 2020. *Tackling the COVID-19 Youth Employment Crisis in Asia and the Pacific*. Bangkok and Manila.

IMF (International Monetary Fund). 2020a. *World Economic Outlook: The Great Lockdown*, April. Washington, DC: IMF. www.imf.org/en/Publications/WEO/Issues/2020/04/14/weo-april-2020

IMF (International Monetary Fund). 2020b. *World Economic Outlook: A Long and Difficult Ascent,* October. Washington, DC: IMF. www.imf.org/en/Publications/WEO/Issues/2020/09/30/world-economic-outlook-october-2020

Jellinek, Lea and Bambang Rustanto. 1999. *Survival Strategies of the Javanese during the Economic Crisis,* January. Jakarta: World Bank.

Lee, Ayoung and Joonmo Cho. 2016. 'The impact of epidemics on labor market: Identifying victims of the Middle East Respiratory Syndrome in the Korean labor market. *International Journal for Equity in Health* 15(196). doi.org/10.1186/s12939-016-0483-9

Lee, Jong-Wha and Warwick J. McKibbin. 2004. 'Globalization and disease: The case of SARS'. *Asian Economic Papers* 3(1): 113–31. doi.org/10.1162/1535351041747932

Manning, Chris. 1998. *Indonesian Labour in Transition: An East Asian Success Story?* Trade and Development Series. Cambridge: Cambridge University Press.

Manning, Chris. 2000. 'Labour market adjustment to Indonesia's economic crisis: Context, trends and implications'. *Bulletin of Indonesian Economic Studies* 36(1): 105–36. doi.org/10.1080/00074910012331337803

Manning, Chris and Devanto Pratomo. 2018. 'Labour market developments in the Jokowi years'. *Journal of Southeast Asian Economies* 35(2): 165–84. doi.org/10.1355/ae35-2d

Octavia, Joanna. 2020. 'Towards a national database of workers in the informal sector: COVID-19 pandemic response and future recommendations'. *CSIS Commentaries* DMRU-070-EN, 13 May. https://csis.or.id/publications/towards-a-national-database-of-workers-in-the-informal-sector-covid-19-pandemic-response-and-future-recommendations/

OECD (Organisation for Economic Co-operation and Development). 2009. *OECD Employment Outlook 2009: Tackling the Jobs Crisis.* Paris: OECD.

Olivia, Susan, John Gibson and Rus'an Nasrudin. 2020. 'Indonesia in the time of COVID-19'. *Bulletin of Indonesian Economic Studies* 56(2): 143–74. doi.org/10.1080/00074918.2020.1798581

Pane, Deasy and Donny Pasaribu. 2020. 'Indonesia's garment industry in crisis'. *East Asia Forum,* 10 August. www.eastasiaforum.org/2020/08/10/indonesias-garment-industry-in-crisis/

Pratama, Akhdi Martin. 2020. 'Efektifkah bantuan tunai Rp 600.000 bagi karyawan swasta di masa pandemi? *Kompas,* 7 August. https://money.kompas.com/read/2020/08/07/082400926/efektifkah-bantuan-tunai-rp-600000-bagi-karyawan-swasta-di-masa-pandemi?page=all

Pratomo, Devanto Shasta and Chris Manning. 2020. 'Structural change and formal sector employment growth in Indonesia'. *Working Paper in Trade and Development* No. 2020/15. Canberra: Arndt-Corden Department of Economics, Australian National University.

Purnamasari, Ririn and Bambang Suharnoko Sjahrir. 2020. 'High-frequency monitoring of socio-economic impact of COVID-19 on households in Indonesia'. World Bank presentation, ANU Indonesia Project Global Seminar Series, 30 September. www.youtube.com/watch?v=4DYck8WOLxk

Rosenthal, Rachel. 2020. 'Millennials face second age of underemployment'. *Bloomberg,* 23 April. www.bloomberg.com/opinion/articles/2020-04-23/coronavirus-job-stagnation-familiar-to-millennials-awaits

Skoufias, Emmanuel and Asep Suryahadi. 1999. 'Growth and crisis impacts on formal sector wages in Indonesia'. *SMERU Working Paper Series*, December. Jakarta. www.smeru.or.id/en/content/growth-and-crisis-impacts-formal-sector-wages-indonesia

Sparrow, Robert, Teguh Dartanto and Renate Hartwig. 2020. 'Indonesia under the new normal: Challenges and the way ahead'. Bulletin of Indonesian Economic Studies 56(3): 269–99. doi.org/10.1080/00074918.2020.1854079

World Bank. 2010. *Indonesia Jobs Report*. Washington, DC: World Bank.

World Bank. 2020. 'The long road to recovery'. *Indonesia Economic Prospects*, July. Jakarta: World Bank.

7 COVID-19, food security and trade: The case of Indonesia

Arianto Patunru and Felippa Amanta

Abstract

Food security has long been a contentious issue in Indonesia. As the country has graduated into the upper middle income group it still has to deal with ensuring people's access to food. The self-sufficiency ambition exacerbates this situation, as policies taken are often protectionist in nature, resulting in high domestic prices and thus hurting the poor, whose access to affordable food deteriorates. Now, the COVID-19 pandemic may further amplify food insecurity, leading to chronic hunger and lasting developmental challenges. We discuss the impact of the pandemic on Indonesia's food security by examining the global and regional food trade along with Indonesia's domestic food policies. We argue that the COVID-19 pandemic exposes the vulnerability in Indonesia's food systems, especially in terms of declining production trends, inadequate distribution capacity and trade limitations. Needed reforms include inviting more investment, supporting diversification of food supply, easing food trade flows and working with other countries to ensure regional food security.

Introduction

The COVID-19 pandemic is directly affecting food supply and demand globally, raising concerns over a potential food crisis on top of the existing health crisis. Mobility restrictions required to contain the spread of the virus disrupt the increasingly complex and interconnected food supply chain, from food production through processing, distribution and consumption, both domestically and globally. The disruption may result in food shortages, price spikes or price volatility that harms the livelihoods of people working in the supply chain and threatens food security, especially for the vulnerable poor. A joint report by the Food and Agriculture Organization of the United Nations (FAO), International Fund for Agriculture Development (IFAD), United Nations International Children's Fund (UNICEF), World Food Programme (WFP) and World Health Organization (WHO) estimated that, in 2019, 690 million people or 9 per cent of the world's population went hungry, and the COVID-19 pandemic may push another 83 million to 132 million people into chronic hunger (FAO et al. 2020).

Food insecurity risks during and after the pandemic will hit hard in Indonesia where, even before the pandemic, 9 per cent of the population or more than 22 million people were undernourished between 2017 and 2019.[1] The Economist Intelligence Unit's Global Food Security Index ranked Indonesia 62nd out of 113 countries for food security in 2019, below neighbours Singapore (1st), Malaysia (28th), Thailand (52nd) and Vietnam (54th).[2] Indonesia's low rank is mostly because of poor affordability and low quality and safety of food, particularly due to a lack of dietary diversity. More than a third of Indonesians cannot afford a nutritious diet, and the proportion is greater in poorer provinces such as East Nusa Tenggara, Maluku and Papua (WFP 2017). Poor diets lead to a high stunting prevalence that affects 31 per cent of children under five years old, significantly higher than the global stunting prevalence of 21 per cent (Global Hunger Index 2020; FAO et al. 2020). The stunting incidence is also concentrated in poorer provinces, such as East Nusa Tenggara (40.3 per cent), West Sulawesi (40 per cent) and Central Kalimantan (39 per cent) (Databoks 2017).

The COVID-19 pandemic may exacerbate Indonesia's food insecurity even further, leading to more chronic hunger and lasting developmental challenges. This chapter discusses the impact of COVID-19 on food security in Indonesia by looking at global and regional food trade and

---

1 Global Hunger Index 2020, www.globalhungerindex.org/indonesia.html
2 https://foodsecurityindex.eiu.com/Index

Indonesia's domestic food policies. It also explores the potential long-term implications and the reforms needed for a resilient, sustainable food system.

Latest developments of global food trade during COVID-19

Food and agriculture trade is an important component of a support system for food security. World agriculture trade increased more than threefold in value from US$570 billion in 2000 to US$1.6 trillion in 2016 (FAO 2018a). Intra-Asian food trade grew from US$22 billion in 2000 to over US$70 billion in 2018 (Oxford Economics 2020). Countries' dependency on food imports from the international marketplace increased to an average of around 28 per cent globally in 2015–2017 (Schmidhuber 2020). Like many countries, Indonesia is a beneficiary of the global food system, both in importing and exporting agricultural products. In 2018, Indonesia's imports of animal, vegetable and food products reached US$20 billion or 11 per cent of total imports. Exports were even greater at US$38 billion, contributing 21 per cent of Indonesia's total exports, with most coming from palm oil (WITS 2020). Due to the significance of global food trade, the trade disruptions during the COVID-19 pandemic raised the alarm for potential food insecurity.

The World Trade Organization predicts that global merchandise trade will plunge by between 13 per cent and 32 per cent in 2020 (WTO 2020), which is more severe than the drop during the global financial crisis of 2008–2009. Evidence of this decline was seen in April 2020 when container shipping fell by 5.9 per cent year on year and new export orders contracted sharply (World Bank 2020a). Early analysis of trade data shows that food and agriculture trade is more resilient than trade in other sectors. During the first quarter of 2020, while sectors such as textiles and apparel, automotive, machinery and communication equipment saw a decline in trade, the food and agriculture sector grew 2 per cent compared to the first quarter of the previous year (UNCTAD 2020a). This positive growth should be considered in the context of low agriculture trade to begin with. In 2018, agricultural raw materials exports accounted for less than 2 per cent of total merchandise exports (World Bank 2020b).

The resilience of food and agriculture trade may be attributed to several factors. First, the global supply chain of food and agriculture is less complex than that of manufacturing. There is limited global value chain integration, where production and processing are broken down into several countries, which makes the chain less vulnerable to disruptions. Second, as an essential need, food demand is relatively income-inelastic and so trade continues to flow, especially with the support of world leaders who have vowed to ensure trade flows on essential items including agricultural commodities.[3] Yet food and agriculture trade is still highly exposed to risks and mobility disruptions due to COVID-19.

The COVID-19 pandemic unfolded during an abundant production year where global cereal supply is approaching a record high due to favourable weather conditions. The FAO (2020a) predicts that world cereal production in 2020 will reach around 2.8 billion tonnes, surpassing 2019 production by 3 per cent. Among this, world rice production is forecast to exceed 500 million tonnes in 2020, an almost 2 per cent increase from the previous year. The rice supply is more than enough to cover the global demand with a stock-to-use ratio of 35 per cent. However, the production outlook varies when disaggregated into different agricultural commodities. Fruit and vegetables are labour intensive during harvest season, and many countries such as the United States and Australia rely on seasonal migrant workers. COVID-19–induced mobility restrictions put those countries at risk of labour shortages, which may lead to suboptimal harvest (Schmidhuber et al. 2020).

The food processing industry is also severely impacted by the pandemic. For example, meat-processing abattoirs are particularly vulnerable to COVID-19 transmission because of the cold temperatures, tight spaces on production lines and dry air. The high-risk scenario has led to multiple outbreaks in Australia, the United States, France, Germany and the United Kingdom, leading many abattoirs to suspend operations. In Australia, the world's seventh-largest meat producer in terms of value and Indonesia's top meat import source, national beef production and adult cattle slaughter could drop by 16 per cent and 19 per cent, respectively, from 2019 (MLA 2020).

The distribution of food supply across the global market is also challenged by the mobility restrictions, especially when the pandemic had just started developing. For instance, India imposed a three-week lockdown in March that halted port operations and caused delays in planned food exports (*Bloomberg* 2020). While almost all countries have generally exempted the transport of food and agriculture from lockdown restrictions, logistics are still disrupted due to road closures, blockages, slowdown of operations and reduced transportation capacity. High-value commodities such as fruit, vegetables and fisheries are particularly

---

3 G20 leaders' statement. 'Extraordinary G20 leaders' summit statement on COVID-19'. [26 March 2020]. https://reliefweb.int/report/world/g20-leaders-statement-extraordinary-g20-leaders-summit-statement-covid-19

sensitive to logistics bottlenecks because of their perishability, which can lead to food waste in the supply chain.

Adding to the disruption are trade measures adopted by countries in response to the pandemic. From January to October 2020, the International Trade Centre recorded more than 300 temporary trade measures enacted by 140 countries in relation to the COVID-19 pandemic (ITC 2020). These include 148 export measures that are 96 per cent restrictive in nature and 185 import measures where 80 per cent are liberalising in nature. These statistics expose countries' instinct to hoard supplies by protecting domestically sourced supply while opening access to foreign supply. These trade measures mostly affect personal protective equipment such as masks and medical and pharmaceutical products, but are also found in food and agriculture products.

Specifically on food and agriculture products, 28 countries introduced restrictive export measures, such as limited export quotas or even total export prohibitions. These measures anticipate potential domestic food supply shortages as the pandemic is prolonged without a clear end in sight. Importantly, India and Vietnam, the world's first- and third-biggest rice exporters, respectively, are among the countries that closed their exports. Indian rice traders suspended signing new export contracts amid the lockdown uncertainty (Jadhav and Bhardwaj 2020). Meanwhile, Vietnam introduced an export quota for rice (ITC 2020). These export restrictions, especially if applied in the form of quantitative restrictions, could create instability in both the exporting country and the world market (Martin and Glauber 2020).

The turn of events by exporting countries is reminiscent of the food price crisis in 2007–2008 when the rice price nearly tripled from October 2007 to April 2008. During the crisis, India and Vietnam's export restricting policies triggered a chain reaction for importing countries such as the Philippines to panic buy, which resulted in skyrocketing prices (Alavi et al. 2012: 38). The food price crisis pushed 130 million people around the world into poverty. The circumstances of the 2007–2008 crisis and the current pandemic are different, particularly as the 2019–2020 food and agriculture supply is abundant while input costs and oil prices are low (Schmidhuber and Qiao 2020). Yet the sudden protectionist moves are concerning, since additional shocks to supply could cause even more uncertainty amid the pandemic. Early calculations suggest that escalating export protectionism during COVID-19 could raise world food prices by 18 per cent on average (Espitia et al. 2020). As countries start to adapt and engage in diplomacy to weather the pandemic, Vietnam relaxed its export ban into an export quota, and then terminated the measure in May 2020, while Indian traders have started signing rice export contracts again.

On the import side, restrictive measures are introduced mostly to reduce health risks, especially on food and agriculture products from China. In the early days of the pandemic, the transmission risk of the coronavirus (SARS-CoV-2) through food and agriculture products was still unknown, and countries took a precautionary step of prohibiting food imports from China for sanitary and phytosanitary reasons. However, this was an exceptional case of short duration. The majority of world import measures on food and agriculture are liberalising in nature, mostly in the form of tariff reductions. Countries enacted liberalising measures to ensure access to food items, particularly for commodities they cannot produce themselves. Indonesia is one of these countries, which we will discuss in more detail below.

Amid the prolonged trade disruption, global food prices remain relatively steady. The upward pressure caused by the compounding trade disruption is balanced by downward pressure from plentiful supply and, for some high-value commodities, by reduced demand. The FAO Food Price Index shows that global food prices have been relatively stable for the past five years (Figure 7.1). Recently there was a slight drop in the beginning of the pandemic between March and May, followed by a modest rebound. The meat price index has seen the greatest drop compared to cereal, dairy and sugar indices, dropping as much as 9.4 per cent in September 2020 compared to the corresponding month in 2019. The World Bank's commodity data reported that the rice price increased by up to 14 per cent between March and April 2020, then fell slightly in May and June but remained above pre–COVID-19 prices (Figure 7.2). This is likely due to a spike in demand that has subsequently eased (FAO 2020b: 26).

Food security in Indonesia amid COVID-19

While global rice production is experiencing a positive trend, Indonesia's rice production is not as fortunate (Figure 7.3). After continued increases for many years, rice production in 2019 experienced an almost 8 per cent drop from 2018, largely due to extreme drought. In the first half of 2020, rice production in Indonesia is estimated to be around 16.8 million tonnes, 9.7 per cent lower than the same period in 2019, continuing the declining trend (Ministry of Agriculture 2020). While the supply is more than enough to cover domestic demand in the first semester with a 6.4 million tonne surplus, there are concerns with rice supply towards the end of the year and early 2021 as the dry season typically contributes only 35 per cent to annual production (WFP 2020).

Figure 7.1   FAO Food Price Index, January 1990 to September 2020
(2014–2016 = 100)

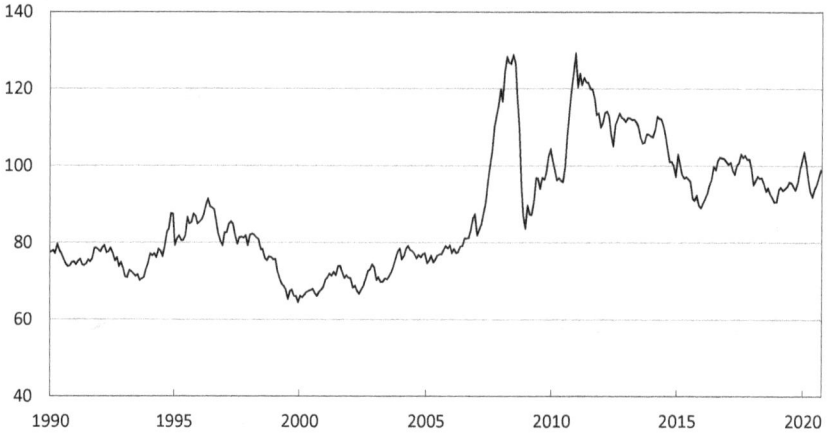

Source: FAO Food Price Index, www.fao.org/worldfoodsituation/foodpricesindex/en

Figure 7.2   Rice commodity prices, Thailand and Vietnam, January 2019 to
September 2020 (US$/tonne)

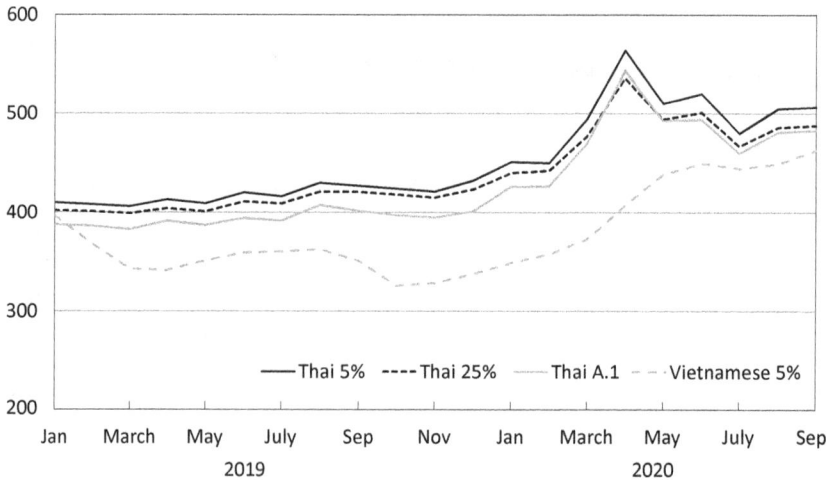

Note: Thailand 5% broken, 25% broken and A.1 (100% broken) white rice prices, milled, are indicative survey prices, government standard, f.o.b. Bangkok. Vietnam 5% broken white rice price, milled, is indicative survey price, minimum export price, f.o.b. Hanoi.

Source: World Bank (2020c).

Figure 7.3   Rice production in Indonesia and in the world, 1961–2019
(milled, million tonnes)

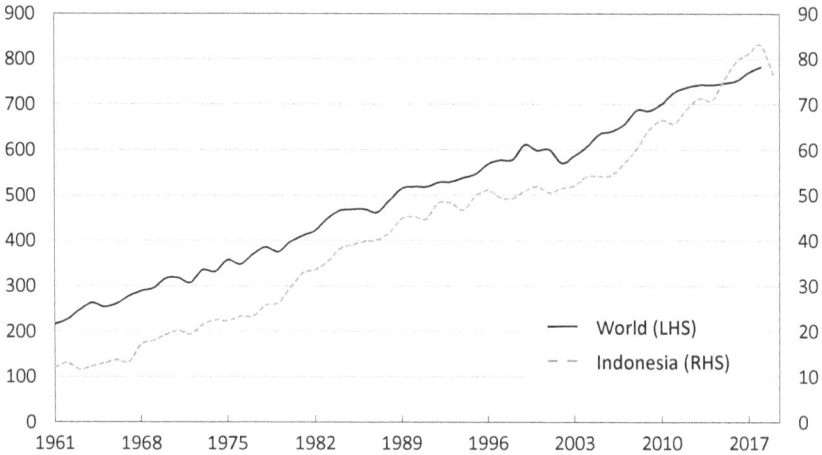

Note: In 2018 BPS adjusted its sampling method (Ruslan 2019), resulting in a 40% difference in estimates of production relative to those using the previous sampling method. We apply this difference to the new estimates of 2018 and 2019 to make them comparable to that of the preceding years.

Source: BPS (Badan Pusat Statistik, Statistics Indonesia); FAO.

Concern for the rice supply is even higher in eastern parts of Indonesia. Rice production remains concentrated in the western part of Indonesia, where in 2019 Java Island contributed 56 per cent of total domestic rice production and Sumatera region contributed 20 per cent (BPS 2020a). Interestingly, many of the rice-producing regions, for example, the provinces in Java, show a relatively high degree of fatality rates due to COVID-19 (Figure 7.4). If the pandemic continues, therefore, it is possible that the future production of rice in Indonesia will be further depressed.

While people in some places in eastern Indonesia typically eat other staple crops such as sago, maize and cassava, rice consumption has been increasing and even overtaking local foods as the primary staple food (Arifin et al. 2018). Yet distribution to eastern Indonesia is disrupted because of the regional large-scale social restrictions (*pembatasan sosial berskala besar*, PSBB) that formally started in April. Also in April, President Joko Widodo raised the issue of staple food shortages in most of Indonesia's provinces, with garlic, sugar, chilli and eggs deficit in more than twenty provinces, while rice is deficit in seven provinces (Rahman 2020a). Although the local PSBB regulations were relaxed around June, the remaining health protocols, procurement challenges and reduced capacity

Figure 7.4   Rice-producing regions and COVID-19

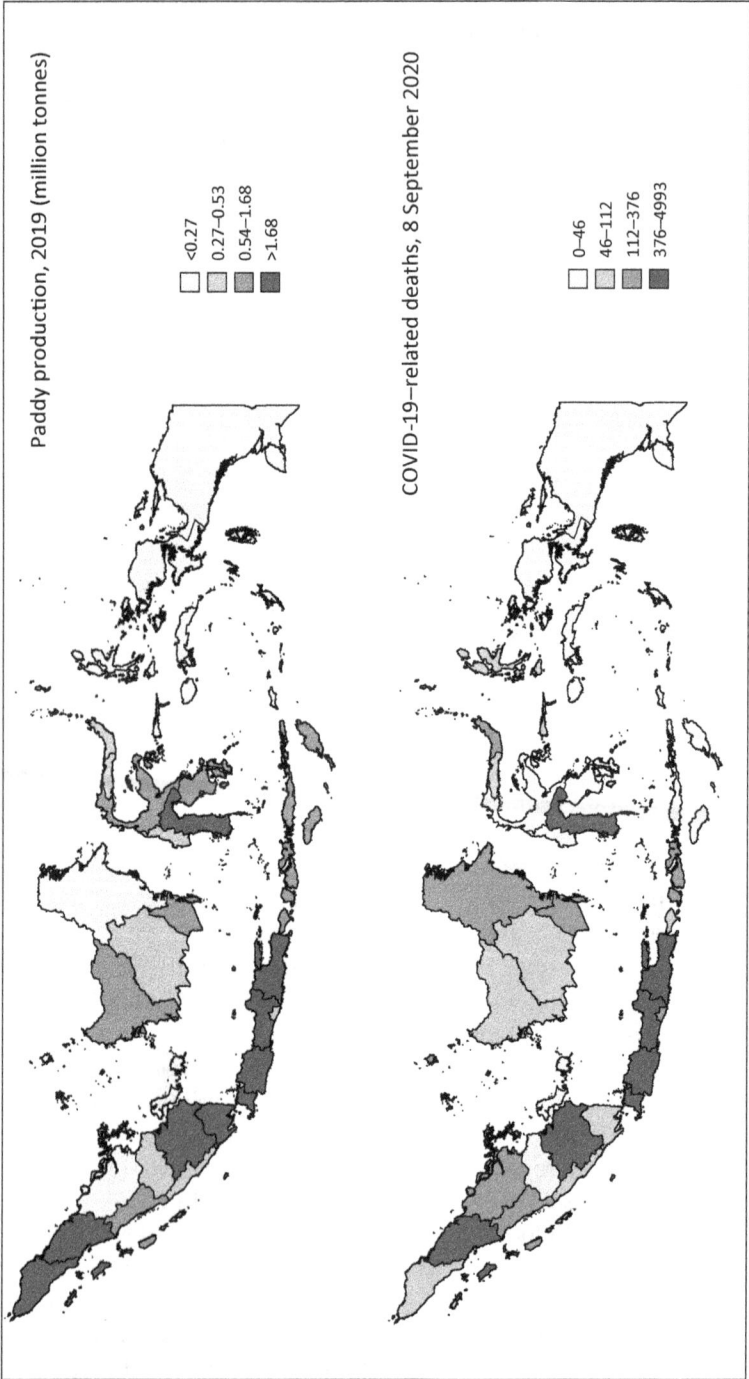

Source: BPS (Badan Pusat Statistik, Statistics Indonesia); LaporCOVID19.org continue to hinder distribution. The Minister of Agriculture stated in a virtual press briefing in July that only six ships are delivering food to eastern Indonesia each month, compared to 48 ships per month before the pandemic. Furthermore, truck drivers who deliver to COVID-19 hot spots must also be quarantined according to COVID-19 travel protocols, adding to the delay (Rahman 2020b).

Even before the pandemic, the prices of some key foods had been volatile. As COVID-19 started to affect economic activities, prices continued to increase. But in the last two quarters many food items showed a slight drop in price (Figure 7.5). This reflected a downturn in the economy in

Figure 7.5 Food prices in the lead-up to the pandemic outbreak, January 2018 to August 2020 (January 2018 = 100)

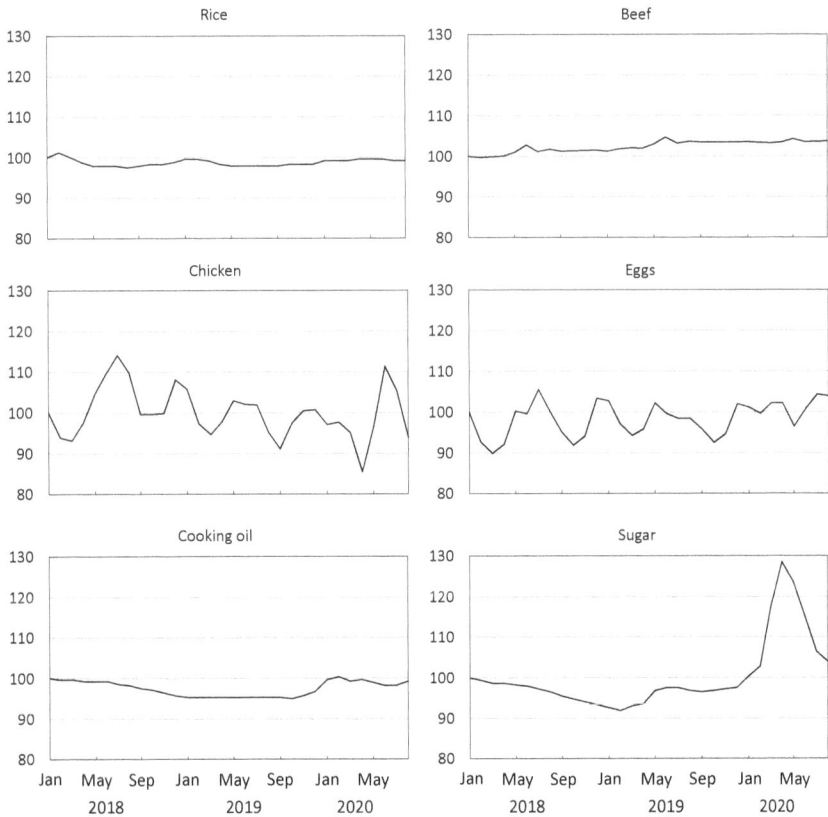

Source: PIHPS Nasional (2020).

general, as the demand shock kicked in. Nevertheless, total consumption expenditure for food did not drop in the last two quarters, unlike those for other needs, as shown in Figure 7.6. This confirms that the price and income elasticities of food are lower than those of other commodities.

The PSBB regulations have also disrupted farmers' access to inputs and markets. Farmers reported challenges in getting labour and subsidised fertilisers, as well as increased input prices (AIP-PRISMA 2020). At the same time, closures of hotels, restaurants and catering businesses has led to significantly reduced food demand, leaving many farmers with no buyers and with lower purchasing prices. As a result, Indonesian farmers' terms of trade declined and even dipped below 100 in May and June, which means the prices they pay for input costs are higher than the prices they receive (BPS 2020b) (Figure 7.7). Farmers fared slightly better from July, coinciding with the relaxation of the regional PSBB and reopening of restaurants and malls, although their terms of trade were still lower than the rate in 2019. Smallholder farmers are already disproportionately poor, with an 18 per cent poverty rate, which is double the national poverty rate (FAO 2018b).

Figure 7.6   Consumption expenditure, March 2018 to June 2020 (March 2018 = 100)

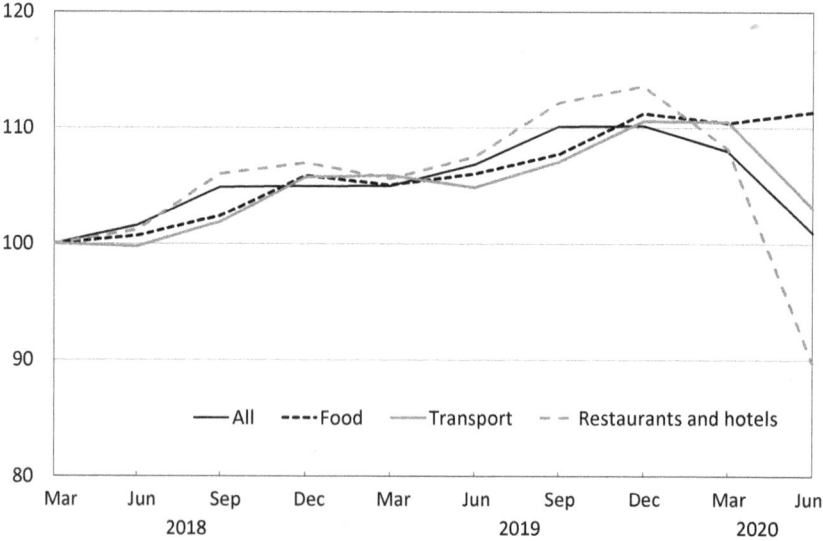

Source: BPS (Badan Pusat Statistik, Statistics Indonesia).

Figure 7.7   Farmers' terms of trade, January 2019 to September 2020
(2018 = 100)

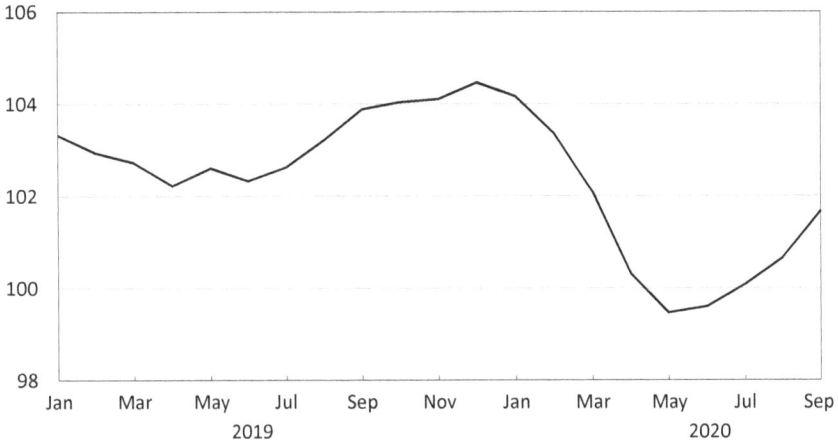

Source: BPS (Badan Pusat Statistik, Statistics Indonesia).

In addition to domestic supply disruption, Indonesia is also affected
by the global trade turmoil, especially for agricultural products that rely
on imports. In 2018, Indonesia sourced 94 per cent of its garlic, 69.9 per
cent of its sugar, 28.4 per cent of its meat and even 6.2 per cent of its rice
from abroad (WFP 2020) (Table 7.1). Despite the popular self-sufficiency
narrative, Indonesia has been a net rice importer for the past decade except
for three brief periods when exports were greater than imports (Patunru
forthcoming). As the provinces are experiencing shortages of sugar,
garlic, meat and rice, the need to expedite food imports is complicated
not only by the global trade disruption, but also by Indonesia's own
protectionist policies.

The relationship of food trade to food security is contested in Indonesia
where a self-sufficiency discourse is dominant. Law No. 18/2012 on Food
mandated that food imports are allowed only when domestic supply is
insufficient. To enforce this, Indonesia imposes trade barriers in both tariff
and non-tariff form to restrict food imports. In 2018, the simple average
of import tariff with the most favoured nation applied for agricultural
products was 8.6 per cent (WTO et al. 2019: 16). Of non-tariff measures
in 2019, 433 were imposed on agro-food products, including quantitative
restrictions, sanitary and phytosanitary measures, and technical barriers
to trade (Table 7.2). Marks (2017) estimated that, in 2015, non-tariff measures
on agriculture together amounted to an effective rate of protection of
41 per cent. This year, the number of non-tariff measures imposed has

Table 7.1 Indonesia's import reliance, 2018

Commodity	Import dependency ratio (%)*	Top source	Top source share of total imports of commodity (%)
Rice	6.2	Thailand	35
Beef	28.4	Australia	49
Sugar	69.9	Thailand	80
Soybean	72.5	United States	98
Wheat	100.0	Australia	24
Garlic	93.7	China	100

* Import dependency ratio is import divided by the sum of production and export minus import.

Source: BPS (Badan Pusat Statistik, Statistics Indonesia).

Table 7.2 Indonesian non-tariff measures on agro-food products

Non-tariff measure	2019	2020
Export-related measures	72	76
Other measures	7	7
Pre-shipment inspection	23	23
Price control measures	8	9
Quantity control measures	31	31
Sanitary and phytosanitary	219	235
Technical barriers to trade	73	85
Total	433	466

Source: TRAINS: The global database on non-tariff measures, https://trains.unctad.org

increased by more than 7 per cent, which likely correlates with a greater effective rate of protection. The biggest contributor to the effective rate of protection is the quantitative restriction or quota, which effectively limits the amount of import.

The impact of trade restrictions on domestic prices can be illustrated with the cases of rice and beef (Figures 7.8 and 7.9). Throughout 2019, the Indonesian average rice price at Rp 11,762 per kilogram was more than double the average international price of Rp 5,947 per kilogram. Meanwhile, the average domestic beef price is about 60 per cent more

Figure 7.8   Domestic and world price of rice, 1995 to March 2020 (rupiah/kg)

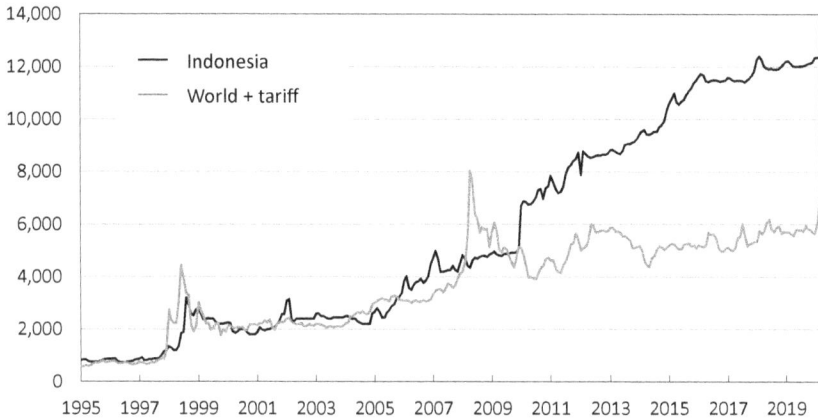

Note: The domestic price series is represented by the wholesale prices of rice variety IR-64 and the world price series is represented by the wholesale prices of rice variety Thai 25 per cent broken. The world price is converted into Indonesian rupiah, adding a US$20/tonne shipping and handling cost, US$5/tonne import profit and the ongoing, specific tariffs (Rp 430/kg from January to December 2006, Rp 550/kg from January to November 2007 and Rp 450/kg from December 2007 onward).

Source: BPS (Badan Pusat Statistik, Statistics Indonesia); Bank of Thailand.

Figure 7.9   Domestic and world price of beef, 2011–2019 (rupiah/kg)

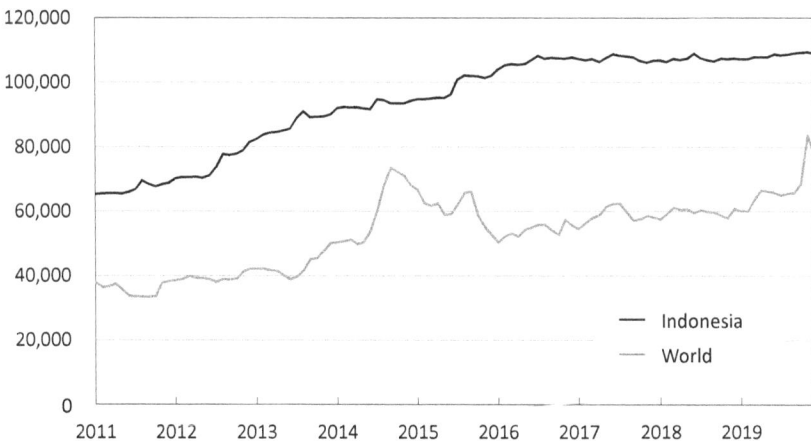

Note: Indonesian price is retail beef price; international price is beef (Australia, New Zealand), chucks and cow forequarters, frozen boneless, 85 per cent chemical lean, c.i.f. United States port (east coast), ex-dock.

Source: BPS (Badan Pusat Statistik, Statistics Indonesia); World Bank.

expensive than the international price (PIHPS Nasional 2020; World Bank 2020c). Patunru (forthcoming) discusses the trade measures that are likely to cause the significant price dispersion between domestic and imported rice. In the case of beef, Respatiadi and Nabila (2017) provide similar discussion.

In addition, trade restrictions often caused import delays resulting in price spikes, such as in the case of garlic and onion (KPPU 2020). Garlic and onion imports are restricted through a quota that requires a recommendation letter from the Ministry of Agriculture and an import licence from the Ministry of Trade (Table 7.3). This system has previously led to a corruption case of a lawmaker convicted of receiving bribes in exchange for an import licence (Adjie 2020). In 2020, the complex import

Table 7.3 Import regulations on food: Garlic and onion

Regulation	Requirement
Ministry of Agriculture Regulation No. 38/2017 on Import Recommendation for Horticulture Products	Importers must receive an Import Recommendation for Horticulture Products (Rekomendasi Impor Produk Hortikultura, RIPH) from the Minister of Agriculture. For garlic, importers must commit to cultivating 5 per cent of the total import volume in Indonesia and submit a report of previous cultivation efforts, if applicable. (Article 18.2) RIPH is issued twice per year. Importers can apply for RIPH only in specific times outside the pre-harvest, harvest and post-harvest periods, as decided by the Directorate General. (Articles 6 and 10)
Ministry of Agriculture Regulation No. 24/2018 Changes to No. 38/2017	The time limit for RIPH issuance in Articles 6 and 10 is removed. Importers can now apply for RIPH at any time. The requirements remain the same as Regulation No. 38/2017.
Ministry of Trade Regulation No. 44/2019 on Import Requirement for Horticulture Products	Importers must obtain an import licence from the Minister of Trade. The required documents are (Article 6): 1. Nomor Induk Berusaha (Business Identification Number) 2. Proof of cold storage ownership 3. Proof of ownership of transportation suitable for horticulture 4. Letter of statement of condition of cold storage and transport 5. RIPH Importers must also conduct a pre-shipment inspection in the exporting country, conducted through Laporan Surveyor (Surveyor Report). (Articles 17–19)
Ministry of Trade Regulation No. 27/2020 Changes to No. 44/2019	Temporary exemption of import licence and Surveyor Report requirements for onion and garlic shipped before 31 May 2020.

process led to import delays, causing the garlic price to shoot up by 49 per cent to Rp 57,350 per kilogram and in some weeks increasing to more than Rp 70,000 per kilogram between December and March (KPPU 2020). Faced with global trade disruption during the pandemic, the import restriction only limits Indonesia's ability to proactively anticipate or remedy food shortages. In response, the Ministry of Trade temporarily eliminated import licensing requirements for garlic and onion in March. As a result, garlic prices dropped back to Rp 40,650 per kilogram as of 23 April 2020 (PIHPS Nasional 2020). The import liberalisation strategy is a departure from Indonesia's usual self-sufficiency policy. As such, it was short-lived. The trade liberalising measure was only temporary until 31 May 2020 and was not extended once the price stabilised.

Indonesia's broader response to the potential food crisis during the pandemic remains consistent with its self-sufficiency discourse. In response to concerns over food supply later in 2020 or in 2021, the government turns inward, that is, towards increasing domestic production instead of looking to trade. President Joko Widodo announced the creation of a food estate in Kalimantan with a target to develop 165,000 hectares into farmland, and later appointed defence minister Prabowo Subianto to oversee the development (Fachriansyah 2020; Parama 2020). Large-scale food estates have long been the policy of choice for the Indonesian government, starting with President Suharto's Mega Rice Program, President Yudhoyono's Merauke Integrated Food and Energy Estate, and President Widodo's 500,000 hectares of food estate in Kalimantan in 2015, even though the models have been repeatedly criticised for failing to achieve the intended production targets, creating serious environmental problems, disenfranchising local populations, and even contributing to poverty among the local populations (Neilson 2018: 82–83).

To help ease food insecurity for the vulnerable poor during COVID-19, the Indonesian Ministry of Social Affairs expanded its Staple Food Card Program (Kartu Sembako) from 15 million families to 20 million beneficiary families. The subsidy also increased from Rp 150,000 to Rp 200,000 per family per month, and can be used to purchase rice, eggs, vegetables, fruit and legumes (SKRI 2020). While this is welcome assistance, a recent study shows that it loses its effectiveness if food prices remain expensive (Ilman 2020).

Long-term implications

The COVID-19 pandemic's impact on food security is apparent, in terms of both access and dietary diversity. People outside Java are more vulnerable to food shortages if distribution problems are not addressed. While people in rural areas may adapt to local food sources for subsistence, this option is difficult for people living in non-farming areas or for the urban poor. The lack of physical and financial access to food may cause millions of people to experience hunger. This effect has started to surface. A high-frequency survey by the World Bank covering more than 4000 respondents found that, in the first two weeks of May 2020, 31 per cent of households experienced a shortage of food and 38 per cent of households ate less than they should (Purnamasari and Ali 2020). While a slight improvement was observed in August 2020 after PSBB regulations were relaxed, the numbers are still concerning at 24 per cent and 30 per cent, respectively (Purnamasari and Sjahrir 2020). These disadvantaged households are predominantly poor, female-headed and located outside Java, and are more likely in households experiencing income shocks, which suggests affordability issues.

Dietary quality will likely worsen. People who have lost their income will shift their consumption to cheaper, less nutritious food such as rice, as was evident during the Asian financial crisis, leading to problems such as increased prevalence of anaemia in children (Block et al. 2004; Headey and Ruel 2020). This will aggravate the already poor diet where rice makes up 70 per cent of Indonesians' daily dietary energy needs, while consumption of fruit, vegetables and meat is still low. If dietary quality is not addressed, increases in stunting can also be expected given the high correlation between unaffordability of a healthy diet and child stunting (FAO et al. 2020: 86, 113).

The implication of Indonesia's food policy goes beyond food security; it also affects poverty. The relationship between food and poverty is double-edged. Poverty prevents people from accessing quality food and, at the same time, high food prices prevent people from escaping poverty. On average, Indonesians spend almost half of their expenditure on food and beverages.[4] An early estimate suggests that the pandemic may increase the poverty rate from 9.2 per cent in 2019 to 9.7 per cent in the mildest scenario, or to 16.7 per cent in the most severe scenario at the end of 2020, which means between 1.3 million and 19.7 million more Indonesians could be pushed into poverty, wiping away decades of progress in poverty reduction (Suryahadi et al. 2020). High food prices will undermine any poverty reduction efforts after COVID-19.

---

4 World Bank Global Consumption Database—Indonesia, http://datatopics. worldbank.org/consumption/country/Indonesia

Moving forward: Building a resilient food system

The COVID-19 pandemic exposes the vulnerability in Indonesia's food systems, in particular its declining production trend, inadequate distribution capacity and trade limitations. Indonesia now faces food insecurity risks amid the pandemic with potentially long-lasting implications for poverty and nutrition. In the meantime, the climate crisis is already putting a strain on Indonesia's food systems, which could aggravate food insecurity in the long run. Policy reforms in the food and agriculture sector will be crucial to ensure a more robust and resilient food system.

More investment will be necessary to strengthen Indonesia's domestic agriculture production, especially for research and development and technology towards sustainable agriculture. Investment in Indonesia's agriculture in 2016 was a meagre Rp 400 trillion, coming mostly from farmers themselves and less than 5 per cent from foreign direct investment (ADB 2019). The United Nations Conference on Trade and Development estimated that global foreign direct investment will decrease by up to 40 per cent in 2020 and foreign direct investment to Asia could decline by around 30–45 per cent (UNCTAD 2020b). Facing this pessimistic outlook, the Indonesian government must proactively attract foreign direct investment to support Indonesia's agriculture by simplifying its regulatory framework (Patunru and Surianta 2020).

In addition to supporting domestic agricultural production, diversification of food supply is also needed. Relying on domestic production alone increases exposure to domestic production risks. Yet current trade restrictions such as the quantitative restrictions have hampered Indonesia's ability to source food from the global market in times of crisis. Furthermore, trade restrictions have kept domestic food prices high compared to international prices, which prevents the poor from accessing food and at the same time undermines poverty reduction efforts. Indonesia could benefit from reducing its food and agriculture import restrictions, such as by simplifying the non-tariff measures across the ministries and agencies and reforming its import licensing regime in the Ministry of Trade.

Reforms to open up to investment and to food trade may come in the omnibus law on job creation that was passed in October 2020. The law changed provisions in the food law to now allow imports, with consideration of farmers' and fishers' interests. It also removes limits and barriers to foreign investment in the horticulture, plantation and livestock sectors, and eases restrictions to inputs like seeds and veterinary drugs. This is a major breakthrough in an otherwise restricted sector and can potentially boost Indonesia's food security by opening access to the global market. However, many of the changes in the omnibus law are to be clarified in following government regulations, so policy and procedural changes as well as its implementation are still to be anticipated.

Aside from reforming its own policies, Indonesia could also work with other countries to ensure regional food security. The ASEAN Economic Community (AEC), for example, has a major focus on the agriculture sector. In response to the 2008 food price crisis, the AEC established ASEAN Plus Three Emergency Rice Reserve (APTERR), which could be useful in times of crisis. This initiative, however, needs significant improvement. Beyond that, the AEC through its ASEAN Trade in Goods Agreement provides the opportunity for greater integration to the market (Patunru and Ilman 2020). Greenville (2018) estimated that rice market integration in ASEAN could lead to a 5 per cent reduction in the number of households experiencing undernourishment, with gains in food security for Indonesia.

To conclude, a self-sufficiency food policy is not useful, especially in times of crisis, and may risk exacerbating food insecurity risks. During and after a crisis, regional or global cooperation to maintain a flow of food trade is crucial for food security. Indonesia can support this by reassessing and reforming its own domestic policies to open up to global food trade.

References

ADB (Asian Development Bank). 2019. *Policies to Support Investment Requirements of Indonesia's Food and Agriculture Development during 2020–2045*. October. Manila: ADB.

Adjie, Moch. Fiqih Prawira. 2020. 'Former PDI-P lawmaker sentenced to seven years in prison in garlic import permit bribery case'. *Jakarta Post*, 7 May. www.thejakartapost.com/news/2020/05/07/former-pdi-p-lawmaker-sentenced-to-seven-years-in-prison-in-garlic-import-permit-bribery-case.html

AIP-PRISMA (Australia–Indonesia Partnership for Promoting Rural Incomes through Support for Markets in Agriculture). 2020. 'Impact of COVID-19 on agriculture (farmers perspective)'. 29 April. https://aip-prisma.or.id/data/public/uploaded_file/2020-05-29_09-44-01am_PRISMA_Report_COVID-19_Study_-_Farmers_Perspective_(English).pdf

Alavi, Hamid R., Aira Htenas, Ron Kopicki, Andrew W. Shepherd and Ramon Clarete. 2012. *Trusting Trade and the Private Sector for Food Security in Southeast Asia*. Washington, DC: World Bank.

Arifin, Bustanul, Noer Azam Achsani, Drajat Martianto, Linda Karlina Sari and Ahmad Heri Firdaus. 2018. 'Modeling the future of Indonesian food consumption: Final report'. Jakarta: World Food Programme. www.wfp.org/content/2018-modeling-future-indonesia-food-consumption

Block, Steven A., Lynnda Kiess, Patrick Webb, Soewarta Kosen, Regina Moench-Pfanner, Martin W. Bloem and C. Peter Timmer. 2004. 'Macro shocks and micro outcomes: Child nutrition during Indonesia's crisis'. *Economics & Human Biology* 2(1): 21–44. doi.org/10.1016/j.ehb.2003.12.007

Bloomberg. 2020. 'Indian ports in confusion as virus lockdown hits operations'. *Bloomberg*, 25 March. www.bloomberg.com/news/articles/2020-03-25/indian-ports-declare-force-majeure-amid-national-virus-lockdown

BPS (Badan Pusat Statistik). 2020a. 'Luas panen, produksi, dan produktivitas padi menurut provinsi 2018–2020'. www.bps.go.id/indicator/53/1498/1/luas-panen-produksi-dan-produktivitas-padi-menurut-provinsi.html

BPS (Badan Pusat Statistik). 2020b. 'NTP (Nilai Tukar Petani) menurut provinsi (2018 = 100) 2020'. www.bps.go.id/indicator/22/1741/1/ntp-nilai-tukar-petani-menurut-provinsi-2018-100-.html

Databoks. 2017. 'Di mana provinsi dengan stunting tertinggi 2017?' Databoks. https://databoks.katadata.co.id/datapublish/2018/04/08/di-mana-provinsi-dengan-stunting-tertinggi-2017

Espitia, Alvaro, Nadia Rocha and Michele Ruta. 2020. 'COVID-19 and food protectionism: The impact of the pandemic and export restrictions on world food markets'. *Policy Research Working Paper* No. 9253. Washington, DC: World Bank. http://hdl.handle.net/10986/33800

Fachriansyah, Rizki. 2020. 'Prabowo to oversee development of food estate program, Jokowi says'. *Jakarta Post*, 14 July. www.thejakartapost.com/news/2020/07/14/prabowo-to-oversee-development-of-food-estate-program-jokowi-says.html

FAO (Food and Agriculture Organization of the United Nations). 2018a. *The State of Agricultural Commodity Markets 2018: Agricultural Trade, Climate Change and Food Security.* Rome: FAO.

FAO (Food and Agriculture Organization of the United Nations). 2018b. 'Small family farms country factsheet: Indonesia'. www.fao.org/3/i8881en/I8881EN.pdf

FAO (Food and Agriculture Organization of the United Nations). 2020a. 'FAO cereal supply and demand brief'. www.fao.org/worldfoodsituation/csdb/en/

FAO (Food and Agriculture Organization of the United Nations). 2020b. 'Crop prospects and food situation'. *Quarterly Global Report* No. 2, July. www.fao.org/3/ca9803en/CA9803EN.pdf

FAO, IFAD, UNICEF, WFP and WHO (Food and Agriculture Organization of the United Nations, International Fund for Agriculture Development, United Nations International Children's Fund, World Food Programme and World Health Organization). 2020. *The State of Food Security and Nutrition in the World 2020: Transforming Food Systems for Affordable Healthy Diets.* Rome: FAO. https://doi.org/10.4060/ca9692en

Greenville, Jared. 2018. 'ASEAN rice market integration: Findings from a feasibility study'. *OECD Food, Agriculture and Fisheries Papers* No. 117. Paris: OECD Publishing. doi.org/10.1787/8ca16e31-en

Headey, Derek and Marie Ruel. 2020. 'The COVID-19 nutrition crisis: What to expect and how to protect'. In *COVID-19 and Global Food Security*, edited by Johan Swinnen and John McDermott, 38–41. International Food Policy Research Institute.

Ilman, Assyifa Szami. 2020. 'Effects of high food prices on non-cash food subsidies (BPNT) in Indonesia: Case study in East Nusa Tenggara'. *CIPS Policy Paper* No. 26. www.cips-indonesia.org/bpnt-case-study-in-ntt

ITC (International Trade Centre). 2020. 'COVID-19 temporary trade measures'. 6 October. www.macmap.org/covid19

Jadhav, Rajendra and Mayank Bhardwaj. 2020. 'Exclusive: Indian rice exports suspended on supply chain disruption–industry'. Reuters, 4 April. www.reuters. com/article/us-health-coronavirus-india-food-exclusi-idUSKBN21L1XX

KPPU (Komisi Pengawas Persaingan Usaha, Commission for the Supervision of Business Competition). 2020. 'Perkembangan komoditi bawang putih di awal 2020'. Siaran Pers No. 7/KPPU/PR/II/2020.

Marks, Stephen V. 2017. 'Non-tariff trade regulations in Indonesia: Nominal and effective rates of protection'. *Bulletin of Indonesian Economic Studies* 53(3): 333–57. doi.org/10.1080/00074918.2017.1298721

Martin, Will J. and Joseph W. Glauber. 2020. 'Trade policy and food security'. In *COVID-19 and Trade Policy: Why Turning Inward Won't Work*, edited by Richard E. Baldwin and Simon J. Evenett, 89–101. London: CEPR Press.

Ministry of Agriculture. 2020. 'Kementan: Tidak benar stok beras menipis'. http:// bkp.pertanian.go.id/blog/post/kementan-tidak-benar-stok-beras-menipis

MLA (Meat & Livestock Australia). 2020. 'Industry projections 2020: Australian cattle – April update.' www.mla.com.au/prices-markets/Trends-analysis/ cattle-projections/

Neilson, Jeff. 2018. 'Feeding the bangsa: Food sovereignty and the state in Indonesia'. In *Indonesia in the New World: Globalisation, Nationalism and Sovereignty*, edited by Arianto A. Patunru, Mari Pangestu and M. Chatib Basri, 73–89. Singapore: ISEAS – Yusof Ishak Institute.

Oxford Economics. 2020. *Mapping Asia's Food Trade and the Impact of COVID-19*. Singapore: Oxford Economics.

Parama, Mardika. 2020. 'Government to develop 165,000 hectares land in Central Kalimantan for food-estate program'. *Jakarta Post*, 11 June. www. thejakartapost.com/news/2020/06/11/government-to-develop-165000-hectares-land-in-central-kalimantan-for-food-estate-program.html

Patunru, Arianto A. Forthcoming. 'Is greater openness to trade good? What are the effects on poverty and inequality?' In *Globalization, Poverty, and Income Inequality: Insights from Indonesia*, edited by Richard Barichello, Arianto A. Patunru and Richard Schwindt. Vancouver: University of British Columbia Press.

Patunru, Arianto A. and Assyifa Szami Ilman. 2020. 'Political economy of rice policy in Indonesia: A perspective on the ASEAN Economic Community'. *CIPS Discussion Paper* No. 6. www.cips-indonesia.org/political-economy-rice-policy

Patunru, Arianto A. and Andree Surianta. 2020. 'Attracting FDI post COVID-19 by simplifying Indonesia's regulatory framework'. *CIPS Policy Brief*, 20 May. www.cips-indonesia.org/post/policy-brief-attracting-fdi-post-covid-19-by-simplifying-indonesia-s-regulatory-framework

PIHPS Nasional (Pusat Informasi Harga Pangan Strategis Nasional, National Strategic Commodity Price Centre). 2020. https://hargapangan.id

Purnamasari, Ririn and Rabia Ali. 2020. 'High-frequency monitoring of households: Summary of results from survey round 1, 1–17 May 2020'. *Indonesia COVID-19 Observatory Brief* No. 3. World Bank, 26 June. https://openknowledge.worldbank.org/handle/10986/34740

Purnamasari, Ririn and Bambang Suharnoko Sjahrir. 2020. 'High-frequency monitoring of socio-economic impact of COVID-19 on households in Indonesia'. World Bank presentation, ANU Indonesia Project Global Seminar Series, 30 September. www.youtube.com/watch?v=4DYck8WOLxk

Rahman, Dzulfiqar Fathur. 2020a. 'Virus, climate change cause food shortages in parts of Indonesia'. *Jakarta Post*, 8 May. www.thejakartapost.com/news/2020/05/06/virus-climate-change-cause-food-shortages-in-parts-of-indonesia.html

Rahman, Dzulfiqar Fathur. 2020b. 'Pandemic disrupts food distribution across country, minister says'. *Jakarta Post*, 15 July. www.thejakartapost.com/news/2020/07/14/pandemic-disrupts-food-distribution-across-country-minister-says.html

Respatiadi, Hizkia and Hana Nabila. 2017. 'Beefing up the stock: Policy reform to lower beef prices in Indonesia'. Jakarta: Center for Indonesian Policy Studies. https://repository.cips-indonesia.org/publications/271870/beefing-up-the-stock-policy-reform-to-lower-beef-prices-in-indonesia

Ruslan, Kadir. 2019. 'Improving Indonesia's food statistics through the area sampling frame method'. *CIPS Discussion Paper* No. 7. www.cips-indonesia.org/area-sampling-frame-method

Schmidhuber, Josef. 2020. 'COVID-19: From a global health crisis to a global food crisis?' *Food Outlook*, June. Rome: FAO. www.fao.org/3/ca9509en/covid.pdf

Schmidhuber, Josef and Bing Qiao. 2020. *Comparing Crises: Great Lockdown versus Great Recession*. Rome: FAO. https://doi.org/10.4060/ca8833en

Schmidhuber, Josef, Jonathan Pound and Bing Qiao. 2020. *COVID-19: Channels of Transmission to Food and Agriculture*. Rome: FAO. https://doi.org/10.4060/ca8430en

SKRI (Sekretariat Kabinet Republik Indonesia). 2020. 'Atasi dampak COVID-19, Kemensos berikan bansos reguler dan nonreguler'. 9 May. https://setkab.go.id/atasi-dampak-covid-19-kemensos-berikan-bansos-reguler-dan-nonreguler/

Suryahadi, Asep, Ridho Al Izzati and Daniel Suryadarma. 2020. 'Estimating the impact of COVID-19 on poverty in Indonesia'. *Bulletin of Indonesian Economic Studies* 56(2): 175–92. doi.org/10.1080/00074918.2020.1779390

UNCTAD (United Nations Conference on Trade and Development). 2020a. 'Global trade continues nosedive, UNCTAD forecasts 20% drop in 2020'. 11 June. https://unctad.org/news/global-trade-continues-nosedive-unctad-forecasts-20-drop-2020

UNCTAD (United Nations Conference on Trade and Development). 2020b. *World Investment Report 2020: International Production beyond the Pandemic*. New York: United Nations Publications. https://unctad.org/en/PublicationsLibrary/wir2020_en.pdf

WFP (World Food Programme). 2017. 'Food security monitoring bulletin – Indonesia. Special focus: Food affordability and Ramadan'. Volume 6, April. Jakarta: WFP. https://documents.wfp.org/stellent/groups/public/documents/ena/wfp291748. pdf?_ga=2.181577763.564713101.1604921287-289071716.1602485830

WFP (World Food Programme). 2020. 'Indonesia. COVID-19: Economic and food security implications'. www.wfp.org/publications/indonesia-covid-19-economic-and-food-security-implications

WITS (World Integrated Trade Solution). 2020. 'Indonesia product exports and imports 2018'. https://wits.worldbank.org/countrysnapshot/en/IDN/textview

World Bank. 2020a. *Global Economic Prospects, June 2020.* Washington, DC: World Bank. www.worldbank.org/en/publication/global-economic-prospects

World Bank. 2020b. 'Agricultural raw materials exports (% of merchandise exports)'. https://data.worldbank.org/indicator/TX.VAL.AGRI.ZS.UN

World Bank. 2020c. 'Commodity Markets Monthly Prices'. www.worldbank.org/en/research/commodity-markets

WTO (World Trade Organization). 2020. 'Trade set to plunge as COVID-19 pandemic upends global economy'. Press release, 8 April. www.wto.org/english/news_e/pres20_e/pr855_e.htm

WTO, ITC and UNCTAD (World Trade Organization, International Trade Centre and United Nations Conference on Trade and Development). 2019. *World Tariff Profile 2019.* Geneva: WTO. www.wto.org/english/res_e/publications_e/world_tariff_profiles19_e.htm

8 Improving Indonesia's targeting system to address the COVID-19 impact

Vivi Alatas

Abstract

In an increasingly complex environment of COVID-19, improving Indonesia's targeting system is needed more than ever. Both the poor and the bottom middle class need support during the current crisis. However, improving Indonesia's targeting system is technically and politically challenging. Support is needed from different stakeholders, and we need to ensure the system will improve the accuracy of targeting. Targeting accuracy could be improved by better collecting poor household data and better selecting the beneficiaries from those data. Better collection of data relies on ensuring the right households are surveyed. Accurately identifying the poor and the bottom half of the population from among those surveyed will lead to better selection of beneficiary households. Improving the selection method without improving the data collection will not improve the exclusion error. Improving data collection without improving the selection method will not address the changing environment. There are several choices in improving data collection and selection methods, each with different advantages. Because there is no best method for all situations, a mixed-method approach is recommended.

Introduction

COVID-19 is a double malady that creates not only health shocks but also economic shocks. In Indonesia, with businesses closed and large-scale mobility restrictions imposed after the COVID-19 outbreak, the World Bank estimated 24 per cent of households' breadwinners had stopped working by early May 2020 (Purnamasari and Ali 2020). Among household breadwinners who continued working, 64 per cent experienced reduced income and 32 per cent experienced food shortages. There was a significant improvement from May to August 2020, with only 10 per cent of breadwinners not working. Those experiencing food shortages also decreased, from 32 per cent to 24 per cent.[1] Wealthier and female-headed households experienced faster improvement than others. However, 13 per cent of households are experiencing worsening food shortages, mostly in the poorest 40 per cent of the population and outside Java.

It is not only the poor who need help. Households in the bottom middle class are also experiencing hardship. Indonesia's major household social assistance programs are critical in providing a safety net for affected households. Via Presidential Regulation No. 72/2020, the Indonesian government has allocated Rp 203.9 trillion for various programs (Table 8.1).

Considering limited budgets and the uncertainty of when COVID-19 will cease, the programs' impacts depend on accurate targeting. In an increasingly complex environment of COVID, improving Indonesia's targeting system is needed more than ever.

The World Bank high-frequency monitoring survey showed a significant reliance on government assistance. As of May 2020, 55 per cent of households relied on government assistance, with higher reliance among households with older females, lower-educated households, and those in the bottom 40 per cent of the population. By August 2020, based on Round 3 of the World Bank survey, 89 per cent of the bottom 40 per cent of the population had received at least one social assistance or relief measure.[2] However, within each social assistance program there are still significant exclusion errors and deserving households who have not benefited from the program. The Staple Food Card (Kartu Sembako) and the Family Hope Program (Program Keluarga Harapan, PKH) rely on

---

1 'Indonesia: High-frequency monitoring of COVID-19 impacts on households and individuals, Round 3 (August 2020)', a phone survey supported by the World Bank.
2 'Indonesia: High-frequency monitoring of COVID-19 impacts on households and individuals, Round 3 (August 2020)', a phone survey supported by the World Bank.

Table 8.1 Government social assistance programs

Social assistance program	Budget (rupiah trillion)
Family Hope Program (Program Keluarga Harapan, PKH)	37.4
Staple Food Card (Kartu Sembako)	43.6
Social assistance for Jakarta and its surrounding cities	6.8
Social assistance for the rest of the country	32.4
Pre-employment Card (Kartu Prakerja)	20.0
Village Funds Direct Cash Assistance (Bantuan Langsung Tunai Dana Desa)	31.8
Electricity bill discount program	6.9
Food in-kind transfer program	25.0

the Integrated Database for Social Welfare (Data Terpadu Kesejahteraan Sosial, DTKS), a registry that collects information about the bottom 40 per cent of individuals, to determine beneficiaries. Only 34 per cent of the bottom 30 per cent of the population have received assistance from PKH and/or the Kartu Sembako (Figure 8.1). In addition, the DTKS has limitations. The data cover only 17 per cent of the middle 50 per cent of the population. Therefore, the DTKS data were not adequate to ensure an effective response to help vulnerable households to cope with the economic impact of COVID-19. Moreover, data from the National Socioeconomic Survey (Survei Sosio-Ekonomi Nasional, Susenas) 2019 also indicated the need to improve the DTKS data. Although Figure 8.2 shows a progressive targeting, substantial beneficiaries still came from the upper 40 per cent of the population.

The COVID-19 battle is ongoing, and households continue to need support. Improving the targeting system is important in helping Indonesia address both current and future shocks. There are several benefits of having an improved targeting system. Any shocks—financial, fuel, food prices or pandemic—can happen. Well-targeted programs can help affected households manage those shocks. The targeting system is also an essential instrument in reforming policies that can allow the government to compensate those affected. Indonesia has had several experiences with compensation programs for fuel subsidies. The targeting system is also crucial for better and progressive fiscal spending in addressing poverty and inequality.

Figure 8.1 Beneficiaries of social welfare by program (%)

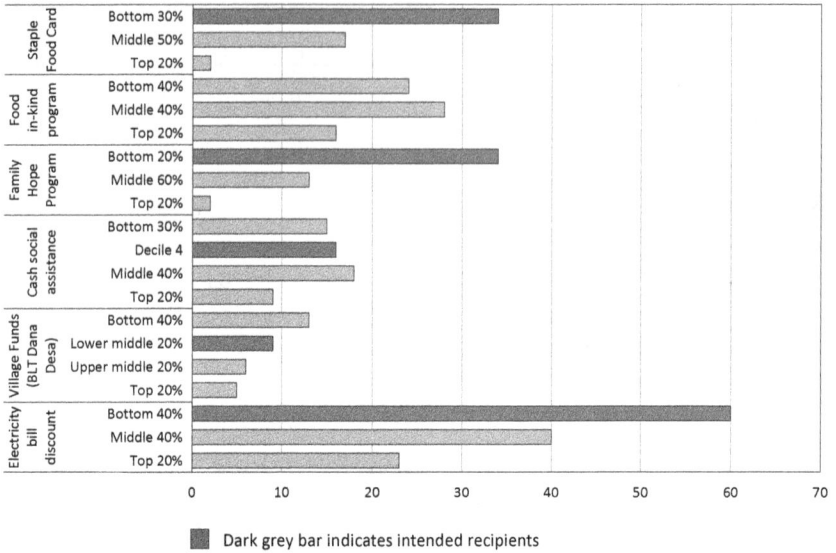

Dark grey bar indicates intended recipients

Source: 'Indonesia: High-frequency monitoring of COVID-19 impacts on households and individuals, Round 3 (August 2020)', a phone survey supported by the World Bank.

Figure 8.2 Coverage of social assistance program by decile (%)

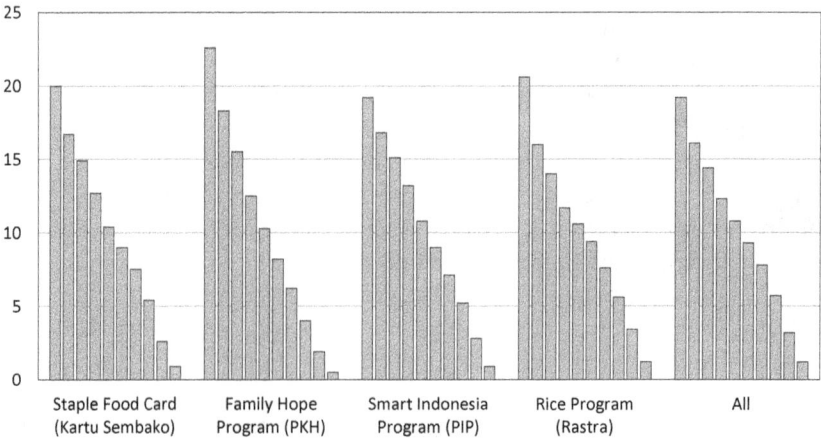

Note: Deciles are ordered left to right from 1 (poorest) to 10 (richest) for each program.
Source: Susenas (2019).

Nevertheless, it is not easy to establish and maintain a targeting system. Indonesia is a complex targeting environment. It is the world's largest archipelago and fourth most populous country. It has a considerable, decentralised budget and operational control over more than 500 districts. The high vulnerability of poverty creates additional challenges in distinguishing the poor and near-poor because Indonesian poverty is very fluid, with high entry and exit rates. Also, optimising targeting methods is subject to a degree of path dependency because various social poverty programs have used the current data with its high degree of exclusion and inclusion errors.

Improving targeting needs buy-in from all stakeholders. In the first place, implementation at central levels requires line ministries buy-in of all program elements. Similarly, implementation at local levels requires local government, local leaders and community buy-in. Further, continued political support requires parliamentary cooperation. Several factors determine this buy-in. The first factor is the credibility of the institution in charge of implementation. Effective collaboration among different institutions with clear roles and responsibilities can increase acceptance. Another important factor is the rigour of the targeting methods. Targeting methods need to be technically correct, with comprehensive and feasible operating procedures.

The main ingredient of a national targeting system is a unified registry of potential beneficiaries. Improving the registry requires data collection and selection decisions. Collection methods are needed to determine which households to assess. There are several choices for collection methods (World Bank 2012). Geographical targeting can be used to determine areas to survey, such as pockets of poverty. It is also quite common to rely on community referrals to select which households to visit. There is also a choice of revisiting and updating pre-existing lists from the existing social protection programs. Some countries allow self-assessment of anyone who thinks themselves poor to apply.

Selection methods are needed to assess households and determine beneficiaries. While some countries may have the necessary information to use a means-testing method, others need to use proxy means testing (PMT) by using a scoring system of indicators correlated with income or consumption. When budgets allow, it is also common to use a categorical selection method, where all households with specific demographic characteristics qualify. Communities can also have a role through community selection, either through village meetings or through the discretion of village heads or village elites. Lastly, the program rule can allow self-selection, with anyone who applies able to enter the program.

A mix of methods can be used in different areas or contexts, given there is no best method for all situations. Indonesia has been using various mixed methods (World Bank 2012). For example, the 2005 BLT Dana Desa (Bantuan Langsung Tunai Dana Desa, Village Funds Direct Cash Assistance) mainly used community selection, self-assessment and pre-existing lists to collect data, while it used PMT and community selection to determine beneficiaries. In theory, the village head is supposed to nominate potential beneficiaries for the data collection method, in addition to the family planning data list. In practice, mostly only village head nominations were used. The 2008 BLT Dana Desa was supposed to use consultative community meetings to update the list for households that had moved or were no longer poor, and for people who had died. In reality, mostly only village officials participated in the meetings. And community meetings did not improve the inclusion error. Households that had moved and people who had died were removed from the list, but households that were no longer poor were not removed from the list.

Improving the collection system

How should new households be identified? We can use a mixed-method approach to collect data. Three main methods can be used and matched to the local district context. In the poorest districts, in pockets of poverty, it is most useful to include all households by doing survey sweeps. In other areas, a combination of an on-demand system and community nominations can be used. An on-demand system allows households who feel they need to be on the list to apply.

Survey sweeps

A survey sweep collects data for all households in a particular area. In the poorest districts, it is most useful to visit all households. This method ensures no exclusion error due to missed households during data collection (exclusion can still occur through model error). Although this involves an extra cost, it is usually relatively little extra to visit all households within the same poor subdistricts. A World Bank (2012) study showed that conducting survey sweeps resulted in a significant improvement in targeting accuracy. To help identify the poorest subdistricts, we can estimate poverty maps from census data using an econometric model. The exact number of subdistricts to sweep will come from the poverty map classification analysis, subject to budget constraints.

Community nominations

In other areas, community meetings can help identify poor households currently excluded from the DTKS and affluent households that are currently in the DTKS by mistake. The advantage of such meetings is that communities will better understand the targeting of social assistance programs. Moreover, community participation in the process helps reduce inclusion and exclusion errors. Equally important, involving the community increases satisfaction with targeting outcomes and reduces local conflict.

Nonetheless, these meetings require careful guidance, socialisation and implementation. Community meetings are culturally typical in Java but less so in other parts of Indonesia. In less densely populated areas, such as Papua and inland Kalimantan, different testing procedures and processes will be required.

Community targeting has potential strengths. With community involvement, we can rely on local knowledge of low-economic-status households, as community members may have better information about recent shocks and unobserved characteristics not collected in household surveys. Community involvement may lead to greater support as final beneficiary lists may be closer to community opinions. Participation in the process may increase satisfaction, even if some may disagree with the outcome. Increased satisfaction will also strengthen community buy-in of the targeting outcomes.

However, there are potential weaknesses in community targeting. We cannot ignore the possibility of corruption, nepotism or political exploitation. A community leader in determining beneficiaries might include relatives and friends or include specific individuals or households for political leverage. The community may not focus on targeting, and may wish to avoid dissent. The community may use criteria different from that specified for the program. Furthermore, the concept of community can be quite different between rural areas and urban areas.

Whether community targeting will do better than using a PMT scoring system is an empirical question. The government, J-PAL[3] and the World Bank conducted randomised control trials to test several different targeting methods. In the first treatment, beneficiary selection used PMT scores up to a village quota based on poverty mapping estimates. In the second treatment, a facilitator helped the community rank all households

---

3   The Abdul Latif Jameel Poverty Action Lab (J-PAL) is a research centre in the Massachusetts Institute of Technology whose aim is to reduce poverty by ensuring that policy is based on scientific evidence. www.povertyactionlab.org/

in each village. Households with the lowest ranking up to the village quota received benefits.

There are several main findings of these targeting experiments (Alatas et al. 2012). PMT provided more accurate estimates of household consumption, particularly for those near the poverty line. However, community targeting was more accurate at identifying households with the lowest consumption levels (Figure 8.3). Also, satisfaction in outcomes from community targeting was higher than that from PMT. Outcomes from community targeting correlated 10 percentage points higher than those of PMT to self-assessment of one's poverty level (as surveyed before the research project). Community satisfaction, and hence buy-in, was significantly higher when villagers were involved in the targeting process. Community-led approaches better incorporate local knowledge and definitions of poverty that may not be captured by PMT, reducing the exclusion error of the very poor. Data capture by elites was also tested: in half of the villages, only community elites chose beneficiaries, while in the other half of villages the whole community was invited to a meeting. There was no evidence of elite capture, with no difference in mistargeting outcomes (Alatas et al. 2019). Elite households and their relatives were less likely to be selected, regardless of actual consumption levels. However, benefit levels were low (Rp 30,000 or about US$3).

Figure 8.3 Comparison of proxy means testing and community-targeting methods for determining poverty, by decile

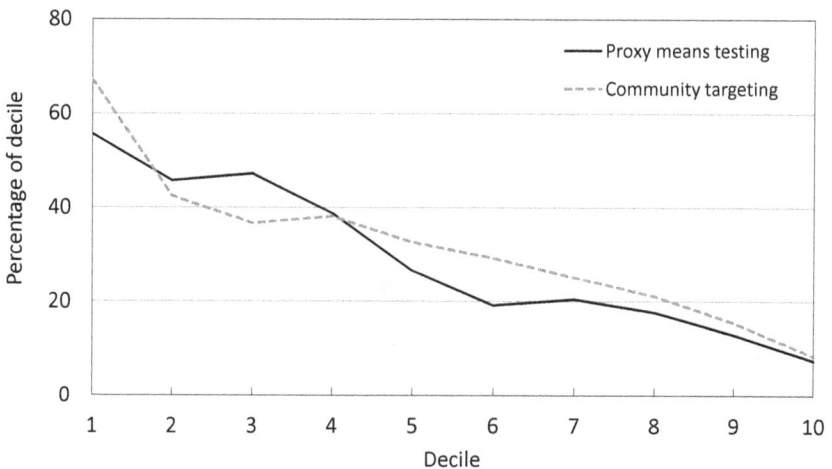

Source: Alatas et al. (2012).

In improving the targeting system, communities can have several roles. Communities can improve the data collection process with a standardised protocol about who should participate, and a transparent procedure. To avoid crowded meetings during the COVID-19 pandemic, smaller meetings could be conducted, inviting only village representatives, which is more straightforward, safer and cheaper. Community meetings can help verify preliminary beneficiary lists by adding excluded poor households up to a fixed quota. Community meetings can also help to resolve appeals and serve as an offline on-demand mechanism. Households excluded from initial beneficiary lists could appeal through the program's complaints and grievances process. In principle, the Village Funds Program (Dana Desa) could facilitate the community role as long as it has a better standard of operating procedures and monitoring systems in place than currently.

On-demand applications

The goal is not just to improve targeting now. There is a need to ensure the targeting system is continuously maintained and used across time. It needs to ensure Indonesia can react quickly to any emergency. On-demand targeting can reduce the cost of surveying many households while still allowing affected poor and vulnerable households to apply for subsequent verification.

Other countries' experience shows that 10–15 per cent of total target households apply through on-demand applications (World Bank 2012). We can quickly increase coverage needed during the COVID-19 crisis if we use an on-demand application. The implementation itself can be online or offline. During COVID-19, we need to maximise the online mechanism and also involve community targeting to ensure better coverage. Furthermore, technology can help make the application available anytime and verify the list with other data.

We can use data from several sources to verify claims. Verification with other data can prune applicants with high electricity and mobile phone use from the data. The value of land and building tax (*pajak bumi dan bangunan*) gives proxies of dwelling prices and hence applicants' economic status. Cross-referencing with other databases, such as those for property tax, mortgages, car loans and electricity use, will allow the screening out of non-poor households from the data. If people know there will be a verification process, it can further discourage upper middle class households from applying. World Bank–J-PAL–Government of Indonesia experiments have shown that with proper socialisation in place, affluent households, sometimes selected by PMT models as beneficiaries, actually self-select themselves by not applying (Alatas et al. 2016).

Improving the selection system

We need to improve both collection and selection processes. Improving collection without improving selection will not give us a better ability to distinguish the bottom middle class from the upper middle class. Improving the selection method without improving collection will not give us the bigger coverage necessary and significant reduction of exclusion error.

Accurate and sound PMT models are at the heart of the selection model. International experience and field experiments in Indonesia show that PMT is one of the most accurate targeting mechanisms. The use of PMT means that assessments are objective and replicable. They also ensure horizontal equity across households. A poor household in one district has the same chance of being assessed as eligible for programs as a poor household in another district. Relying only upon local officials or communities to assess households means that very different criteria may be used in different places, and the chances of the poor getting assistance can depend on where they live.

PMT models need to be updated over time. The current DTKS PMT models were developed in 2015. We need more recent data to update the models and to assess whether the current statistical approaches are still the most accurate.

In improving PMT, three problems need to be addressed. The first problem is unobserved characteristics if we use only the existing PMT variables or those collected through the Susenas household surveys. Considering the need to expand coverage, we need better data to distinguish transient versus chronic poor, the upper deciles from middle deciles, and bottom deciles. Other data sources can be used to improve the selection model. Google Street Data can be used to get better data to assess and categorise neighbourhoods. GPS data of each household can provide additional variables such as access to facilities and spatial data. The land agency data can improve neighbourhood assessment by using spatial characteristics, landownership and land value predictions. Satellite data can show areas that are illuminated at night, and areas of vegetation.[4] Deep learning methods can classify dwelling characteristics from photographs.

The second problem is small sample size. The desire to have a different model for a different district can create a dilemma of choosing specificity versus precision. We can encounter an overfitting model when we rely on

---

4 Vegetation extent provides an estimate of the degree of urban/rural land and area used for agriculture as a main source of income in a neighbourhood.

a relatively small number of observations with a large number of variables in a district.[5] We need to strike a better balance of where to disaggregate the model. The third problem is the need to more accurately model where a household sits in the overall distribution of expenditure. There is potential for improvement in exploring more sophisticated methods like machine learning and deep learning. A machine learning approach can help in finding a model with better accuracy.

The focus of improvement needs to be balanced. Focusing mostly on using sophisticated machine learning and deep learning methods will not improve unless we also address unobserved characteristics, small sample sizes and better collection methods.

Moving to dynamic updating

The ultimate goal is to move from static and infrequent updating to dynamic updating with on-demand application and graduating households throughout the year. The incorporation of unique identification numbers—NIK (Nomor Identifikasi Kependudukan)—will allow cross-referencing with other databases, such as those for property tax, mortgages, car loans, electricity use, phone use and other data. The cross-referencing will then allow dynamic screening out of non-poor households from the registry.

Dynamic updating can be done either in real time or through frequent batch processing. Some countries require households to recertify themselves every one or two years (e.g. Brazil), staggered across households to smooth the workload. Details such as address and new family members can be updated at any time. Updating that would affect economic status should only be allowed periodically (once a year, for example), but the on-demand application can happen at any time. Dynamic updating has the advantage that as households' demographic or economic circumstances change, they can update their details in the DTKS, making them either automatically eligible for new programs or waitlisted. Buy-in from communities, local governments and line ministries tends to be higher as well. The disadvantage is that office infrastructure, including a reliable internet connection, is required at a local level, and can be difficult to establish in remote areas.

A related function for maintaining the targeting system is an effective grievance redress system. When a household feels unfairly excluded from a program (or if a wealthy household is unfairly included), a system is

---

5 An overfitting model is a condition where a statistical model begins to describe the random error in the data rather than the relationships between variables. This problem occurs when the model is too complex.

needed to receive and evaluate a complaint. When a dynamic updating system exists, a grievance redress system can largely piggyback this process. Households can apply to be assessed or re-assessed, and this occurs alongside regular updating.

Summary recommendations

The benefits of moving towards improving the targeting system are clear. Having a national targeting system reduces costs, improves the impact of social programs, and helps Indonesia respond better in addressing current and future shocks. The availability of such a system facilitates the implementation of complementary programs for beneficiaries and expansion of coverage when there is a need to help beyond just the poor households. The system also facilitates the implementation of dynamic entry and exit strategies for social programs using on-demand application and cross-checking with other data.

Indonesia does not need to start from scratch because the current DTKS data already include around 40 per cent of all Indonesian households. This makes the DTKS a good initial dataset to build upon in developing a proper targeting system with a registry of not only poor and vulnerable Indonesians but also the bottom middle class. The DTKS data and the system can be improved by conducting the following four steps: (1) identifying pockets of poverty to do survey sweeping, (2) setting up a proper on-demand application system that is linked to other data to verify claims, (3) involving communities with standardised procedures and (4) addressing the three problems to improve PMT, described above. With political willingness, Indonesia can have a sound targeting system that can help ensure whatever the storm, Indonesia has the instruments to respond and cope.

References

Alatas, Vivi, Abhijit Banerjee, Rema Hanna, Benjamin A. Olken and Julia Tobias. 2012. 'Targeting the poor: Evidence from a field experiment in Indonesia'. *American Economic Review* 102(4): 1206–40. doi.org/10.1257/aer.102.4.1206

Alatas, Vivi, Abhijit Banerjee, Rema Hanna, Benjamin A. Olken, Ririn Purnamasari and Matthew Wai-Poi. 2016. 'Self-targeting: Evidence from a field experiment in Indonesia'. *Journal of Political Economy* 124(2): 371–427. doi.org/10.1086/685299

Alatas, Vivi, Abhijit Banerjee, Rema Hanna, Benjamin A. Olken, Ririn Purnamasari and Matthew Wai-Poi. 2019. 'Does elite capture matter? Local elites and targeted welfare programs in Indonesia'. *AEA Papers and Proceedings* 109: 334–39. doi.org/10.1257/pandp.20191047

Purnamasari, Ririn and Rabia Ali. 2020. 'High-frequency monitoring of households: Summary of results from survey round 1, 1–17 May 2020'. *Indonesia COVID-19 Observatory Brief* No. 3. World Bank, 26 June. https://openknowledge.worldbank.org/handle/10986/34740

World Bank. 2012. *Targeting: Poor and Vulnerable Households in Indonesia*. Jakarta: World Bank. https://openknowledge.worldbank.org/handle/10986/26700

9 COVID-19 and health systems challenges of non-communicable diseases

Firman Witoelar and Riyana Miranti

Abstract

Prior to the COVID-19 pandemic, Indonesia's health system was already facing some daunting challenges: the increasing burden of non-communicable diseases (NCDs), including mental disorders, that threatens to drain the financial sustainability of the universal health system, and the persistent problems of maternal health, and infectious and nutritional diseases. Health and economic costs of NCDs from labour supply and productivity loss are likely to be high and increasing. This chapter discusses the channels through which the COVID-19 pandemic may have medium- and long-term impacts on NCDs and their risk factors. The immediate and long-term effects of the disruption of services, the 'long-haul' effects and the effects on mental health may further increase the burden that NCDs place on the Indonesian health system. Indirect effects through income loss and job loss, and long-term tolls on health workers, present challenges for those with NCDs to access services. The effects of the pandemic on NCDs are likely to be heterogeneous across socioeconomic gradients and may exacerbate the existing health inequities.

Introduction

At the end of August 2020, Indonesia was in the midst of a health crisis, with the COVID-19 pandemic showing no clear sign of slowing down. Official figures reported the number of positive cases had surpassed 120,000, with more than 7400 confirmed deaths.[1] Several key economic indicators have also shown that the crisis has hit the economy in full force. By the first quarter of 2020, gross domestic product (GDP) growth had slowed markedly, and official poverty numbers had risen from 9.2 per cent in September 2019 to 9.8 per cent in March 2020 (Olivia et al. 2020). A number of non-representative rapid surveys have suggested that the employment shocks have been severe (Windya 2020; Purnamasari and Sjahrir 2020).

But the pandemic was first and foremost a health crisis. It has challenged the resilience of health systems in countries around the world, including Indonesia. By many accounts, the Indonesian government's immediate health response in dealing with the pandemic has been inadequate (Djalante et al. 2020; Olivia et al. 2020). The delayed response, lack of data transparency and logistical bottlenecks surrounding protective equipment and testing plagued the initial response and continued to be a problem even until August 2020. The government's overstretched resources meant that other health services and programs have had to be sacrificed. These services range from routine but essential child and maternal health services including immunisation and programs to reduce stunting; programs to fight other infectious diseases; and routine services for non-communicable diseases (NCDs) and long-term ailments such as cardiovascular diseases, diabetes, cancers and respiratory diseases. The disruptions and reallocation of resources away from these services can have lasting health impacts.

This chapter discusses the likely effects of the pandemic, both direct and indirect, to health outcomes that are related to NCDs, including mental disorders. We focus on NCDs for two reasons. First, there is mounting evidence that the risk and severity of COVID-19 is correlated with NCDs. Second, for several years now, NCDs have taken over as the largest contributor of the burden of disease in Indonesia. Because of their long duration, NCDs may have large economic impacts beyond the monetary costs to treat them. We also know that many NCDs can be prevented and the diseases can largely be treated. While health policy priority must be to control and to stop the pandemic, given the

---

1 Official numbers from the Minister of Health, 31 August 2020, accessed via corona tracker, www.coronatracker.com/country/indonesia/

reasons above, it is important to shed light on the potential setback to the prevention and management of NCDs. We argue that NCDs should be a key factor in any post-pandemic health recovery plans or health reforms.

We begin by looking at health outcome challenges that Indonesia faced before the pandemic. We first describe the epidemiological transition that Indonesia has been going through for the past three decades. We then discuss the increased importance of NCDs as burdens of disease and the economic costs of NCDs. We briefly outline how NCDs are managed within the Indonesian health system. The second half of the chapter discusses how the pandemic has affected NCD services, drawing from international experience as well as the limited data we have on Indonesia. We then examine the likely medium- and long-term threat faced by Indonesia in terms of prevention and control of NCDs. We conclude with discussion and offer some policy insights.

Health challenges on the eve of COVID-19

Epidemiological transition

On the eve of COVID-19, Indonesia already faced enormous challenges in the health sector. Despite progress in the past decades, critical issues remain. Stunting, and maternal and infant mortality rates are still high, particularly for a country with the level of economic development of Indonesia. Indonesia is still struggling to contain infectious diseases including tuberculosis, malaria and dengue. For example, despite achieving a high success rate in tuberculosis treatment at around 90 per cent nationwide, there are still significant disparities across regional Indonesia (Miranti 2018). In the meantime, for the past three decades, NCDs have become the largest contributors of Indonesia's disease burden.[2] Figure 9.1 shows the epidemiological transition between 1990 and 2019. In 1990, the top three contributors of the burden of disease in terms of DALYs were respiratory infections and tuberculosis, maternal and neonatal illness, and enteric infections. By 2019, seven of the top ten diseases were NCDs, including the top three. These increases in burden of disease partly offset the improvement in other health outcomes (Mboi et al. 2018).

---

2 Burden of disease is commonly summarised by disability-adjusted life year (DALY), which quantifies the number of healthy life years that are lost to illness and premature death. DALY comprehensively quantifies physical and psychosocial health impacts of various diseases, conditions and risk factors, and therefore is highly useful for setting public health priorities.

Figure 9.1 Changes in the burden of disease, 1990–2019

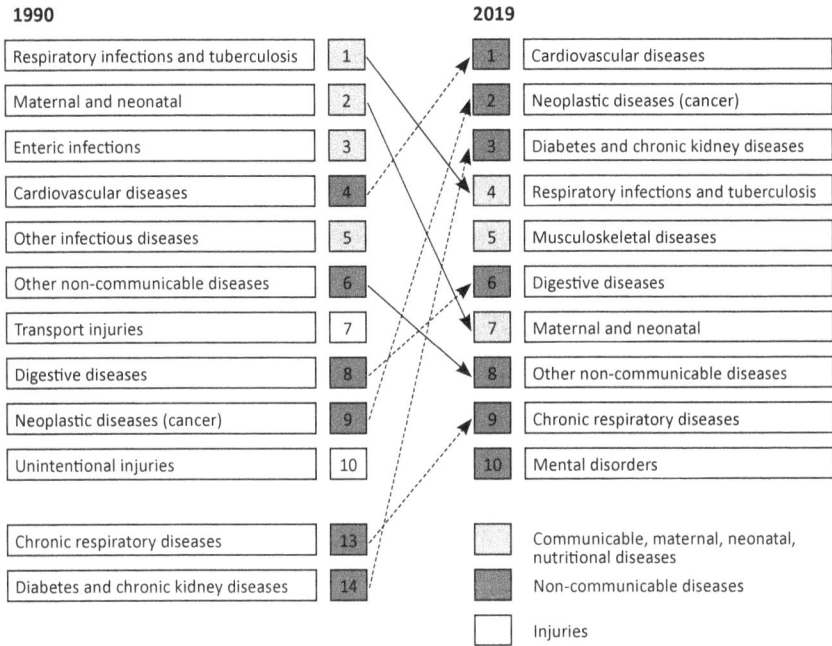

Source: Global Burden of Disease Collaborative Network, http://ghdx.healthdata.org/gbd-results-tool

Data from the nationally representative health surveys RISKESDAS show that the prevalence of diabetes mellitus, stroke and chronic kidney disease increased over the period 2013 to 2018 (MoH 2013, 2018). Along with the increase in NCDs, risk factors of NCDs also increased. The percentage of people aged 18 and older with measured hypertension increased from 25.2 per cent to 34.1 per cent, obesity increased from 14.8 per cent to 21.8 per cent and physical inactivity increased from 26.1 per cent to 33.5 per cent over the period. The prevalence of smoking, which has always been high, especially among adult males (around 60 per cent), shows no sign of decreasing. The epidemiological transition has also been observed among the same individuals in a longitudinal sample spanning up to 21 years (Witoelar et al. 2012, 2018). These numbers prompted some experts to state that Indonesia is on the verge of an NCD epidemic (Kusuma et al. 2019), even prior to the COVID-19 pandemic. Note that many NCD risks are behavioural risk factors such as unhealthy diet, physical inactivity and smoking, which are generally modifiable. Metabolic risk factors or a cluster of conditions involving biochemical processes involved in the body's normal functioning that increase the risk of NCDs, such as elevated blood pressure, obesity and high blood sugar, can also be affected by external factors, including policies.

Economic costs of NCDs

The increase in NCDs as burdens of disease translates to an increase in economic costs of NCDs. NCDs progress slowly and have long duration, increasing frequency of use of health services and health expenses, and often affecting people throughout their productive age. Using data from the Indonesia Family Life Survey (IFLS) 1993–2007, it was estimated that, in addition to indirect burden, hypertension, diabetes, heart problems and stroke account for 8 per cent of out-of-pocket health expenditure (Finkelstein et al. 2014). When conditions get worse, NCDs are likely to result in catastrophic spending. Chronic diseases including NCDs, in particular cardiovascular disease, kidney failure and cancer, constitute the largest case-based payment from the Healthcare and Social Security Agency (Badan Penyelenggara Jaminan Sosial Kesehatan, BPJS-K) at hospital level (Prabhakaran et al. 2019). A model developed by Bloom et al. (2015) uses measures of the burden of disease to estimate economic loss due to labour supply lost and loss of outputs. In terms of output loss, they estimated that NCDs will cost US\$4.5 trillion between 2012 and 2030, five times Indonesia's GDP in 2012.

Health infrastructure and geographical disparity

After the onset of the pandemic in early 2020, discussions on the ability of a health system to deal with COVID-19 centred on flattening the epidemic curve to prevent health systems from being overwhelmed.[3] Crude measures of health system capacity such as number of hospital beds or

---

3 Several different indices that were designed to measure a health system's capacity to provide a comprehensive and effective health response to public health shocks, and to absorb and recover from the shocks, were found to be wanting. For example, the Global Health Security Index measures countries' capacity and readiness to face outbreaks (www.ghsindex.org/). Adherence to the World Health Organization's International Health Regulations on a country's capacity to prevent, protect against and control diseases measures health system robustness. While these measures are useful in measuring health capacity, it is clear from what has transpired in the first half of 2020 around the world that what is being done with health capacity matters more. It is evident that countries that consistently ranked at the top in these indices, such as the United States (ranked 1 in the Global Health Security Index; Indonesia ranked 37), have not necessarily fared well at controlling the pandemic.

doctors per population show the supply-side challenges that Indonesia is facing. As Indonesia was moving towards universal health care, it was understood that growth in the number of trained doctors has not been able to keep up with population growth, and there has been increasing concern about the quality of health workers produced (Rokx et al. 2010). There are also issues with quality, which is hard to measure and for which data are very limited. Survey-based health vignettes administered to health providers in several rounds of the IFLS suggest there was high variation in quality between types of health providers and between regions (Rokx et al. 2010). More recent evidence shows that the average knowledge of health providers to deliver services for diabetes in primary care facilities may have declined between 2007 and 2014 (Stein et al. 2020). This could have important consequences because primary care services play the key role in prevention and early diagnosis of NCDs.

At the subnational level, significant regional disparities exist in health infrastructure and outcomes. Suparmi et al. (2018) calculated the Public Health Development Index (PHDI), combining measures of health infrastructure and outcomes, across 30 public health indicators at the provincial and district level in Indonesia. They found significant regional disparities across the index, with the provinces in western regions of Indonesia tending to have higher overall PHDI scores compared to the eastern areas. Significant variations in province averages were also observed for several subindexes, including for the NCD subindex, which was lowest in South Sulawesi and highest in Lampung (Suparmi et al. 2018). The variations in NCD prevalence do not necessarily overlap with variations in income or urbanicity. As an illustration, Figure 9.2 shows the percentage of adults with hypertension—a key risk factor of NCDs—in Indonesia.

Socioeconomic correlates of NCDs

The pattern of epidemiological transition experienced by Indonesia is not unique. Other low- and middle-income countries have also experienced increases in NCDs before a complete decline in infectious diseases. NCDs, which used to be associated with ageing populations, higher incomes and sedentary and urbanised lifestyles, are now associated with poverty as well. In many countries, poor individuals face higher risks of NCDs due to a worse disease environment and lower access to prevention, diagnostic and care services. Heterogeneous conditions affecting NCDs means that the link between NCDs and socioeconomic correlates is never straightforward.

Figure 9.2 Geographical variations in hypertension (%)

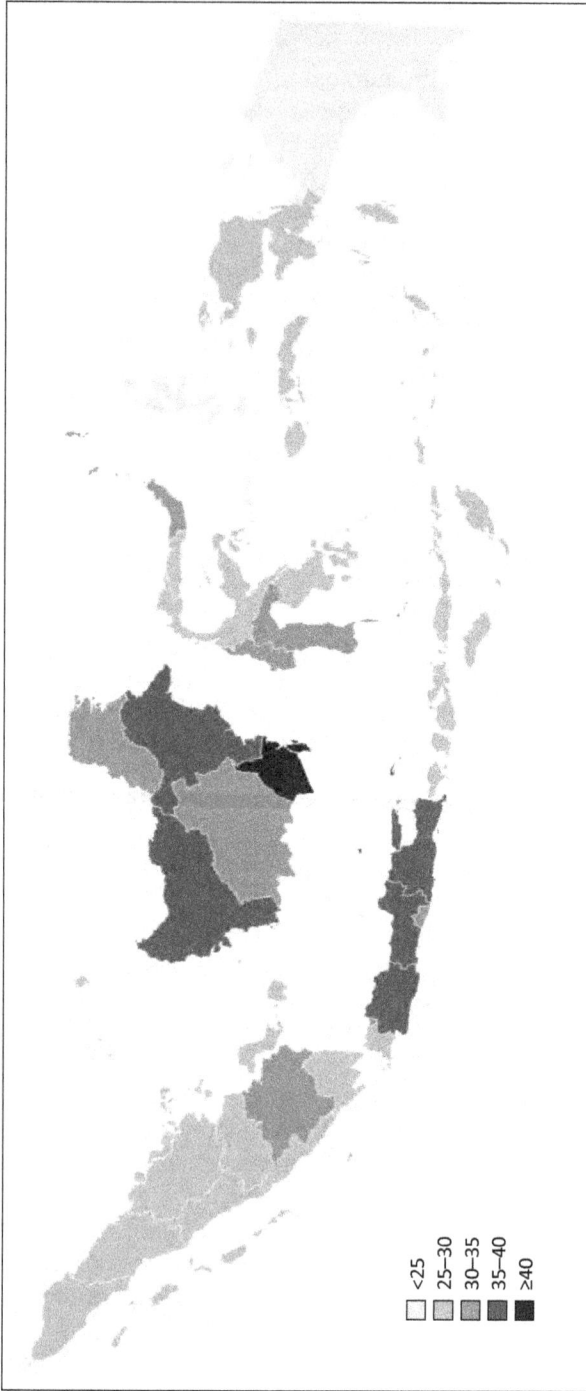

	<25
	25–30
	30–35
	35–40
	≥40

Source: MoH (2018).

The lack of strong association between low socioeconomic status and NCDs is also found in Indonesia. Using data from IFLS5, we found the prevalence for hypertension to be relatively similar across education groups and consumption quintiles (Figure 9.3a). At the same time, by comparing self-reported diagnosis with actual measurement, it was evident underdiagnosis of hypertension is correlated with socioeconomic status: hypertensive individuals with more schooling and from the higher per capita expenditure quintile are more likely to be diagnosed and receive treatment (Figure 9.3b)..These findings were also evident in an earlier round of the IFLS (Witoelar et al. 2012). Data from IFLS5 also suggest that individuals from the 4th and 5th per capita expenditure quintile are less likely to be diagnosed with depression, and the correlation is stronger among women.

The problem of underdiagnosis is important because many underlying factors of NCDs are modifiable through lifestyle changes and when detected at an early stage are easier to treat with medication.

Figure 9.3 Socioeconomic correlates of hypertension and underdiagnoses of hypertension

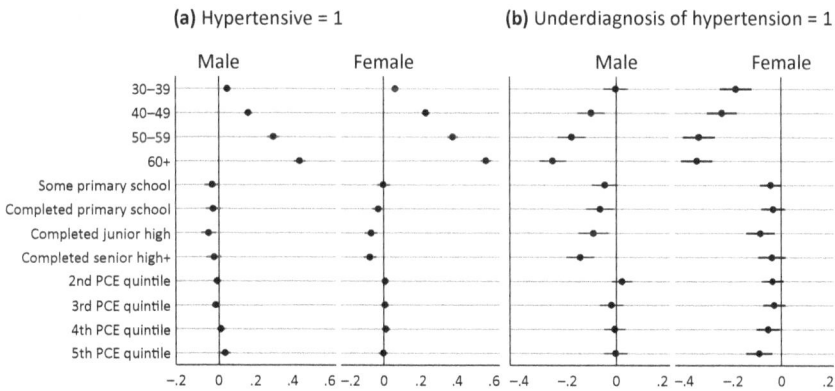

Note: Figure 9.3 shows the regression coefficients obtained by estimating a linear probability model of hypertension (Figure 9.3a) among adults 25 years and older interviewed in IFLS5 on age groups, education variables, household per capita expenditure (PCE) quintiles, province and urban dummy variables interactions, and birth cohort dummy variables. Omitted categories are the 25–29 age group, no schooling and the 1st PCE quintile (the poorest). Standard errors are clustered at the enumeration area level.

Source: Authors' calculation using data from the Indonesia Family Life Survey 5 (2014).

NCD management system in Indonesia

Since early 2000 Indonesia's health system governance has been decentralised. The role of the Ministry of Health is mainly to regulate and ensure overall availability of resources (Mahendradhata et al. 2017). The Directorate of Non-communicable Diseases, established in 2005, was tasked to lead and formulate policies to prevent and control NCDs. At the frontline, NCD management is spearheaded by *puskesmas*, community-level health providers, and their networks. Screening, detecting and managing NCDs is one of the core functions of *puskesmas* as the primary health care provider. A study to assess the supply-side readiness to address NCDs in Indonesia suggests that while the majority of *puskesmas* were ready to screen, diagnose and treat primary hypertension and chronic respiratory disease, only around 54 per cent were ready to diagnose and monitor Type I diabetes mellitus (World Bank 2014). At the community level, in 2006, the government initiated *posbindu*, community-based NCD prevention posts modelled after *posyandu*, the community-based health service that has been at the frontline in delivering basic services related to child and maternal health, family planning and sanitation since the 1980s. Coverage of *posbindu* was low until mid-2015 when the government re-energised it through a flagship program established by the Ministry of Health organised around three 'pillars': promoting a healthy lifestyle paradigm, strengthening healthcare services and improving the national insurance scheme. *Posbindu* falls under the second pillar while also tasked with promoting the first pillar. By 2018, around 44 per cent of villages in Indonesia had a *posbindu*. In addition, a chronic disease management program offered to civil servants since 2010, *prolanis*, has been expanded to all patients, following the implementation of universal health care. Rigorous evaluation of how these different initiatives have affected NCD outcomes has been limited.

COVID-19 and NCDs

Interplay of COVID-19 and NCDs

Evidence is mounting that there is an interaction between the severity of COVID-19, underlying health issues and comorbidities, and age (Clark et al. 2020). People with chronic diseases are more vulnerable to COVID-19 and fatalities disproportionately affect those with chronic illnesses, the most common of which were hypertension and diabetes. In countries with population ageing, more individuals live with chronic diseases and are more likely to be adversely affected from COVID-19 (Cummings et al. 2020; Guan et al. 2020). In addition to comorbidities, age has been an important correlate, and evidence in China suggests that high body mass index is also associated with higher severity of COVID-19 (Kluge et al. 2020). There is still little evidence on the effects of smoking on COVID-19 outcomes, although it has been suggested that any condition that causes a person to be immunocompromised, including smoking, increases risk of severe illness from COVID-19 (Drope et al. 2020; WHO 2020c).

Quality of data on COVID-19 in Indonesia has been a problem due to lack of testing and transparency. Using the available data, we show a simple association between COVID-19 cases and the NCD index before the pandemic at the provincial level in Indonesia (Figure 9.4). We constructed the NCD index based on selected available NCDs and their risk data: the prevalence of hypertension (measured), diabetes, obesity, mental health and injury.[4] Figure 9.4 shows a relatively positive association between these two indicators, with a Spearman rank correlation of 0.164. Provinces that had a high NCD index (such as DKI Jakarta and North Sulawesi) prior to the pandemic tend to have more COVID-19 cases.

Another possible direct channel between COVID-19 and the increased burden of NCDs is through the long-term effects of COVID-19. Studies are ongoing on long-term health consequences of COVID-19 infections, with symptoms including crushing fatigue and lung damage as well as inflammation and damage to the heart muscle (Marshall 2020). Those who survived COVID-19 may suffer from COVID-19–related NCDs in the long term.

Indirect effects of NCDs: Possible channels

In addition to worsened health outcomes for those with NCDs, the pandemic is likely to have indirect long-term adverse consequences on NCDs through different channels. One channel is through the decline in NCD services coverage. A decline in utilisation may occur because of the decline in the demand for services due to mobility restrictions and people not taking risks. On the supply side, the provision of NCD services is determined by physical health infrastructure including supplies and availability of health workforce, all of which were disrupted in the onset of

---

4 The index is calculated using principal component analysis, a technique to transform a set of correlated data into a smaller set of uncorrelated components. Two domains are established to capture the different nature of the data: (1) prevalence of hypertension (measured), diabetes and obesity and (2) prevalence of mental health and injury that disturbs daily activities. The two domains are then averaged and combined into a composite NCD index. Then the NCD index is ranked with the higher value indicating a more serious NCD condition.

Figure 9.4 NCD prevalence in 2018 and confirmed COVID-19 deaths,
31 August 2020

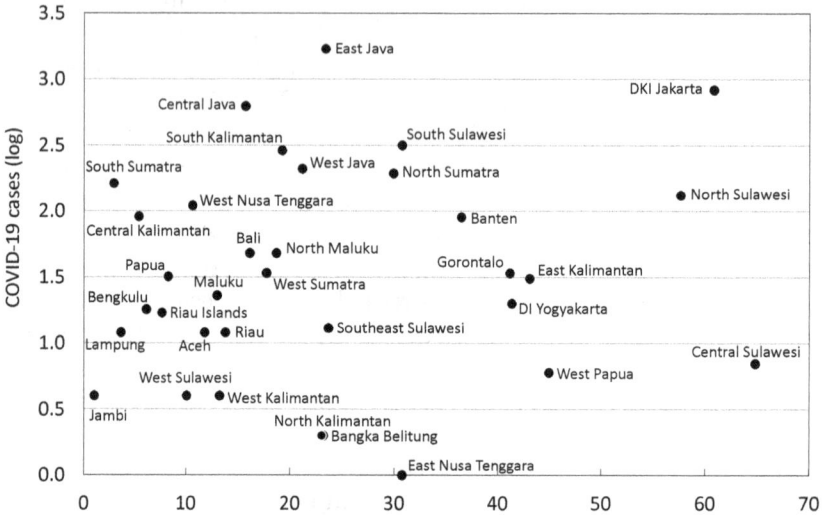

Source: Authors' calculations, based on MoH (2018).

the pandemic. Another important channel is through a decline in income that reduces budgets for food and health care. Correlations between NCDs and socioeconomic factors can have long-term impacts on the widening NCD outcomes between different income groups. Income loss and job loss also increase the likelihood of insurance cover dropouts. In addition to hastening the progression and worsening the outcomes of existing NCDs, the pandemic threatens to increase new cases of NCDs in the long term through diversion of resources including infrastructure, health workers and other resources.

Disruption of services for NCDs care

In May 2020, the World Health Organization conducted a rapid assessment survey of service delivery for NCDs during the COVID-19 pandemic in 155 countries. Around 53 per cent of the countries in the survey had partially or entirely disrupted services for hypertension treatment, and disruptions were reported for treatment for diabetes and diabetes-related complications (almost 50 per cent), cancer treatment (42 per cent) and cardiovascular emergencies (31 per cent) (WHO 2020a). In many countries surveyed, including Indonesia, only limited access for NCD emergencies was available. Other services, such as cancer treatment, diabetes management, hypertension management and palliative care were partially interrupted due to limited stocks of essential medicines and medical diagnostic facilities. Public screening for NCD risk factors, usually conducted in community-based health facilities, had ceased in order to reduce the transmission risk of COVID-19 (WHO 2020a). More than 90 per cent of the countries responding to the survey reported that ministry staff had been reassigned from NCDs work.

The lockdown mobility restrictions and the mobilisation of health personnel to combat COVID-19 have prohibited patients from doing check-ups, follow-ups or prescription refills as access to health services and general physicians is limited (Kretchy et al. 2020; Lim et al. 2020). Patients have not been encouraged to visit hospital unless it is an emergency (Nachimuthu et al. 2020). Thus, one may argue that demand for NCD treatments seems to decline, but it is actually hidden because of the forceable situation. In a pilot study in India, Nachimuthu et al. (2020) found that only 28 per cent of the participants were checking their blood glucose levels regularly during the pandemic. Hofman and Madhi (2020) also observed a 48 per cent decline in tuberculosis testing in South Africa.

In April 2020, a month after the first official case was announced in Indonesia, the Directorate of Non-communicable Diseases issued a memorandum for province and district health officials on the management for people with NCDs and risk factors during the pandemic (MoH 2020; WHO 2020b). Local health officials were to urge communities and especially people with NCDs and risk factors of NCDs to observe mobility restrictions and to monitor their health status at home during the mobility restrictions. The memo also encourages the use of telemedicine services. By April 2020, *puskesmas*, which had been given additional tasks to promote health and prevent and monitor NCDs, had become a frontline in the battle against the pandemic. Public screening for NCD risk factors has all but completely stopped, to reduce the risk of COVID-19 transmission.

Figure 9.5 shows the decline in services for advanced medical treatments for Indonesia and selected provinces, indicating a sharp decline in April 2020 when the impact of COVID-19 started to be felt. Declines in health contacts were mostly at primary care level, in particular *puskesmas*, outpatient clinics and private practice. In the meantime, indirect primary care health contacts through telemedicine increased from around 3207 in March 2020 to 390,000 in May and 494,000 in July (BPJS 2020).

Disruptions caused by mobility restrictions are likely to affect individuals with different socioeconomic backgrounds differently. Healthcare-seeking behaviour and healthcare utilisation are higher for those with more or cheaper access to health services. Even though there

Figure 9.5 Disruption of health services, October 2019 to May 2020

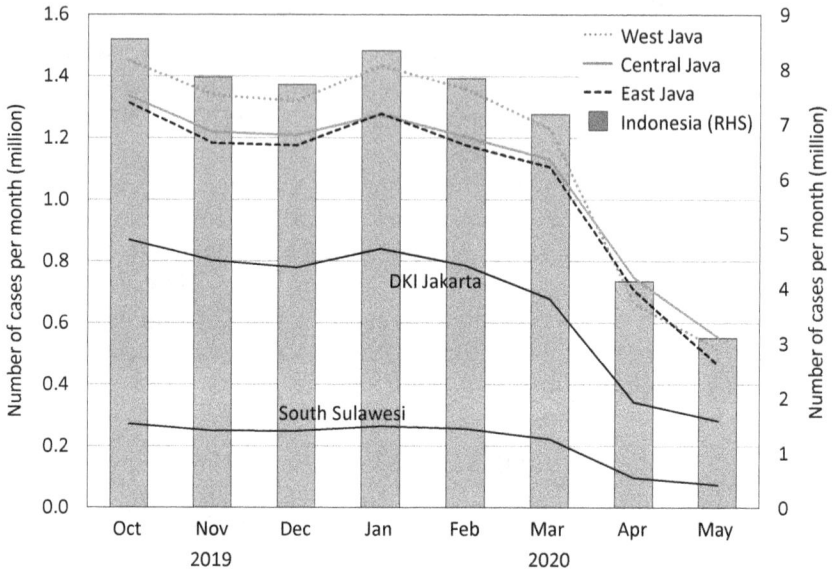

Source: Sparrow et al. (2020a).

are limited correlations between socioeconomic factors and prevalence of NCDs and risk factors as we discussed above, it is clear that underdiagnosis and undertreatment of these diseases is more critical among individuals from lower-income households, exacerbating the existing inequities.

Indirect effects through income and job loss

Early estimates from Suryahadi et al. (2020) suggest that an additional 5.9 million to 8.5 million people will become poor if Indonesia's economic growth drops from 5 per cent to 2 per cent and further to 1 per cent by the end of 2020. A number of rapid surveys have suggested that food security has started to be an issue as some households have started missing meals or have a shortage of food (Windya 2020). Disruptions to affordable, healthier food may cause households to shift to less nutritious but cheaper food, with potentially long-term impacts on NCD risk factor management. Disruptions in nutrition have potentially even longer-term impacts in terms of human capital development. Mobility restrictions may inhibit the physical activities that are a vital component of the management of NCD risk factors.

Income loss and job loss have also caused a significant drop in health insurance participation. It is estimated that, by July 2020, the number of active memberships in JKN (Jaminan Kesehatan Nasional, Indonesia's national health insurer) had dropped by 5.3 million—2.4 per cent of all membership (Sparrow et al. 2020b). For those with NCDs, loss of insurance cover may prevent them from routine care, hastening the progress of the illness and increasing the likelihood of incurring catastrophic health expenses.

Immediate and long-term impacts on mental health

As discussed earlier, reduced physical activity and access to unhealthy foods is likely to worsen the quality of life of people living with NCDs during the pandemic (Kraef et al. 2020). There are also mental health impacts of COVID-19. People living with NCDs can experience more stress and anxiety about being infected with the virus or worry that their health will be worsening as they are not able to access their regular NCD health protocols or management.

Data from the Ministry of Health shows that 6.8 per cent of Indonesians had suffered from anxiety disorders during the pandemic, with 14,619 people receiving treatment from members of the Indonesian Clinical Psychologists Association (IPK Indonesia) from March to August 2020 (*Jakarta Post* 2020). It was reported that the most common disorders experienced were learning difficulties, anxiety, stress, mood disorders and depression. The pandemic affects the mental health of individuals and communities directly (for those suspected or diagnosed with COVID-19) and indirectly (for example, through job loss, lockdown and school closures). The impacts translate into a range of mental health and wellbeing issues such as anxiety, distress and psychological trauma, as well as anxiety from non-compliance with public health regulations. Harlianty et al. (2020) found that awareness of COVID-19 correlates with community compliance. They found that groups that have a higher risk of experiencing anxiety and thus need more attention to build awareness are younger people, the less educated and the unemployed. Young people seem to be particularly vulnerable. Ardan et al. (2020) found that around 40 per cent of 248 university students in East Kalimantan experienced some form of anxiety.

With respect to longer-term impacts on mental health, Abdullah (2020) proposes four types of psychological trauma related to COVID-19, which link to threat and fear. The first trauma is social withdrawal, where those who are affected directly, such as suspected coronavirus patients, or indirectly, such as someone who has lost their job because of COVID-19, have isolated themselves socially from their peers and family. Social withdrawal may also happen to medical professionals whose tasks have taken a huge toll (Pereira-Sanchez et al. 2020). The second trauma is uncontrolled behaviour or hysteria, where individuals refuse to be tested because they fear being quarantined and separated from their family. The third trauma is related to violence, particularly against disadvantaged women and children. In an abusive environment, working and studying from home has increased women's and children's vulnerability to experience violence at home. The final trauma refers to collective violence where a community has a panic response to the pandemic and individuals who have been diagnosed with COVID-19 may experience discrimination.

Longer-term impacts: Toll on health workforce

There have been reports from several countries of substantial numbers of casualties among the health workforce working on the frontline against the pandemic. A scoping review suggests that, by April 2020, around 153,000 healthcare workers worldwide had been infected and around 1410 had died due to COVID-19 (Bandyopadhyay et al. 2020). While infected cases were mainly among women (71.6 per cent) and nurses (38.6 per cent), most deaths were mainly among men (70.8 per cent) and doctors (51.4 per cent). The Indonesian Medical Association estimated between 200 and 300 of Indonesia's 160,000 doctors had been infected by the virus (WHO 2020b). In Indonesia, as of mid-September 2020, around 115 doctors and 82 nurses had died because of COVID-19.

The pandemic has also taken a toll on the mental health of health workers around the world. A meta-analysis of 13 studies with a total of 33,000 health workers showed an increase in depression, anxiety and insomnia among health workers (Pappa et al. 2020). In Indonesia, a study on 644 health workers showed 55 per cent were suffering from anxiety and 24 per cent from depression (Irwandy 2020). Data are not available yet but some of the early casualties among doctors are specialists in respiratory diseases, diabetes and other chronic diseases.

Inadequacies in the quantity and quality of the health workforce in Indonesia, apparent even before the pandemic, may become larger, partly because of the direct casualties during the pandemic. Given the extraordinary burden faced by the frontline health workforce, recruitment may prove to be challenging in the future.

Conclusions

Non-communicable diseases presented a challenge to the Indonesian health system prior to the COVID-19 pandemic. In this chapter we have shown different channels in which the pandemic may further increase the burden that NCDs place on the Indonesian health system. The disruption of services and reallocation of resources away from NCDs, the 'long-haul' effects and the effects on mental health threaten to hasten the progress of existing cases of NCDs, and add new cases. Income and job loss during the pandemic reduce access to health cover and services including NCD care. NCDs are prevalent across different socioeconomic gradients and the pandemic threatens to increase existing inequities.

Burden of disease metrics provide a useful tool for prioritisation among diseases and NCDs should be prioritised. Translating the burden of disease into economic costs in terms of labour supply and lost output can help make the costs more explicit. Considering the urgent need to control the pandemic and competing needs for other health services, putting a priority on NCDs entails a difficult trade-off. Because of the modifiable nature of some risk factors, NCD prevention at the community level through promotion of healthy lifestyle, early detection and monitoring may prove to be more cost-efficient in the long run. There is an argument to strengthen the current approach to deal with NCDs at the primary level through community-based networks, but rigorous evaluations are needed.

The emphasis on primary care to address NCDs also means that investing in high-quality healthcare workers who work at the frontline or in primary care, such as paramedics, nurses or midwives, may promise higher social benefits than investing in specialists for whom high private returns may be available.

The pandemic offers an opportunity to make a crucial decision about one of the most harmful key factors, smoking. Indonesia has the second-highest prevalence of adult men smoking in the world (66.6 per cent) and increasing numbers of 10–14 year olds are smoking (MoH 2018). Indonesia is one of only eight countries in the world that has not signed and adopted the World Health Organization Framework Convention on Tobacco Control. The conflicting interests of various ministries, as well as local government opposition to tobacco control regulations, provide a challenge in addressing one of the key risk factors of NCDs (Astuti et al. 2020).

Longer-term changes may likely include increased use of telemedicine. The use of services from Indonesia's largest telehealth firms such as Alodokter, GrabHealth and Halodoc has increased during the pandemic

(Potkin and Widianto 2020). The pandemic has also shown the need for better and more transparent health information systems including routine administrative data for monitoring NCDs.

References

Abdullah, Irwan. 2020. 'COVID-19: Threat and fear in Indonesia'. *Psychological Trauma: Theory, Research, Practice, and Policy* 12(5): 488–90. doi.org/10.1037/tra0000878

Ardan, M., Ferry Fadzlul Rahman and Godefridus Bali Geroda. 2020. 'The influence of physical distance to student anxiety on COVID-19, Indonesia'. *Journal of Critical Reviews* 7(17): 1126–32. www.jcreview.com/?mno=26200

Astuti, Putu Ayu Swandewi, Mary Assunta and Becky Freeman. 2020. 'Why is tobacco control progress in Indonesia stalled? A qualitative analysis of interviews with tobacco control experts'. *BMC Public Health* 20(527). doi.org/10.1186/s12889-020-08640-6

Bandyopadhyay, Soham, Ronnie E. Baticulon, Murtaza Kadhum, Muath Alser, Daniel K. Ojuka, Yara Badereddin, Archith Kamath, et al. 2020. 'Infection and mortality of healthcare workers worldwide from COVID-19: A scoping review'. *medRxiv* 5 June. doi.org/10.1101/2020.06.04.20119594

Bloom, D.E., S. Chen, M. McGovern, K. Prettner, V. Candeias, A. Bernaert and S. Cristin. 2015. *Economics of Non-Communicable Diseases in Indonesia*. World Economic Forum.

BPJS (Badan Penyelenggara Jaminan Sosial). 2020. 'Pandemi COVID-19, angka kontak FKTP ke peserta harus tetap terjaga'. Press release, 19 September.

Clark, Andrew, Mark Jit, Charlotte Warren-Gash, Bruce Guthrie, Harry H.X. Wang, Stewart W. Mercer, Colin Sanderson, et al. 2020. 'Global, regional, and national estimates of the population at increased risk of severe COVID-19 due to underlying health conditions in 2020: A modelling study'. *Lancet Global Health* 8(8): E1003–17. doi.org/10.1016/S2214-109X(20)30264-3

Cummings, Matthew J., Matthew R. Baldwin, Darryl Abrams, Samuel D. Jacobson, Benjamin J. Meyer, Elizabeth M. Balough, Justin G. Aaron, et al. 2020. 'Epidemiology, clinical course, and outcomes of critically ill adults with COVID-19 in New York City: A prospective cohort study'. *The Lancet* 395(10239): 1763–70. doi.org/10.1016/S0140-6736(20)31189-2

Djalante, Riyanti, Jonatan Lassa, Davin Setiamarga, Aruminingsih Sudjatma, Mochamad Indrawan, Budi Haryanto, Choirul Mahfud, et al. 2020. 'Review and analysis of current responses to COVID-19 in Indonesia: Period of January to March 2020'. *Progress in Disaster Science* 6(100091). doi.org/10.1016/j.pdisas.2020.100091

Drope, Jeff, Zach Cahn, Cliff Douglas and Alex Liber. 2020. 'What do we know about tobacco use and COVID-19?' *Tobacco Atlas*, 21 April. https://tobaccoatlas.org/2020/04/21/what-do-we-know-about-tobacco-use-and-covid-19/

Finkelstein Eric A., Junxing Chay and Shailendra Bajpai. 2014. 'The economic burden of self-reported and undiagnosed cardiovascular diseases and diabetes on Indonesian households'. *PLoS ONE* 9(6): e99572. doi.org/10.1371/journal.pone.0099572

Guan, Wei-jie, Zheng-yi Ni, Yu Hu, Wen-hua Liang, Chun-quan Ou, Jian-xing He, Lei Liu, et al. 2020. 'Clinical characteristics of coronavirus disease 2019 in China'. *New England Journal of Medicine* 382: 1708–20. doi:10.1056/NEJMoa2002032

Harlianty, Rully Afrita, Tria Widyastuti, Hamid Mukhlis and Susi Susanti. 2020. 'Study on awareness of Covid-19, anxiety and compliance on social distancing in Indonesia during coronavirus disease 2019 (COVID-19) pandemic'. *Research Square* preprint, 20 July. doi.org/10.21203/rs.3.rs-44598/v1

Hofman, Karen and Shabir Madhi. 2020. 'The unanticipated costs of COVID-19 to South Africa's quadruple disease burden'. *South African Medical Journal* 110(8): 698–99. doi.10.7196/SAMJ.2020.v110i8.15125

Irwandy. 2020. '4 gelombang besar pandemi Covid-19 menghantam sistem pelayanan kesehatan'. *The Conversation*, 16 July. https://theconversation.com/4-gelombang-besar-pandemi-covid-19-menghantam-sistem-pelayanan-kesehatan-142049

Jakarta Post. 2020. 'Mental health services disrupted in 93% of countries during COVID-19 pandemic: WHO'. *Jakarta Post*, 8 October. www.thejakartapost.com/news/2020/10/08/mental-health-services-disrupted-in-93-of-countries-during-covid-19-pandemic-who.html

Kluge, Hans Henri P., Kremlin Wickramasinghe, Holly L. Rippin, Romeu Mendes, David H. Peters, Anna Kontsevaya and Joao Breda. 2020. 'Prevention and control of non-communicable diseases in the COVID-19 response'. *The Lancet* 395(10238): 1678–80. doi.org/10.1016/S0140-6736(20)31067-9

Kraef, Christian, Pamela Juma, Per Kallestrup, Joseph Mucumbitsi, Kaushik Ramaiya and Gerald Yonga. 2020. 'The COVID-19 pandemic and non-communicable diseases—A wake-up call for primary health care system strengthening in sub-Saharan Africa'. *Journal of Primary Care & Community Health* 11: 2150132720946948. doi.org/10.1177/2150132720946948

Kretchy, Irene A., Michelle Asiedu-Danso and James-Paul Kretchy. 2020. 'Medication management and adherence during the COVID-19 pandemic: Perspectives and experiences from low- and middle-income countries'. *Research in Social and Administrative Pharmacy* preprint, 15 April. doi.org/10.1016/j.sapharm.2020.04.007

Kusuma, Dian, Nunik Kusumawardani, Abdillah Ahsan, Susy K. Sebayang, Vilda Amir and Nawi Ng. 2019. 'On the verge of a chronic disease epidemic: Comprehensive policies and actions are needed in Indonesia'. *International Health* 11(6): 422–24. doi.org/10.1093/inthealth/ihz025

Lim, Michael Anthonius, Ian Huang, Emir Yonas, Rachel Vania and Raymond Pranata. 2020. 'A wave of non-communicable diseases following the COVID-19 pandemic'. *Diabetes & Metabolic Syndrome: Clinical Research & Reviews* 14(5): 979–80. doi.org/10.1016/j.dsx.2020.06.050

Mahendradhata, Yodi, Laksono Trisnantoro, Shita Listyadewi, Prastuti Soewondo, Tiara Marthias, Pandu Harimurti and John Prawira. 2017. *The Republic of Indonesia Health System Review*, Health Systems in Transition, Vol. 7, No. 1. WHO Regional Office for South-East Asia. https://apps.who.int/iris/handle/10665/254716

Marshall, Michael. 2020. 'The lasting misery of coronavirus long-haulers'. *Nature* 585: 339–341. doi.org/10.1038/d41586-020-02598-6

Mboi, Nafsiah, Indra Murty Surbakti, Indang Trihandini, Iqbal Elyazar, Karen Houston Smith, Pungkas Bahjuri Ali, Soewarta Kosen, et al. 2018. 'On the road to universal health care in Indonesia, 1990–2016: A systematic analysis for the Global Burden of Disease Study 2016'. *The Lancet* 392(10147): 581–91. doi.org/10.1016/S0140-6736(18)30595-6

Miranti, Riyana. 2018. 'Poverty, inequality and public health in Indonesia: Does wealthier mean healthier?' In *Routledge Handbook of Sustainable Development in Asia*, edited by Sara Hsu, 299–319. Abingdon: Routledge. doi.org/10.4324/9781351008204-14

MoH (Ministry of Health). 2013. *National Report on Basic Health Research – RISKESDAS 2013*. Jakarta: National Institute of Health Research and Development.

MoH (Ministry of Health). 2018. *National Report on Basic Health Research – RISKESDAS 2018*. Jakarta: National Institute of Health Research and Development.

MoH (Ministry of Health). 2020. 'Tentang penanganan orang dengan faktor risiko dan penyandang PTM selama masa pandemi COVID-19'. SE Dirjen P2P No. HK.01.07/I/3402/2020.

Nachimuthu, Sukanya, R. Vijayalakshmi, M. Sudha and Vijay Viswanathan. 2020. 'Coping with diabetes during the COVID-19 lockdown in India: Results of an online pilot survey'. *Diabetes & Metabolic Syndrome: Clinical Research & Reviews* 14(4): 579–82. doi.org/10.1016/j.dsx.2020.04.053

Olivia, Susan, John Gibson and Rus'an Nasrudin. 2020. 'Indonesia in the time of COVID-19'. *Bulletin of Indonesian Economic Studies* 56(2): 143–74. doi.org/10.1080/00074918.2020.1798581

Pappa, Sofia, Vasiliki Ntella, Timoleon Giannakas, Vassilis G. Giannakoulis, Eleni Papoutsi and Paraskevi Katsaounou. 2020. 'Prevalence of depression, anxiety, and insomnia among healthcare workers during the COVID-19 pandemic: A systematic review and meta-analysis'. *Brain, Behavior, and Immunity* 88: 901–7. doi.org/10.1016/j.bbi.2020.05.026

Pereira-Sanchez, Victor, Frances Adiukwu, Samer El Hayek, Drita Gashi Bytyçi, Jairo M. Gonzalez-Diaz, Ganesh Kudva Kundadak, Amine Larnaout, et al. 2020. 'COVID-19 effect on mental health: Patients and workforce'. *Lancet Psychiatry* 7(6): E29–30. doi.org/10.1016/S2215-0366(20)30153-X

Potkin, Fanny and Stanley Widianto. 2020. 'Indonesia leans on healthtech startups to cope with virus surge'. Reuters, 10 April. https://www.reuters.com/article/us-health-coronavirus-indonesia-technolo-idUSKCN21S02F

Prabhakaran, Shreeshant, Arin Dutta, Thomas Fagan and Megan Ginivan. 2019. *Financial Sustainability of Indonesia's Jaminan Kesehatan Nasional: Performance, Prospects, and Policy Options*. Washington, DC: Palladium, Health Policy Plus, and Jakarta: Tim Nasional Percepatan Penanggulangan Kemiskinan (TNP2K).

Purnamasari, Ririn and Bambang Suharnoko Sjahrir. 2020. 'High-frequency monitoring of socio-economic impact of COVID-19 on households in Indonesia'. World Bank presentation, ANU Indonesia Project Global Seminar Series, 30 September. www.youtube.com/watch?v=4DYck8WOLxk

Rokx, Claudia, John Giles, Elan Satriawan, Puti Marzoeki, Pandu Harimurti and Elif Yavuz. 2010. *New Insights into the Provision of Health Services in Indonesia: A Health Workforce Study*. Washington, DC: World Bank. doi.org/10.1596/978-0-8213-8298-1

Sparrow, Robert, Teguh Dartanto and Renate Hartwig. 2020a. 'Economic update'. Presentation to the Economic Dimensions of COVID-19 in Indonesia: Responding to the Crisis conference, 7–10 September. Canberra: Crawford School of Public Policy, Australian National University.

Sparrow, Robert, Teguh Dartanto and Renate Hartwig. 2020b. 'Indonesia under the new normal: Challenges and the way ahead'. *Bulletin of Indonesian Economic Studies* 56(3): 269–99. doi.org/10.1080/00074918.2020.1854079

Stein, Dorit T., Nikkil Sudharsanan, Shita Dewi, Jennifer Manne-Goehler, Firman Witoelar and Pascal Geldsetzer. 2020. 'Change in clinical knowledge of diabetes among primary healthcare providers in Indonesia: Repeated cross-sectional survey of 5105 primary healthcare facilities'. *BMJ Open Diabetes Research & Care* 8(1): e001415. doi.org/10.1136/bmjdrc-2020-001415

Suparmi, Nunik Kusumawardani, Devaki Nambiar, Trihono and Ahmad Reza Hosseinpoor. 2018. 'Subnational regional inequality in the public health development index in Indonesia'. *Global Health Action* 11(suppl): 41–53. doi.org/10.1080/16549716.2018.1500133

Suryahadi, Asep, Ridho Al Izzati and Daniel Suryadarma. 2020. 'Estimating the impact of COVID-19 on poverty in Indonesia'. *Bulletin of Indonesian Economic Studies* 56(2): 175–92. doi.org/10.1080/00074918.2020.1779390

WHO (World Health Organization). 2020a. 'Rapid assessment of service delivery for noncommunicable diseases (NCDs) during the COVID-19 pandemic'. PowerPoint presentation. www.who.int/publications/m/item/rapid-assessment-of-service-delivery-for-ncds-during-the-covid-19-pandemic

WHO (World Health Organization). 2020b. 'Coronavirus disease 2019 (COVID-19): Indonesia'. *Situation Report* 19. WHO, 5 August. www.who.int/docs/default-source/searo/indonesia/covid19/who-situation-report-19.pdf?sfvrsn=531a8fe6_2

WHO (World Health Organization). 2020c. 'Smoking and COVID-19'. *WHO Scientific Brief*, 30 June. www.who.int/news-room/commentaries/detail/smoking-and-covid-19

Windya, Colley. 2020. 'Monitoring the social impact of the COVID-19 pandemic in Indonesia'. J-PAL Southeast Asia, 10 November. www.povertyactionlab.org/blog/11-10-20/monitoring-social-impact-covid-19-pandemic-indonesia

Witoelar, Firman, John Strauss and Bondan Sikoki. 2012. 'Socioeconomic success and health in later life: Evidence from the Indonesia Family Life Survey'. In *Aging in Asia: Findings from New and Emerging Data Initiatives*, edited by James P. Smith and Malay Majmundar, 309–41. Washington, DC: National Academies Press.

Witoelar, Firman, John Strauss and Bondan Sikoki. 2018. 'Health transitions over the course of 21 years'. Paper presented to the Population Association of America Annual Meeting, May. Denver.

World Bank. 2014. *Supply-Side Readiness for Universal Health Coverage: Assessing the Depth of Coverage for Non-Communicable Diseases in Indonesia*. Jakarta: World Bank.

10 Consequences of the COVID-19 pandemic on human capital development[1]

Budy P. Resosudarmo and Milda Irhamni

Abstract

An outbreak the size of the COVID-19 pandemic would surely significantly impact not only the economy but also human capital development. In Indonesia, however, the true size of this pandemic and its human capital impact is unclear since the number of COVID-19 tests has been low. In this chapter we attempt to estimate the true magnitude of the pandemic and outline a conceptual framework to understand channels from which the COVID-19 pandemic will affect human capital development, particularly in health and education, in Indonesia. We find that the number of casualties due to the pandemic could be much larger than those formally announced. The pandemic is expected to increase cases of other morbidities, maternal deaths, and less healthy babies and children. In the long run, there is evidence that a pandemic of this size could increase overall mortality cases.

1 The authors would like to thank Ratih Kertawarhani and Ginanjar Panggalih for their assistance in preparing this chapter. All mistakes are the authors' responsibility.

Introduction

By mid-October 2020, there were around 349,000 formally confirmed cases of COVID-19 in Indonesia and the number of confirmed casualties was approximately 12,000.[2] The pandemic has been spreading to all provinces and the numbers are increasing. Figure 10.1 shows the regional spread of COVID-19 by mid-October 2020. Most confirmed cases are in Java and the Bali Islands. This is understandable since about 58 per cent of Indonesians live in Java and the Bali Islands. Approximately 22 per cent of Indonesians live in Sumatra, but only 15 per cent of cases are on that island. It is predicted, hence, the spread of the pandemic in Sumatra is smaller than the spread of the pandemic in Java and the Bali Islands.

The spread of the pandemic in remote areas of Indonesia, Sulawesi and eastern Indonesia has been relatively equal to the proportion of the population in those areas. However, the number of cases in Sulawesi and eastern Indonesia has increased since July 2020. Hence there are indications that the speed of the pandemic spread in these areas was faster than in other parts of Indonesia between July and October this year. Health facilities and public health programs have been typically weaker outside Java and the Bali Islands, so there is a significant possibility that the pandemic might stay much longer in remote areas of Sulawesi and eastern Indonesia.

The size of the pandemic in Indonesia is unclear since the number of COVID-19 tests has been low. For example, the number of tests per thousand persons in Indonesia by mid-August 2020 was only 2–3 per cent of those numbers in developed countries such as Australia and the United States.[3] The number of tests per capita in Indonesia so far has also been smaller than those in India, the Philippines, Vietnam and Thailand. It is likely, therefore, the spread of the pandemic is much larger than the situation formally announced by the government.

Since 3 April 2020, through the enactment of Presidential Regulation (Peraturan Presiden, Perpres) No. 54/2020, the Indonesian government has tried to control the spread of the COVID-19 pandemic by allocating more funding in the public health budget. On 24 June 2020, through Perpres No. 72/2020, the government increased the health budget to Rp 87.6 trillion. The implementation of programs to manage the pandemic is not

---

2 https://covid19.go.id/

3 These data were from Our World in Data, University of Oxford (https://ourworldindata.org/grapher/full-list-cumulative-total-tests-per-thousand-map?time=latest). Due to the fluid nature of the pandemic, the numbers keep changing.

Figure 10.1 Regional distribution of confirmed cases of COVID-19,
mid-October 2020

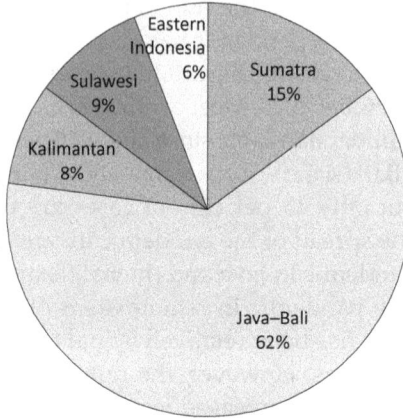

Source: Ministry of Health, https://data.kemkes.go.id/covid19/index.html

without challenges. First, the state of the country's public health sector just
before the outbreak was not strong. For example, the number of physicians
per capita in Indonesia was lower than that in India, Thailand and the
Philippines. Second, Indonesia is still not able to control several major
endemics, such as tuberculosis, dengue and malaria. Third, disbursing
the public health budget for COVID-19 has not happened smoothly.
By mid-July 2020, only about 7 per cent of the COVID-19 public health
budget was disbursed. Almost none of the medical expenses for handling
COVID-19 (Rp 65.8 trillion) has been disbursed. Clearly, Indonesia needs
to do much to improve its public health sector capacity.

An outbreak the size of the COVID-19 pandemic is likely to significantly
affect not only the economy but also human capital development. The
case of the influenza pandemic during 1918–1920, also known as the
1918 influenza or Spanish Flu pandemic, serves as an example. Data for
43 countries indicated that approximately 39 million people, about 2 per
cent of the world population, died due to this disease (Barro et al. 2020).
In Java alone, the estimated death toll due to the 1918 influenza pandemic
was at least 1.5 million people (Brown 1987; Chandra 2013).

Apart from mortality cases, a pandemic this size would be expected
to also affect quality of life. For example, a public health study among
primary school students in Mali between 2007 and 2008 shows that
contracting malaria negatively impacts children's school achievements

and cognitive performance (Thuilliez et al. 2010). It is therefore important for Indonesia to understand what the short- and long-term impacts of the COVID-19 pandemic might be on its population's human capital development. By understanding possible human capital impacts of the COVID-19 pandemic, necessary and appropriate policies could then be developed to mitigate negative impacts.

This chapter discusses potential impacts of the current pandemic on human capital development in Indonesia. To do this, we focus our observations on Indonesians' health and educational performances, using these as proxies of human capital development. To achieve this goal, we first present an estimate of the magnitude of the pandemic in Indonesia. Second, we outline a conceptual framework to understand channels from which the COVID-19 pandemic could affect health and educational performances. Third, we provide a literature review with evidence on the impacts of disease outbreaks on human capital performances in various regions across the world to support the conceptual framework. Finally, we conclude on what the possible impact of the current COVID-19 pandemic on human capital development in Indonesia might be.

Expected magnitude of COVID-19

It is difficult to accurately estimate the number of COVID-19 cases in Indonesia without adequate numbers of tests. The number of COVID-19 tests per thousand persons in Indonesia, at least until mid-August 2020, was one of the lowest among lower–middle income countries in the region, and lower than those in Mexico, Brazil and several Asian countries (Figure 10.2). The gap is even more pronounced when compared to test numbers in several developed countries.

Given the low number of COVID-19 tests per thousand persons and that Indonesia has never strictly imposed the social distancing policy, and disbursement of the COVID-19 public health budget has been slow, it is difficult to know the precise size and spread of the pandemic throughout the country. This section aims to provide some back-of-the-envelope estimations of the size of the pandemic in the country if the numbers of tests were much higher than they are currently.

COVID-19 cases

Literature estimating the spread of and casualties due to a pandemic is widely available. One study uses a dose-response function model that links the number of casualties in a region to the total population being

Figure 10.2 COVID-19 tests per thousand people in several countries,
mid-August 2020

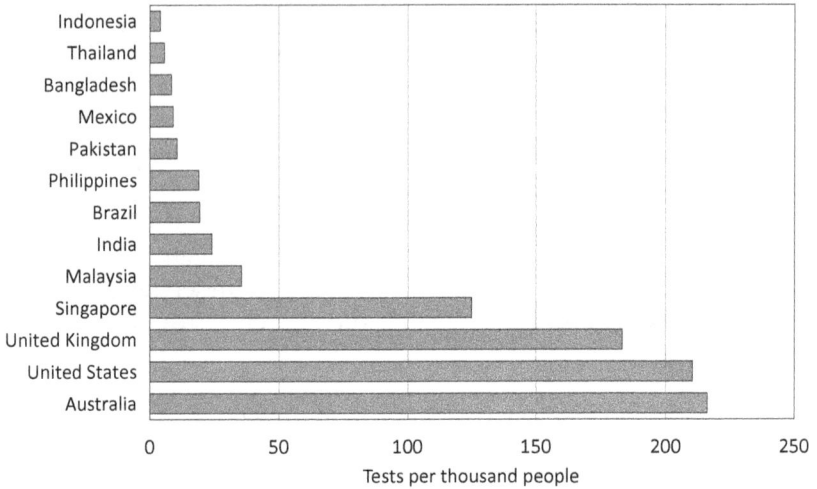

Source: Our World in Data, University of Oxford, https://ourworldindata.org/coronavirus

exposed and the probability of an individual in that region being infected
(Resosudarmo and Napitupulu 2004):

$$h_i = r_i \cdot pop_i \tag{1}$$

where h_i is the number of infected persons or casualties caused by a
certain disease in region i, r_i is the probability of a person in region i
being infected and pop_i is the population in region i being exposed to a
certain disease. Since the number of infected persons is known only if
detected or being tested, we modify equation (1) to become

$$h_i = (t_i)^\sigma \cdot X_i \cdot pop_i \tag{2}$$

where h_i is the number of infected persons detected, t_i is the number of
tests, σ is the elasticity of a person being infected per testing, and X_i is a
vector of region i's characteristics. It is expected that σ is less than 1.

Appendix 1 presents discussion and results of estimating equation (2)
with its variations using daily COVID-19 testing, confirmed cases and
deaths from 1 January 2020 until 24 August 2020 for approximately
100 countries around the world, using data from the World Bank's World
Development Indicators and the University of Oxford's Our World in

Data. Analysis of the data indicates that, on average across countries around the world, a 1 per cent increase in the total number of tests on any given day increases the total number of confirmed COVID-19 cases by approximately 0.3 per cent. Using these figures, the number of confirmed cases can be estimated if Indonesia increases its number of COVID-19 tests per person by a certain date.

An estimate of the total number of confirmed cases due to COVID-19 as total tests increase in Indonesia can be seen in Figure 10.3. By 20 August 2020, the total number of tests per thousand people was 4.1 tests and the total number of confirmed COVID-19 cases was about 145,000. If by that date the number of tests per thousand people in Indonesia was approximately 210 per thousand people instead, or about the same as those in the United States (210 tests) or United Kingdom (183 tests), it is estimated that the number of confirmed COVID-19 cases would be about 560,000 or 0.2 per cent of the population. This estimate does not seem to overestimate the possible true condition in Indonesia, if it is compared to the numbers of confirmed cases by 20 August in the United States and United Kingdom, which were approximately 1.7 per cent and 0.5 per cent of their populations, respectively.

Figure 10.3 Estimated COVID-19 cases and tests per thousand people

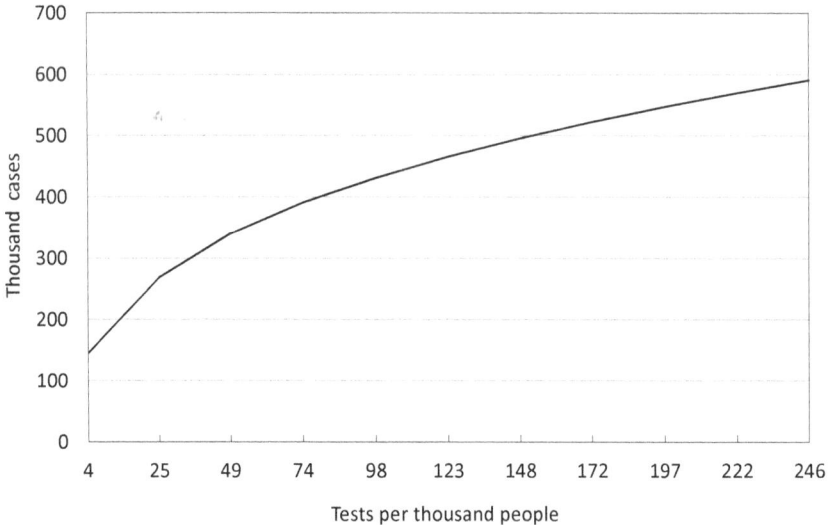

Source: World Development Indicators, World Bank (https://databank.worldbank.org/source/world-development-indicators); Our World in Data, University of Oxford (https://ourworldindata.org/coronavirus).

Since it is likely that the number of COVID-19 tests should be as high as those in the United States and United Kingdom in order to reveal a more accurate estimate of the spread of the pandemic, we argue that the size of the pandemic in Indonesia by 20 August 2020 would be about 560,000, or approximately four times the formal reported cases. Important to note is that these numbers are increasing as the spread of the pandemic is ongoing in the country. Using the rate of transmission by the end of August 2020, the numbers are expected to double in 40 days.

To validate our estimate of the number of COVID-19 cases, we compare this number with a result from a household phone survey conducted from 15 May to 20 June 2020 among 342 random households in Jakarta, in collaboration with Rus'an Nasrudin and Pyan Amin of the University of Indonesia. The household survey revealed that the percentage of the Jakarta population very possibly infected by COVID-19 was 0.5 per cent.[4] Meanwhile, the government reported confirmed cases was 0.15 per cent of Jakarta's population, which is about nine times lower than the number from the household survey. Hence estimating that the actual numbers of COVID-19 cases in Indonesia could be as high as four times the formal reported numbers seems to be accurate.

COVID-19 mortality

To estimate the number of deaths due to COVID-19 by the end of August 2020, we used a similar function as the one used for estimating the total number of COVID-19 cases. Figure 10.4 shows that if the number of COVID-19 tests in Indonesia by 20 August was approximately 210 per thousand people, similar to those in the United States and United Kingdom, it is estimated that the number of confirmed COVID-19 deaths would be about 47,000 or 0.2 per 10,000 people. In other words, the deaths due to COVID-19 by 20 August 2020 in Indonesia might be seven times higher than the formal reported number.

Note that by 20 August 2020, total deaths due to COVID-19 in the United States and United Kingdom were reported to be 173,000 and 41,000 (or 5 and 6 deaths per 10,000 of their populations), respectively. It can hence be argued that the estimates in this chapter could be relatively accurate.

---

4 'Very possible' is defined as those diagnosed as (1) patients under surveillance (PDP) and those living with them, (2) people under surveillance (ODP) having any symptoms or in contact with PDP and (3) having symptoms and having ever been in contact with PDP.

Figure 10.4 Estimated COVID-19 deaths and tests per thousand people

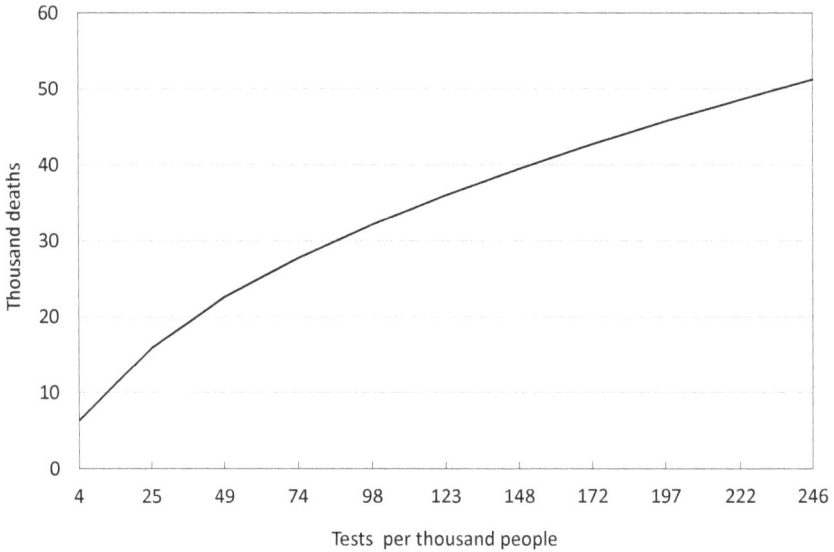

Source: World Development Indicators, World Bank (https://databank.worldbank.org/source/world-development-indicators); Our World in Data, University of Oxford (https://ourworldindata.org/coronavirus).

From disease outbreaks to human capital development

To understand channels from which the COVID-19 pandemic could affect human capital development, we developed a conceptual framework linking the pandemic to health and educational outcomes (Figure 10.5).

Immediate impacts of the pandemic

The immediate (or initial) impacts of the COVID-19 pandemic to the world's population can be grouped into direct and indirect. The direct and foremost is that it causes numbers of COVID-19 illnesses. By mid-October 2020, the number of COVID-19 cases worldwide had reached more than 44 million.[5] The rate of infection is continuing to rise globally despite slowdown in some countries and regions.

The first indirect immediate impact of the pandemic is limited mobility, as governments across the world impose measures to restrict human movements and encourage social distancing. The limited mobility ranged

---

5 www.worldometers.info/coronavirus/

Figure 10.5 Possible mechanisms of COVID-19 impacts to human capital development

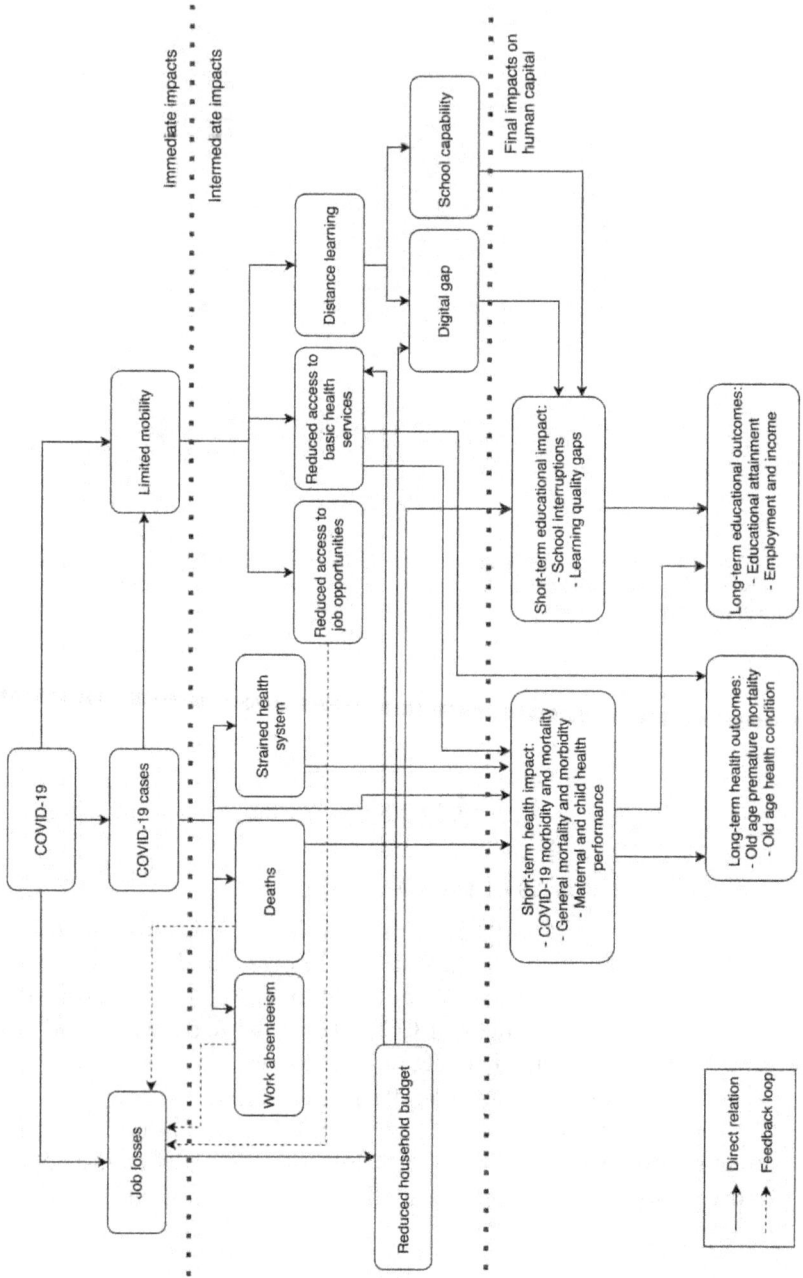

from a full lockdown and very strict social distancing requirements, as employed in China during the first wave of the outbreak (Maier and Brockmann 2020), to allowing relatively free human movement and public health campaigns encouraging social distancing, as employed by the government in South Korea (Campbell 2020). Higher cases of COVID-19 tend to push authorities to impose stricter human movement and social distancing rules.

The second indirect immediate impact of the COVID-19 pandemic is an increase in job losses as the economy struggles to keep up with the public health crisis of such scale. The International Labour Organization predicted that the COVID-19 pandemic may threaten around 25 million jobs globally (UN News 2020).

Intermediate impacts of the pandemic

The intermediate impacts are defined as the consequential impacts from the immediate impacts of the COVID-19 pandemic. Cases of COVID-19 illness have consequential impacts on households and health service institutions. For households, illness due to COVID-19 creates work absenteeism and can result in death. Both chronic work absenteeism and deaths can further exacerbate the problems of job losses. For health institutions, large numbers of COVID-19 cases strain their daily health services, and this can reduce the quality of their health services.

Consequential impacts of limited mobility also include, for students, the requirement to conduct distance learning. This requirement to conduct distance learning induces two issues. First is a digital gap issue, that is, some students have access to digital facilities and can easily participate in a distance learning system, but other students have limited or no access to digital facilities and so cannot fully participate in distance learning. The second issue is schools' limited capacity in conducting distance learning: some schools are not able to properly organise a distance learning system. Limited mobility can also limit access to jobs, which again will further accentuate the problems of job loss.

Lastly, consequential impacts of job losses can further constrain household budgets, which then can indirectly contribute to the digital gap for family members to participate in a distance learning system, as well as reduced ability to access health services.

Impacts on human capital

All the consequential impacts from the COVID-19 pandemic will eventually have some consequences for human capital development, particularly health and educational performances. Health and educational performance can be categorised into short- and long-term issues. First, family member COVID-19 illnesses and deaths can directly translate to short-term morbidity and mortality cases due to COVID-19.

Second, in the short term, lower health services and reduced access to health services could induce cases of morbidity and mortality in general, that is, non–COVID-19 cases. Among these COVID-19 and other morbidity cases, it is important to pay attention to maternal and child health outcomes, since these could be the channel for future health problems for women and their children. This is particularly important for a country like Indonesia that is still struggling with stunting, wasting and maternal mortality.

Long-term health issues include a possibility for those infected by COVID-19 and other diseases in the short term to face a higher probability of premature mortality and/or to contract health issues in their older age. Furthermore, those, particularly children, who cannot properly access health services and get adequate nutrition due to constrained household budgets during the COVID-19 pandemic might, in their older age, confront a higher probability of premature mortality and/or health issues. Maternal nutrition and stress during the pandemic may also influence birth outcomes that can be carried on to adulthood.

Educational performance can be affected by the digital gap, a constrained household budget and limited school capacity in delivering distance learning, causing school interruptions and learning differences in the short term. Some individuals facing digital gaps and/or a constrained household budget might not be able to perform well or may even stop schooling, at least for a while. Further, schools that are unable to properly conduct digital learning produce lower-quality graduates.

These short-term educational performances, together with the health effects of COVID-19, could induce several long-term educational consequences, such as adult educational attainment, employment and income.

Given that this study is conducted while the COVID-19 pandemic is in full swing, the magnitude of the pandemic's impact is unclear. The extent of the impacts, however, is highly contingent on government capacity and responses towards this public health crisis.

Literature on disease outbreak calamities

To better understand what the human capital consequences of the COVID-19 pandemic might be, we collected evidence on the human capital consequences of several large disease outbreaks over the past 100 years. We first focus on the 1918 influenza pandemic, because several academics predict that the current COVID-19 pandemic could be as large (e.g. Barro et al. 2020). Aside from the 1918 influenza pandemic, we also look briefly at 2003 SARS, 2009 swine flu, malaria and COVID-19 itself.

Short-term health outcomes

In the case of the 1918 influenza, in a recent comprehensive analysis, Barro et al. (2020) estimate that the size of casualties from this pandemic was approximately 2.1 per cent of the world population. They further predict that if this casualty rate is applied to the current world population, it will give us an estimate of around 150 million deaths worldwide. In the case of Indonesia, the estimate of mortality cases due to the 1918 influenza pandemic was about 1.5 million (3 per cent) or more in Java alone (Brown 1987; Chandra 2013). This death rate is consistent with the estimates of Barro et al. (2020) and indicates it is possible that the current COVID-19 pandemic could infect a very large portion of the Indonesian population and cause massive casualties.

Another impact of a large pandemic is an increase in cases of other diseases. For example, Duarte et al. (2017) report that during the 2009 swine influenza in Chile, missed working days due to general health cases increased by 800 per cent, a minimum of a 0.2 per cent reduction in labour supply. The impacts of influenza pandemics on maternal and child health conditions have also been recorded in the literature. For example, during the 2009 swine flu pandemic, Doyle et al. (2013) observed that children born to women with swine flu illness during pregnancy were at increased risk for low birth weight, premature birth and infant death, after adjusting for other factors. Roberton et al. (2020) provide an estimate of the impact of COVID-19 on maternal and under-5 child deaths for low income and middle income countries. They estimate that the current pandemic could increase maternal deaths by 8.3–38.6 per cent and child deaths by 9.8–44.7 per cent.

Long-term health outcomes

In the case of the 1918 influenza pandemic, studies show that exposure to the virus while in utero has health consequences in adulthood and old age. For example, Almond and Mazumder (2005) found that individuals born in 1919 (and hence possibly exposed to the pandemic while in utero) in the United States were more likely to have a range of functional limitations (trouble hearing by 19 per cent, trouble speaking by 35 per cent, trouble lifting by 13 per cent and trouble walking by 17 per cent), and more likely to contract illnesses such as diabetes, stroke, cancer, heart problems, hypertension and stomach problems in adulthood. A study by Myrskylä et al. (2013) found that early childhood exposure to the 1918 influenza, as well as exposure in late gestation and at birth, reduced life expectancy by 0.6 years at age 70 years in a population with a 75-year life expectancy.

There is currently no conclusive evidence of fetal transmission of COVID-19. A study by Dashraath et al. (2020) indicates more promising results compared to SARS and MERS.[6] However, because these early studies have a small number of cases and a short study period, it remains unclear what the possible long-term impacts of this specific recent pandemic are, especially for adult outcomes due to exposure to COVID-19 in early childhood.

Short-term educational outcomes

There is early evidence that the current COVID-19 pandemic may disturb children's education. In a survey of 1500 students in the United States, Aucejo et al. (2020) found that 13 per cent of students had delayed graduation, 40 per cent lost a job internship or a job offer and 29 per cent expect to earn less at age 35 due to COVID-19. Furthermore, Azevedo et al. (2020) predict that the income shock due to the pandemic could force about 7 million students in 157 countries, from primary up to secondary education, to drop out. In higher education, COVID-19 has disrupted students' learning experiences and expectations.

The current COVID-19 pandemic is also expected to widen learning-quality differences among students with different socioeconomic characteristics. Bacher-Hicks et al. (2020) found that areas in the United States with higher income, better internet access and fewer rural schools experienced a larger increase in search intensity for online learning resources compared to other areas. Their study suggests that the pandemic will likely worsen achievement gaps between students since there are differences in engagement with online resources to compensate for lost school-based learning time.

Long-term educational outcomes

For the influenza pandemic in 1918, Almond (2006) examined the effects of exposure to influenza on long-term educational attainment. His study found the 1919 birth cohort received 18 months less schooling and was 4–5 per cent less likely to complete high school compared to the predicted

---

6 Severe acute respiratory syndrome (SARS), first identified in 2003, and Middle East respiratory syndrome (MERS), first identified in 2012, are viral respiratory diseases caused by coronaviruses.

trend. Lin and Liu (2014), following the study by Almond (2006), examined impacts of in utero exposure to the 1918 influenza pandemic to long-term education and health outcomes in Taiwan. Their study found that exposure to the pandemic reduced years of education, with an estimated 1.8 per cent drop in years of education for the 1919 male cohort. Nelson (2010) tested the fetal origins hypothesis in Brazil and found that individuals who were in utero during the pandemic had fewer years of schooling and were less likely to go to college compared to individuals who were born in the few years before or after the pandemic.

Other studies suggest that exposure to an outbreak or epidemic can affect cognitive performance and literacy. Kelly (2011) examined the impact of fetal exposure to the 1957 Asian influenza pandemic on child development in Britain and found that the exposure had a negative impact on cognitive development. In Mexico, Venkataramani (2012) confirms that early life exposure to malaria eradication is associated with an increase in cognitive test scores.

Final remarks

Using daily data on COVID-19 testing, confirmed cases and deaths from 1 January 2020 until 24 August 2020 for approximately 100 countries around the world, this chapter estimates that the number of COVID-19 cases in Indonesia by 20 August 2020 could have been about 560,000, or four times the official number, and the number of COVID-19 deaths could have been about 47,000, or seven times the official number. These numbers are still growing as the spread of COVID-19 continues. With the rate of transmission at the end of August 2020, it is expected that the numbers would double about every 40 days. Hence, it can be concluded that the magnitude of the COVID-19 pandemic in Indonesia has likely been much larger than the official numbers.

This chapter develops a conceptual framework to understand channels from which the COVID-19 pandemic could affect health and educational performances of Indonesians. Besides being made ill by the virus, the other main channels show how the pandemic can influence human capital development through job losses and limited human mobility. These channels induce short- and long-term issues related to health and educational performances of Indonesian society.

A comprehensive literature survey, particularly related to the 1918 influenza pandemic, indicates that, in the short term, a pandemic this size could infect almost one-third of a country's population and induce casualties in as much as 2 per cent of the population. The COVID-19 pandemic is expected to increase cases of other morbidities, maternal deaths, and less healthy babies and children. It has also been seen to disrupt the learning process and widen learning-quality gaps among children of different socioeconomic status.

In the long run, there is evidence that a pandemic of this size could increase mortality by approximately 8–9 per cent and lead to a less healthy population in old age. Literature also shows that cohorts exposed to a large disease outbreak while in utero received 18 months less schooling and had poorer cognitive abilities than their counterparts who had not been exposed.

These previous calamities due to large disease outbreaks should serve as a warning to Indonesia to implement sensible policies to minimise the impact of the COVID-19 pandemic on human capital development. Although searching for such policies to protect human capital development against the pandemic is beyond the scope of this chapter, we argue that the following policies should be the Indonesian government's top priorities. In the public health arena, more and better testing, effective tracing and comprehensive treatment should be the main priority for the government. Stricter rules on social distancing, enforcement of the rules and regional containment should be implemented throughout the country. Faster disbursement of the health budget and reforming the country's health institutions to strengthen the public health system should also be implemented. These policies are needed to minimise the spread of the pandemic in the country.

In the education sector, by law the government has to allocate at least 20 per cent of its expenditure to education. This education budget should be included in the COVID-19 stimulus budget so it can be disbursed fast and reallocated to aspects of education that could soften the impact of the pandemic. Among others are reallocating the current budget plan on education to expand scholarship programs, such as Schools Operational Assistance (Bantuan Operasional Sekolah, BOS) and Smart Indonesia Program (Program Indonesia Pintar, PIP), to develop digital infrastructure for education, and to support education in remote areas. The budget could also be used to increase the amount of Family Hope Program (Program Keluarga Harapan, PKH) conditional cash support to families with school-aged children. These policies aim to reduce school interruptions and learning-quality differences among various socioeconomic groups.

By minimising the spread of the pandemic, school interruptions and learning-quality differences, it is expected that the impact of the pandemic on human capital development could be minimised as well.

Appendix 1. Correlation between total tests and total infected cases, and total deaths

The specification used in this appendix is a transformation of equation (2) in the chapter:

$$ln(h_{i,d}) = \sigma \cdot ln(t_{i,d}) + \alpha_1 \cdot X_i + \alpha_2 \cdot pop_i + e_{i,d} \qquad \text{(A1)}$$

where $h_{i,d}$ is the number of infected persons detected in country i on day d, $t_{i,d}$ is the number of tests in country i on day d, σ is the elasticity of a person being infected per testing and X_i is a vector of region i's time-invariant characteristics just before the COVID-19 pandemic (the situation in the region during and after the pandemic, including mobility restriction policies, would be endogenously affected by the pandemic, and those variables are not included in the equation). The main issue with equation (A1) is that we could miss some confounding variables, including those that are time-invariant.

To take into account any possible other time-invariant variables not included in X_i and not pop_i, the equation (A1) can be estimated using a fixed effects model as follows:

$$ln(h_{i,d}) = \sigma \cdot ln(t_{i,t}) + \delta_t + \tau_i + e_{i,t} \qquad \text{(A2)}$$

where τ_i is country fixed effects and δ_t are date dummies for each day during the observation.

Using daily data on COVID-19 testing, confirmed cases and deaths from 1 January 2020 until 24 August 2020 for approximately 100 countries around the world (available from the World Bank's World Development Indicators and the University of Oxford's Our World in Data), we estimate equations (A1) and (A2). Tables 10.A1 and 10.A2 present the results. Total tests, cases and deaths are seven-day moving average observations. This approach is to avoid random timings in reporting testing activities, testing results and deaths. Control variables in these estimations are population (2019 population), proxy of urbanisation (2019 population density and 2019 portion of urban population), level of development (2019 purchasing power parity and current GDP per capita), health condition of the society (2017 diabetes prevalence and 2016 portion of smokers) and quality of health services (2017 physicians per thousand head of population).

Models 1 and 3 are same-day correlations between total tests and total cases or total tests and total deaths. Models 2 and 4 are correlations between total tests lagging 14 days and daily total cases or total deaths. Given there is a lag between tests and their results, particularly with deaths, and our preference is to use equation (A2), our main results are Models 4 in Tables 10.A1 and 10.A2. From these tables it can be said that,

Table 10.A1   Correlation between COVID-19 total cases and total tests, using log function

Model	Ordinary least squares		Fixed effects	
	(1)	(2)	(3)	(4)
Total tests	0.908***		1.296***	
	(0.00625)		(0.0108)	
Total tests—lagging 14 days		0.700***		0.343***
		(0.00800)		(0.00992)
With control variables	Yes	Yes	No	No
Date dummies	No	No	Yes	Yes
Country fixed effect	No	No	Yes	Yes
Observations	7,291	6,768	10,243	9,603
R^2	0.882	0.824	0.890	0.688
Number of countries	55	59	83	104

Table 10.A2   Correlation between COVID-19 total deaths and total tests, using log function

Model	Ordinary least squares		Fixed effects	
	(1)	(2)	(3)	(4)
Total tests	1.179***		0.928***	
	(0.00951)		(0.0139)	
Total tests—lagging 14 days		0.972***		0.510***
		(0.0100)		(0.0108)
With control variables	Yes	Yes	No	No
Date dummies	No	No	Yes	Yes
Country fixed effect	No	No	Yes	Yes
Observations	7,004	6,607	9,807	9,305
R^2	0.774	0.692	0.852	0.757
Number of countries	55	57	82	91

Note for both tables: Total tests are in million tests. Total cases are in thousand cases. Both total tests and cases are calculated based on their 7-day moving average numbers. Control variables are 2019 population, 2019 population density, 2019 portion of urban population, 2019 purchasing power parity and current GDP per capita, 2017 diabetes prevalence, 2016 portion of smokers and 2017 physicians per thousand head of population.

Standard errors are in parentheses. * $p < 0.1$; ** $p < 0.05$; *** $p < 0.01$.

in general, if a country increases its number of tests by 1 per cent at a certain date, the number of infections found would be higher by about 0.34 per cent from the current level and the number of deaths due to the pandemic would be higher by about 0.51 per cent from the current level.

The list of variables used in the models is presented in Table 10.A3.

Table 10.A3 Descriptive summary of variables used in this chapter

Variable	Obs.	Mean	Std Dev.	Min.	Max.
7-day moving average total cases (in thousand cases)	10,326	82.8	355.3	0	5,531.4
7-day moving average total deaths (in thousand cases)	10,326	3.7	14.6	0	173.1
7-day moving average total tests (in million tests)	10,326	1.2	4.7	0	69.6
Lag 7-day moving average total tests (in million tests)	8,509	1.0	4.0	0	59.7
2019 population (in million people)	10,113	54.3	162.0	0.36	1,366.4
2019 population density (persons per km^2)	10,113	185.6	314.8	3.2	1,935.9
2019 portion of urban population (%)	10,113	69.1	19.1	17.3	100
2019 purchasing power parity and current GDP per capita	9,916	33,026	24,657	1,662	121,293
2017 diabetes prevalence (% of those aged 20 to 79)	10,113	7.5	3.3	1.8	17.7
2016 smokers (%)	9,775	22.4	9.1	3.9	43.4
2017 physicians (per 1,000 population)	7,660	2.5	1.7	0	8.3

Source: World Development Indicators, World Bank (https://databank.worldbank.org/source/world-development-indicators); Our World in Data, University of Oxford (https://ourworldindata.org/coronavirus).

References

Almond, Douglas. 2006. 'Is the 1918 influenza pandemic over? Long-term effects of in utero influenza exposure in the post-1940 U.S. population'. *Journal of Political Economy* 114(4): 672–712. doi.org/10.1086/507154

Almond, Douglas and Bhashkar Mazumder. 2005. 'The 1918 influenza pandemic and subsequent health outcomes: An analysis of SIPP data'. *American Economic Review* 95(2): 258–62. doi.org/10.1257/000282805774669943

Aucejo, Esteban M., Jacob F. French, Maria Paola Ugalde Araya and Basit Zafar. 2020. 'The impact of COVID-19 on student experiences and expectations: Evidence from a survey'. *NBER Working Paper* No. 27392. doi.org/10.3386/w27392

Azevedo, João Pedro, Amer Hasan, Diana Goldemberg, Syedah Aroob Iqbal and Koen Geven. 2020. 'Simulating the potential impacts of COVID-19 school closures on schooling and learning outcomes: A set of global estimates'. *Policy Research Working Paper* No. 9284. World Bank. doi.org/10.1596/1813-9450-9284

Bacher-Hicks, Andrew, Joshua Goodman and Christine Mulhern. 2020. 'Inequality in household adaptation to schooling shocks: COVID-induced online learning engagement in real time'. *NBER Working Paper* No. 27555. doi.org/10.3386/w27555

Barro, Robert J., José F. Ursúa and Joanna Weng. 2020. 'The coronavirus and the great influenza pandemic: Lessons from the "Spanish Flu" for the coronavirus's potential effects on mortality and economic activity'. *NBER Working Paper* No. 26866. doi.org/10.3386/w26866

Brown, C. 1987. 'The influenza pandemic of 1918 in Indonesia'. In *Death and Disease in Southeast Asia: Explorations in Social, Medical, and Demographic History*, edited by Norman G. Owen, 235–56. Oxford: Oxford University Press.

Campbell, Charlie. 2020. 'South Korea's health minister on how his country is beating coronavirus without a lockdown'. *TIME*, 30 April. https://time.com/5830594/south-korea-covid19-coronavirus/

Chandra, Siddharth. 2013. 'Mortality from the influenza pandemic of 1918–19 in Indonesia'. *Population Studies* 67(2): 185–93. doi.org/10.1080/00324728.2012.754486

Dashraath, Pradip, Jing Lin Jeslyn Wong, Mei Xian Karen Lim, Li Min Lim, Sarah Li, Arijit Biswas, Mahesh Choolani et al. 2020. 'Coronavirus disease 2019 (COVID-19) pandemic and pregnancy'. *American Journal of Obstetrics and Gynecology* 222(6): 521–31. doi.org/10.1016/j.ajog.2020.03.021

Doyle, Timothy J., Kate Goodin and Janet J. Hamilton. 2013. 'Maternal and neonatal outcomes among pregnant women with 2009 pandemic influenza A (H1N1) illness in Florida, 2009–2010: A population-based cohort study'. *Plos One* 8(10): e79040. doi.org/10.1371/journal.pone.0079040

Duarte, Fabian, Srikanth Kadiyala, Samuel H. Masters and David Powell. 2017. 'The effect of the 2009 influenza pandemic on absence from work'. *Health Economics* 26(12): 1682–95. doi.org/10.1002/hec.3485

Kelly, Elaine. 2011. 'The scourge of Asian flu: In utero exposure to pandemic influenza and the development of a cohort of British children'. *Journal of Human Resources* 46(4): 669–94. doi.org/10.3368/jhr.46.4.669

Lin, Ming-Jen and Elaine M. Liu. 2014. 'Does in utero exposure to illness matter? The 1918 influenza epidemic in Taiwan as a natural experiment'. *Journal of Health Economics* 37: 152–63. doi.org/10.1016/j.jhealeco.2014.05.004

Maier, Benjamin F. and Dirk Brockmann. 2020. 'Effective containment explains subexponential growth in recent confirmed COVID-19 cases in China'. *Science* 368(6492): 742–46. doi.org/10.1126/science.abb4557

Myrskylä, Mikko, Neil K. Mehta and Virginia W. Chang. 2013. 'Early life exposure to the 1918 influenza pandemic and old-age mortality by cause of death'. *American Journal of Public Health* 103(7): e83–90. doi.org/10.2105/AJPH.2012.301060

Nelson, Richard E. 2010. 'Testing the fetal origins hypothesis in a developing country: Evidence from the 1918 influenza pandemic'. *Health Economics* 19(10): 1181–92. doi.org/10.1002/hec.1544

Resosudarmo, Budy P. and Lucentezza Napitupulu. 2004. 'Health and economic impact of air pollution in Jakarta'. *Economic Record* 80(S1): S65–75. doi.org/10.1111/j.1475-4932.2004.00184.x

Roberton, Timothy, Emily D. Carter, Victoria B. Chou, Angela R. Stegmuller, Bianca D. Jackson, Yvonne Tam, Talata Sawadogo-Lewis and Neff Walker. 2020. 'Early estimates of the indirect effects of the COVID-19 pandemic on maternal and child mortality in low-income and middle-income countries: A modelling study'. *Lancet Global Health* 8(7): e901–8. doi.org/10.1016/S2214-109X(20)30229-1

Thuilliez, Josselin, Mahamadou S. Sissoko, Ousmane B. Toure, Paul Kamate, Jean-Claude Berthélemy and Ogobara K. Doumbo. 2010. 'Malaria and primary education in Mali: A longitudinal study in the village of Donéguébougou'. *Social Science & Medicine* 71(2): 324–34. doi.org/10.1016/j.socscimed.2010.02.027

UN News. 2020. 'COVID-19: Impact could cause equivalent of 195 million job losses, says ILO chief'. UN News, 8 April. https://news.un.org/en/story/2020/04/1061322

Venkataramani, Atheendar S. 2012. 'Early life exposure to malaria and cognition in adulthood: Evidence from Mexico'. *Journal of Health Economics* 31(5): 767–80. doi.org/10.1016/j.jhealeco.2012.06.003

11 Deepening multidimensional poverty: The impacts of COVID-19 on vulnerable social groups

Sharon Bessell and Angie Bexley

Abstract

In Indonesia, and globally, there is increasing evidence that COVID-19 is having varying negative impacts on different social groups. Those already experiencing poverty are less able to take necessary measures to protect themselves, while vulnerable groups are in danger of being plunged further into poverty. Most notably, there are indications of deleterious impacts on women, particularly in regard to domestic and intimate partner violence, and time burdens. In assessing and projecting the impacts of COVID-19, in developing immediate responses, and in identifying longer-term policy directions, it is important to adopt a multidimensional definition of poverty and to ensure analyses are sensitive to gender and to those groups experiencing deepest deprivation prior to the pandemic. This chapter provides an overview of the implications of COVID-19 for people living in poverty. We draw on data from a 2018 study on multidimensional poverty in South Sulawesi, which used the Individual Measure of Multidimensional Poverty (IMMP) to demonstrate the value of measuring multidimensional poverty at the individual—rather than the household—level, and to identify the social groups that were experiencing multidimensional poverty prior to the COVID-19 pandemic. Those findings now have important implications for projecting how COVID-19 is likely to affect different social groups, and for COVID-19 responses.

Introduction

In Indonesia, and globally, there is increasing evidence that COVID-19 is having different negative impacts on different social groups. Those already experiencing poverty are less able to take necessary measures to protect themselves, while vulnerable groups are in danger of being plunged further into poverty. Projections also indicate the likely emergence of the 'new poor', those groups that had moved out of poverty but remain susceptible to shocks. Most notably, there are indications of deleterious effects on women, particularly in regard to domestic and intimate partner violence, and time burdens.

Projections of poverty indicate the likely impacts of COVID-19 in terms of income, but are less able to provide insights into the ways different social groups are likely to be affected by the combination of health crisis, economic downturn and declining incomes, and mobility restrictions. In projecting and assessing the impacts of COVID-19, in developing immediate responses, and in identifying longer-term policy directions, it is important to adopt a multidimensional definition of poverty and to ensure analyses are sensitive to gender and to those groups experiencing deepest deprivation prior to the pandemic. This chapter highlights the importance of a multidimensional approach and examines ways in which the pandemic is likely to affect the most vulnerable groups.

We draw on the findings of a study of poverty undertaken in Indonesia in 2018, using the Individual Deprivation Measure (renamed the Individual Measure of Multidimensional Poverty in July 2020). The measure assesses the poverty of each adult within the household across fifteen dimensions, and provides deep and nuanced insights into the nature of poverty, how social characteristics intersect to create deep poverty for some groups, and how dimensions interact to compound the experience of poverty. The findings indicate which social groups are vulnerable to impacts of the COVID-19 pandemic.

Assessing the implications of COVID-19 on poverty: The need for multidimensionality

Poverty is most commonly defined and measured as low income or low expenditure. Such money-metric approaches inform the International Poverty Line, introduced by the World Bank in 1990 and based on the national poverty lines of the world's poorest countries. National poverty lines, including in Indonesia, are also based on money-metric definitions. Indonesia's national poverty line uses a basic needs approach to establish the expenditure required to buy essential food items to achieve

2100 kilocalories per person per day and non-food items (including housing, clothing, education and health care). Indonesia has been highly successful in reducing the proportion of the population living below the national poverty line. In 2018, the official poverty rate fell below 10 per cent for the first time. Yet the official poverty rate masks both the extent of poverty and its nature, for three reasons.

First, decisions about the level at which the poverty line is set are necessarily normative, and driven by a range of political considerations. Indonesia's poverty line is low (World Bank 2015; Yusuf and Sumner 2017). According to Hoy (2016), Indonesia's poverty line would be 2.5 times higher if mean consumption was taken into account, in line with cross-country trends. Thus, while the percentage of the population living below the official poverty line has declined over time, a significant proportion of people are just above the poverty line and remain highly vulnerable, particularly in the context of COVID-19.

Second, like many national poverty lines, the data informing Indonesia's poverty line are narrow. Poverty is calculated from data in the Consumption and Expenditure module of the National Socioeconomic Survey (Survei Sosio-Ekonomi Nasional, Susenas). Thus the national poverty line indicates levels of expenditure on important food and non-food items. Achievement is not assessed as part of the information base that contributes to the national poverty line; for example, expenditure on education may not result in functioning levels of literacy and numeracy, and expenditure on healthcare services may not indicate treatment in an adequately equipped clinic (Wisor et al. 2014: 32). Moreover, non-monetary dimensions of poverty, likely to be significant in the context of COVID-19, are not assessed.

Third, Susenas data are collected for the household, and overall expenditure is then divided by the number of household members. This approach assumes that resources are shared equally between all members of the household, which is not necessarily the case. Differences between members, based on gender, age, disability, ability or other characteristics, are masked and as a consequence it is not possible to accurately determine which social groups are most deprived. This creates specific challenges in the context of COVID-19 impacts and responses.

Over the past decade, there has been increased recognition of the value of multidimensional assessment of poverty. Money-metric measures of poverty are unquestionably necessary. There is no serious argument that insufficient income and expenditure are not central characteristics of poverty. Tracking income or consumption reveals trends over time and allows for comparisons, particularly across geographic locations. However, there are limits to the information money-metric measures can provide. The recognition of poverty as a multidimensional phenomenon has enabled more approaches to emerge that complement poverty assessments based on income or consumption and provide policymakers with more nuanced information on which to formulate policy. Assessing multidimensional poverty provides a broader information base, able to reveal the gendered nature of poverty and patterns of social inclusion or exclusion.

One such approach is the Individual Measure of Multidimensional Poverty (IMMP), called the Individual Deprivation Measure (IDM) during its development.[1] The IMMP/IDM represents the multidimensional turn in conceptualising and measuring poverty, reflecting target 2 of United Nations Sustainable Development Goal 1, which is to 'reduce at least by half the proportion of men, women and children of all ages living in poverty in all its dimensions according to national definitions'.[2] It progresses the recommendation of the Commission on Global Poverty, commissioned by the World Bank (2017), that measurement of income or consumption to determine poverty be augmented by additional and alternative indicators.

The IMMP measures poverty across fifteen dimensions, fourteen of which are used to construct a composite index, providing a single IMMP score. It also provides scores for each dimension and enables rich analysis of descriptive statistics. The IMMP assesses both material and non-material poverty. It includes indicators that are sensitive to gender (such as time burdens and unpaid work) and those that are specific to women (such as access to prenatal care and to sanitary products), which are critical to understanding the gendered nature of poverty, but are rarely assessed by mainstream measures of poverty. The findings from the 2018 study in Indonesia reveal ways in which various characteristics, such as sex, age, geographic location and disability, intersect to shape the nature of poverty. As discussed later in this chapter, the findings indicate the groups likely to be most vulnerable in the context of the COVID-19 pandemic. Before turning to those findings, however, we review the emerging information on the impacts of COVID-19, particularly on women, as a backdrop for considering the implications of our study of multidimensional poverty in Indonesia.

---

1 The research that resulted in the IMMP began with an ARC Linkage grant, LP0989385; from 2016 to 2020 the Individual Deprivation Measure Program was funded by the Australian Government Department of Foreign Affairs and Trade. The study in South Sulawesi was undertaken by the ANU IDM team; data collection was undertaken in collaboration with SurveyMETER.

2 https://sdgs.un.org/goals/goal1

Data emerging on poverty and gender in the context of COVID-19

Around the world, the COVID-19 pandemic is exposing and exacerbating existing inequalities—particularly those relating to gender and to socioeconomic status. As unemployment rises and incomes decline, increasing numbers of people are falling into poverty or are highly vulnerable. Moreover, COVID-19 is having different impacts on different social groups. Those in informal or precarious work are especially exposed, and safety nets are often not reaching those most vulnerable. There is increasing evidence of the ways in which women are affected not only by greater income poverty, but by violence and by additional time burdens. These global trends are also playing out in Indonesia.

Estimates of the impact of COVID-19 on poverty globally present a disturbing picture. Sumner et al. (2020), while taking care to note the limitations of their estimates, suggest that a 5 per cent contraction in income or consumption per capita would reverse the achievements of the past 30 years, and potentially see a rise in global poverty for the first time since 1990. Those falling below the extreme poverty line of US$1.90 per day are expected to be concentrated in sub-Saharan Africa and South Asia. However, estimates suggest that in Southeast Asia there will be significant increases in the 'new poor' who fall below US$5.50 per day. In Indonesia, predictions are far from encouraging. With the growth rate estimated to fall to between 1.8 per cent and −3.5 per cent (Suryahadi et al. 2020; World Bank 2020; Yusuf 2020), a reversal in the downward trend in poverty is almost inevitable. Suryahadi et al. (2020) draw on the impacts of the 2005–2006 economic shock[3] to estimate the impacts of COVID-19 on poverty, measured by household expenditure, in Indonesia. In the best-case scenario, they estimate an increase in poverty from 9.2 per cent in September 2019 to 9.7 per cent by the end of 2020, resulting in 1.3 million more people living in poverty. In the worst-case scenario, whereby growth falls to −3.5 per cent, the poverty rate jumps to 16.6 per cent, with 19.7 million more people in poverty (ibid.: 188). Suryahadi et al. (2020: 181) conclude that households at the low end of expenditure distribution will be disproportionately affected. The first round of high-frequency monitoring of households, undertaken in May 2020, indicated significant job losses, marked declines in income among those who continued to work, and decreased food security (Purnamasari and Ali 2020).

---

3 This economic shock was caused by substantial international price rises in fuel and rice.

Estimates of job losses and increasing poverty, particularly monetary poverty, are deeply concerning, but reveal only part of the picture. While rapid assessments have tended to focus on the impacts of COVID-19 on households, it is also important to understand how deepening poverty will impact *within* households and on the most vulnerable groups. It is also important to understand impacts on the gendered patterns of poverty, with indications emerging around the world that declining incomes disproportionately affect women. Drawing on available global information, the United Nations (2020b: 4) argues that the negative impacts on women result because 'women earn less, save less, hold less secure jobs, and are more likely to be employed in the informal sector'. These impacts appear to be playing out in Indonesia. In a small-scale rapid assessment of COVID-19 impacts with 87 respondents in Bali, Kopernik found that female respondents reported a 72 per cent decline in income, compared with a 52 per cent decline reported by men (Gender Observatory 2020). In June 2020, the Australia–Indonesia Partnership for Economic Development, Prospera, highlighted the severe stress on small and micro businesses. According to Prospera, 70 per cent of all businesses owned by women are small scale, generate profits of less than Rp 1.4 million per month, and have limited cash reserves (Gender Observatory 2020). These businesses are extremely vulnerable to collapse due to COVID-19.

Alongside deepening monetary poverty there are indications globally of deepening multidimensional poverty, with especially deleterious impacts for some groups and for the gendered nature of poverty. The stress and anxiety created by the health, social and economic consequences of crisis and disease have been well documented. The entrenched nature of gender roles and responsibilities mean that these consequences are gendered. While impacts on women are wide-ranging, additional time burdens and increases in gender-based violence are especially concerning (Bradbury-Jones and Isham 2020). John et al. (2020) have highlighted the ways in which violence against women and girls was exacerbated during epidemics in recent decades. Gender-based violence is now increasing as a result of COVID-19 (Boserup et al. 2020; Bradbury-Jones and Isham 2020).

In Indonesia, too, there are signs that violence against women is increasing as a result of COVID-19. Jakarta Women's Legal Aid Institute (Lembaga Bantuan Hukum Asosiasi Perempuan Indonesia untuk Keadilan, LBH APIK Jakarta) has reported a dramatic increase in violence cases against women and girls. Prior to the COVID-19 pandemic, LBH APIK received about 60 cases each month. In the period 16 March to 25 July, 327 new cases were reported (Gender Observatory 2020). Among the new cases reported, 117 related to domestic violence and 104 to cyber violence—both of which are considered to be associated with restrictions on movement adopted to address COVID-19. In April–May 2020, the National Commission on Violence Against Women (Komisi Nasional anti Kekerasan Terhadap Perempuan—Komnas Perempuan) conducted an online survey, 'Changes in household dynamics during COVID-19 in 34 provinces in Indonesia', with 2285 respondents. The survey found that violence against women had increased, with women earning less than Rp 5 million per month, informal workers, those in the 31–40 age cohort, and women in the ten provinces with the highest incidence of COVID-19 experiencing the greatest impacts (Komnas Perempuan 2020). The survey results indicated increases in both physical and sexual violence. Muna et al. (2020) argue that women facing domestic violence have greater difficulty in accessing services during the pandemic as crisis centres require a health certificate stating that they have tested negative for COVID-19. As support systems erode, woman across the socioeconomic spectrum are vulnerable to violence (ibid.).

Time burdens have also increased for women in Indonesia, mirroring the situation globally (United Nations 2020b). Komnas Perempuan (2020) found marked increases in women's unpaid work, which includes taking responsibility for home schooling (Syakriah 2020).

While systematic evidence from Indonesia is limited, Mariska (2020) has argued that Indonesian women are especially vulnerable to negative impacts of COVID-19 because of the discrimination they faced before the pandemic. Mariska documents the range of discriminatory laws that have been adopted over the past decade restricting women's freedoms and human rights, and creating conditions of vulnerability that will be exacerbated during the current crisis.

The Individual Measure of Multidimensional Poverty study in Indonesia

The 2018 study of multidimensional poverty in South Sulawesi used the IMMP (then the IDM) and focused on two districts: Jeneponto, and Pangkajene and Islands (Pangkep) (Bexley et al. 2020a, 2020b).[4] A total of 5596 women and men over the age of sixteen were surveyed. The findings demonstrate the value of measuring multidimensional poverty at the

---

4   The authors acknowledge the invaluable contribution of the ANU IMMP/ IDM team—Janet Hunt, Masud Hasan, Trang Pham, Helen Suich and Mandy Yap—to all aspects of the research that underpin this chapter; the contribution of Mark McGillivray to developing the approach to scoring and index construction; and the role of SurveyMETER in data collection. All views are those of the authors.

individual—rather than the household—level, and identify the social groups that were experiencing multidimensional poverty before the COVID-19 pandemic. Those findings now have important implications for projecting how COVID-19 is likely to impact different parts of the population, and for COVID-19 policies.

The overall IMMP index indicates women are more multidimensionally poor than men.[5] However, for some indicators and dimensions men are more deprived, and across all dimensions the gendered nature of poverty is revealed.[6] Significantly, the IMMP reveals the ways in which various characteristics, such as sex, age, geographic location and disability, intersect to shape the nature of poverty.[7] Such intersectional analysis is critical in revealing which social groups are most impacted by multidimensional poverty, and the dimensions in which they are deprived. The findings of the study indicate that people living with disability, and especially women, are more likely to experience multidimensional poverty.

The gendered nature of poverty

While more women than men were multidimensionally poor overall, women were not consistently poorer across all indicators and dimensions. Rather than indicating that poverty is feminised, our results suggest that it is gendered. Both women and men experience multidimensional poverty, but the nature of deprivation is often different, and appears to be shaped by gendered roles and responsibilities.

---

5 The IMMP index is a single score calculated from the data provided through the IMMP survey, which summarises an individual's level of multidimensional poverty across the fourteen dimensions of the IMMP. The variables for which data are collected provide the score for each indicator. Scores for indicators are aggregated to form themes, themes are aggregated to create dimensions, and then dimensions aggregated to create index scores. The components of each level are non-compensatory in nature, that is, a low score in one component (indicator, theme or dimension) cannot be compensated for by a high score in another. The Indonesia dimension scores and index are developed using equal weights geometric mean aggregation. A low index score indicates that an individual experiences a higher level of multidimensional poverty.

6 Unlike many measures of poverty, which use binary poor/non-poor classifications, the IMMP describes individuals' depth of deprivation. Categories used are least deprived, deprived, somewhat deprived and most deprived, using quarters as the cut-off for each category at indicator, theme and dimension.

7 Detailed information on the IMMP methodology and findings is available at https://immp.crawford.anu.edu.au/

The ways in which gendered roles and responsibilities may shape experiences of poverty is evident in relation to food deprivation. This dimension uses the Food Insecurity Experience Scale, developed by the Food and Agriculture Organization of the United Nations, to assess food insecurity. Women in the middle age cohort (25–59 years) were more likely to report being worried about running out of food, likely reflecting their responsibility for caring for and feeding their families. Men also reported experiencing food insecurity, but on different variables. Men in the middle age cohort were more likely to report skipping meals and eating less than they thought necessary. Here it seems that male patterns of employment may affect their ability to access food during the day (Bexley et al. 2020a, 2020b). Overall, almost one-quarter of people experienced food deprivation, indicating high levels of vulnerability that are likely to be exacerbated in a context of rising unemployment and falling incomes. While both women and men experienced food insecurity, the nature of that deprivation is different and requires different responses. High levels of food insecurity prior to COVID-19 caused hardship and stress, both of which are likely to be exacerbated. Given the emerging evidence of violence against women, discussed above, it is critical that close attention be paid to the linkages between hardship and stress—particularly in regard to known problems, such as food insecurity—and violence.

Gender differences were most apparent in regard to time burdens and work. In both Jeneponto and Pangkep, women spent more time than men in paid and unpaid work combined, indicating far higher levels of unpaid domestic work and care roles among women. In Jeneponto, women typically spent 11.5 hours per day in paid and unpaid work—1.5 hours more than men. In Pangkep, the imbalance was greater, with women spending 12 hours per day in paid and unpaid work—2.5 hours more than men. In Pangkep, the widest gender gap in time spent in unpaid work was in the youngest age cohort (16–24 years), with 53.7 per cent of women compared to 36.2 per cent of men undertaking both paid and unpaid work.

Women were far more likely to have a child in their care while performing primary activities—almost 42 per cent of women in Jeneponto cared for children while performing other tasks, compared with just under 12 per cent of men. This suggests that COVID-19–related restrictions on children attending school will result in responsibility for caring for and teaching and supervising children falling largely to women.

It is important to note that men also worked long hours, but women's time burdens were greater. Evidence from around the world indicates that women's time burdens have generally increased during COVID-19, in part due to a greater need to provide care to others. Given the already significant time burdens experienced by women, and the disparity between women and men, COVID-19–related time burdens have the potential to further erode gender equality and impact negatively on women's multidimensional poverty.

Age and multidimensional poverty

As gender shapes the nature of poverty experienced by individuals, so too does age; with age and gender intersecting to provide gendered and generational patterns of poverty.

Research on poverty and wellbeing has established that older people are at a higher risk of social exclusion and loneliness (Guillen et al. 2011; Hao et al. 2017; Montero-López Lena et al. 2019). People with reduced community participation are also likely to not reap the benefits of social interaction and reciprocity. The absence of positive or supportive social relationships may be both a cause and a consequence of poverty, and is associated with shame and stigma. Social exclusion may also heighten vulnerability to poverty (de Haan 2000). Sen (2000: 5) has argued that social relationships have both intrinsic and instrumental value. Exclusion from social relationships limits individuals' opportunities, leading to both social and economic impoverishment.

As countries are affected by the coronavirus, the elderly population in particular is advised to self-isolate. Social isolation can result in serious public health concerns, as social disconnection can put older adults at greater risk of depression and anxiety (Santini et al. 2020). Quarantining older people increases the risks of isolation, loneliness and other forms of deprivation, particularly if they are dependent on others for essential needs.

Our findings show that over 22 per cent of women and men in the oldest cohort (aged 60 years and above) reported depending on others not living with them to help with their basic needs, compared with 10.8 per cent in the youngest cohort. Men in the oldest age cohort (30.3 per cent) were the most likely to report being dependent on others, compared to 15.7 per cent of women. These levels of dependency on others outside the home have significant implications for the poverty and wellbeing of older people in contexts of lockdown or restrictions on movement.

Reciprocity is an important element of social relationships that plays a protective role in times of hardship. When an individual is unable to fulfil social expectations in terms of returning a favour or contributing to social activities, they are no longer able to draw on networks of support. The IMMP individual survey asks respondents whether they are able to return a favour. Here gender differences clearly emerge, with older women twice as likely to report being unable to return a favour. Women in the older age cohort were also least likely of all age and sex cohorts to be able to make a contribution to community events. Moreover, just over 26 per cent of older women, compared with 13 per cent of older men, reported not attending community events, most commonly due to poor health. These findings suggest that both older women and older men were vulnerable to poverty and social isolation before the current pandemic. While older men experience higher levels of dependency on others, older women are more likely to experience social isolation. These existing vulnerabilities are likely to be exacerbated in the context of COVID-19.

The IMMP assesses health status, including mental health. Young people (16–24 years) reported feeling depressed more than both the middle age cohort (25–59 years) and the oldest cohort (60 years and above), and were twice as likely as the older cohorts to experience depression on a daily, weekly or monthly basis. Young men were slightly more likely than young women to report feeling worried, nervous, anxious and depressed. In the context of the pandemic and emerging indications of mental health impacts on young people, the IMMP findings of pre-existing worry, anxiety and depression are of particular concern.

Before the pandemic, Indonesia's unemployment among 15- to 24-year-olds was 17 per cent (World Bank 2020). Youth unemployment has been above 15 per cent since the 1997–1998 Asian financial crisis. In a context of widespread lay-offs and rising unemployment, the situation of young people is especially precarious. Several decades of research internationally has shown the long-term 'scarring' effect of youth unemployment, resulting in lower pay, higher unemployment, fewer life chances and poorer health (McQuaid 2015: 4). The scarring caused by the 'Great Lockdown' associated with COVID-19 is predicted to be particularly deep for young people (ADB and ILO 2020). Combined with existing deprivation in regard to mental health, the current situation of job loss and lockdowns has particularly worrying implications for young people, particularly those with few employment prospects.

While the IMMP results indicate deprivation in social relationships for older people and in mental health status for the youngest cohort, people in middle age were especially deprived in regard to time and work burdens. The vulnerabilities experienced by different age groups suggest that the impacts of COVID-19 will be different. The power of the IMMP is to reveal how deprivation plays out in specific dimensions and across dimensions to shape the experience of multidimensional poverty for women and men of different ages.

Disability and multidimensional poverty

People living with disability are a missing group in poverty assessments, with detailed and nuanced information on the ways disability and poverty interact absent from most mainstream poverty datasets. Those data that are available for Indonesia indicate that people with disability have lower monthly expenditure per capita, lower educational attainment, fewer economic opportunities and reduced access to services. However, available data are rarely disaggregated by sex.

The IMMP individual survey draws on the Washington Group Short Set questions to identify people living with disability. The findings indicate that people with disability are more deprived than those without disability on almost every dimension. There are important gender differences between those people with disability on a number of indicators.

Strikingly, people with disability report contributing through paid and unpaid work at rates as high or higher than those without disability. More people with disability reported having one paid job in the past six months than those without—almost 93 per cent of people with disability compared to almost 85 per cent of those without. Respondents with disability (97.2 per cent) were more likely than those without disability (92.8 per cent) to reporting being engaged in informal work, suggesting greater precarity of work. Within the home, women with disability reported significant hours of unpaid work. Women with disability (81.6 per cent) were more than twice as likely as men with disability (37.5 per cent) to report experiencing injury, illness or mental harm related to unpaid domestic work and care. The picture here is of people with disability making significant contribution through paid work, and women with disability contributing greatly through unpaid domestic work and care. Worryingly, however, despite these levels of contribution, people with disability were more likely to experience food insecurity across all eight variables within the food dimension, and women with disability were most deeply deprived. This raises serious warnings about the likely impacts on people living with disability as paid employment decreases, unpaid work—particularly for women—increases, and food becomes less affordable as incomes fall. Existing poverty is likely to be deepened, with women living with disability extremely vulnerable. The vulnerability of women with disability is deepened in contexts of increased domestic violence.

COVID-19 presents particular risks to people with disability, not only in terms of health impacts but also in accessing medical care. The IMMP findings indicate the poor health status of people with disability prior to

COVID-19, with greater reporting among this group of physical illness and injury, and worry, anxiety and nervousness. People with disability were also more likely than those without to have sought medical care during the past twelve months, and also more likely to report problems with the nature and quality of healthcare services. Women with disability were more likely than any other population group to report not being treated with respect by medical staff.

The challenges facing Indonesia's health system and the implications for coping with COVID-19 have been well documented, as has the failure to learn from previous health crises, including the Avian flu (Djalante et al. 2020). These shortcomings will negatively affect all social groups, but are likely to be particularly severe for people living with disability, given pre-existing health deprivation. The danger is not lost on people living with disability themselves, who have voiced concern that they will be intentionally given lowest priority for medical care, and be allowed to die of COVID-19 due to their pre-existing disability or chronic illness (Saputra 2020).

Vulnerability to coronavirus

While COVID-19 is increasing poverty in Indonesia, those who are already multidimensionally poor face the double impact of deepening deprivation and pre-existing barriers to their ability to adopt measures to stem the spread of the virus and to protect themselves (Bessell and Bexley 2020).

In our study of multidimensional poverty in South Sulawesi, 34 per cent of those surveyed were identified as being in the 'most deprived' category in the sanitation dimension, meaning they lacked access to adequate toilet and handwashing facilities. Deprivation was deeper in rural areas, where 38.7 per cent of survey respondents were in the most deprived category, compared with 16.4 per cent of those in urban areas. While the rural–urban divide is stark, deeper analysis of patterns of deprivation across geographic locations reveals a more disturbing picture. Included in our study were the remote islands to the west and south of the mainland of South Sulawesi. Here, 77 per cent of individuals surveyed were in the most deprived category for the sanitation dimension.

One of the key COVID-19 containment strategies is increased hygiene, particularly regular handwashing with soap or hand sanitising. Over one-quarter of individuals surveyed reported having no place to wash their hands in their house or yard, with striking variation across geographic locations. In urban areas, 8 per cent of people reported having no handwashing facilities at home; in rural areas this increased to 30 per cent, and in the islands of Pangkep, 59 per cent of survey respondents did not have access to handwashing facilities at home.

Alongside regular handwashing, physical distancing and isolating when feeling unwell are central to COVID-19 containment strategies. The ability to physically distance or to isolate is more difficult for people living in contexts of multidimensional poverty, whereby interaction with others is required for the most basic human functions. While only 3 per cent of respondents in urban areas reported not having access to private toilet facilities, 29 per cent of people in rural areas reported no access. Almost 9 per cent of survey respondents reported using only public toilets. In the islands, just over 54 per cent of people reported using only public or shared toilets. Over one-quarter of individuals surveyed reported needing to go out regularly to collect water for household use: 10 per cent in urban areas and one-third in rural areas. Almost 19 per cent of respondents reported that their home was too crowded to live comfortably. Combined, these findings indicate the inability of people to protect themselves and others from coronavirus when living in contexts of poverty, inadequate infrastructure and insufficient basic services. They also highlight the disparities across geographic areas, not only in terms of the urban–rural divide, but also the deep deprivation and vulnerability in remote areas. This brings a disturbing additional dimension to the ways in which COVID-19 will impact on poverty in Indonesia, and highlights that the poor are susceptible not only to deepening economic hardship but also to the virus itself.

Concluding remarks

In launching the Global Humanitarian Response Plan for COVID-19, the United Nations Secretary-General argued that this was the 'moment to step up for the vulnerable' (United Nations 2020a). This can only occur if those who are most vulnerable can be identified. The IMMP data reveal which social groups were experiencing multidimensional poverty before the COVID-19 pandemic and are important in indicating how the poverty and vulnerability of specific groups is likely to be deepened. Age and gender are revealed as important in shaping the nature and depth of multidimensional poverty. People with disability, very often the 'forgotten group', experience deep multidimensional poverty and are especially vulnerable during COVID-19.

Senior officials from Indonesia's National Development Planning Agency (Badan Perencanaan Pembangunan Nasional, Bappenas) have argued that successful responses to the pandemic will require learning from the past, whereby successful social safety-net programs were central to driving down the official poverty rate (Asadullah et al. 2020). However, they note that success in dealing with COVID-19 'depends on the capacity of local governments to efficiently manage existing cash assistance and other safety-net schemes, as well as actively updating databases for better targeting' (Aulia et al. 2020). COVID-19 responses have included the extension of some existing social protection programs and adoption of temporary social protection measures that target poor households, the unemployed and workers who have lost their jobs (Olivia et al. 2020). Yet accurate targeting of social protection interventions was problematic prior to the pandemic and assistance did not always reach those in greatest need (McCarthy and Sumarto 2018; Olivia et al. 2020; see also Alatas, this volume). Moreover, Olivia et al. (2020) have questioned whether COVID-19 social protection measures will reach the transient poor, who are not usually beneficiaries of such programs and may not be easily identified.

If national and local governments are to design effective social protection measures in response to COVID-19, nuanced information on the ways in which multidimensional poverty is affecting different social groups is essential. For people living in multidimensional poverty, COVID-19 is just one more of the many crises they must deal with on a daily basis, but without well-designed interventions their poverty and precarity will deepen. Individual-level and gender-sensitive information on multidimensional poverty, of the kind provided by the IMMP, is essential in determining responses and ensuring that the most vulnerable groups are reached.

References

ADB and ILO (Asian Development Bank and International Labour Organization). 2020. *Tackling the COVID-19 Youth Employment Crisis in Asia and the Pacific.* Bangkok: ILO and Manila: ADB.

Asadullah, M. Niaz, Fisca Miswari Aulia and Maliki. 2020. 'What can Indonesia learn from past policies to prevent another poverty hike during the pandemic?' *The Conversation,* 15 May. https://theconversation.com/what-can-indonesia-learn-from-past-policies-to-prevent-another-poverty-hike-during-the-pandemic-136702

Aulia, Fisca Miswari, Maliki and M. Niaz Asadullah. 2020. 'Without intervention, model shows COVID-19 will drag at least 3.6 million Indonesians into poverty'. *The Conversation,* 15 May. https://theconversation.com/without-intervention-model-shows-covid-19-will-drag-at-least-3-6-million-indonesians-into-poverty-138305

Bessell, Sharon and Angie Bexley. 2020. 'Overcrowded homes and a lack of water leave some Indonesians at risk of the coronavirus'. *The Conversation,* 8 May. https://theconversation.com/overcrowded-homes-and-a-lack-of-water-leave-some-indonesians-at-risk-of-the-coronavirus-136855

Bexley, Angie, Mandy Yap, Sharon Bessell, Monica Costa, Masud Hasan, Janet Hunt, Grace Lovell, Trang Pham and Helen Suich. 2020a. *The Individual Deprivation Measure. Indonesia Country Study: Jeneponto Regency*. Canberra: Crawford School of Public Policy, Australian National University.

Bexley, Angie, Mandy Yap, Sharon Bessell, Masud Hasan, Janet Hunt, Grace Lovell, Trang Pham and Helen Suich. 2020b. *The Individual Deprivation Measure. Indonesia Country Study: Pangkajene and Islands Regency*. Canberra: Crawford School of Public Policy, Australian National University.

Boserup, Brad, Mark McKenney and Adel Elkbuli. 2020. 'Alarming trends in US domestic violence during the COVID-19 pandemic'. *American Journal of Emergency Medicine* 38(12): 2753–55. doi.org/10.1016/j.ajem.2020.04.077

Bradbury-Jones, Caroline and Louise Isham. 2020. 'The pandemic paradox: The consequences of COVID-19 on domestic violence'. *Journal of Clinical Nursing* 29(13–14): 2047–49. doi.org/10.1111/jocn.15296

de Haan, Arjan. 2000. 'Social exclusion: Enriching the understanding of deprivation'. Working Paper. January. Canada: International Development Research Centre.

Djalante, Riyanti, Jonatan Lassa, Davin Setiamarga, Aruminingsih Sudjatma, Mochamad Indrawan, Budi Haryanto, Choirul Mahfud, et al. 2020. 'Review and analysis of current responses to COVID-19 in Indonesia: Period of January to March 2020'. *Progress in Disaster Science* 6(100091). doi.org/10.1016/j.pdisas.2020.100091

Gender Observatory. 2020. 'The Gender Observatory: COVID-19 and the crisis'. June. Jakarta: Kementerian PPN/Bappenas, Australia Government and Mampu. https://www.mampu.or.id/en/knowledge/publication/gender-observatory-covid-19-the-crisis-june-2020/

Guillen, Laura, Lluis Coromina and Willem E. Saris. 2011. 'Measurement of social participation and its place in social capital theory'. *Social Indicators Research* 100(2): 331–50. doi.org/10.1007/s11205-010-9631-6

Hao, Gang, Ghose Bishwajit, Shangfeng Tang, Changping Nie, Lu Ji and Rui Huang. 2017. 'Social participation and perceived depression among elderly population in South Africa'. *Clinical Interventions in Aging* 12: 971–76. doi.org/10.2147/CIA.S137993

Hoy, Chris. 2016. *Projecting National Poverty to 2030*. London: Overseas Development Institute. www.odi.org/publications/10356-projecting-national-poverty-2030

John, Neetu, Sara E. Casey, Giselle Carino and Terry McGovern. 2020. 'Lessons never learned: Crisis and gender-based violence'. *Developing World Bioethics* 20(2): 65–68. doi.org/10.1111/dewb.12261

Komnas Perempuan. 2020. 'Kajian dinamika perubahan di dalam rumah tangga selama COVID-19 di 34 provinsi di Indonesia'. Jakarta: Komnas Perempuan.

Mariska, Made Ayu. 2020. 'Indonesian women were already at risk. Then COVID-19 came'. *The Diplomat*, 1 May. https://thediplomat.com/2020/05/indonesian-women-were-already-at-risk-then-covid-19-came/

McCarthy, John and Mulyadi Sumarto. 2018. 'Distributional politics and social protection in Indonesia: Dilemma of layering, nesting and social fit in Jokowi's poverty policy'. *Journal of Southeast Asian Economies* 35(2): 223–36.

McQuaid, Ronald. 2015. *The Multiple Scarring Effects of Youth Unemployment*, Skills in Focus. Skills Development Scotland and Scottish Funding Council. doi.org/10.13140/RG.2.1.1300.4964

Montero-López Lena, María, Diego Luna-Bazaldúa and Laura Ann Shneidman. 2019. 'Loneliness in the elderly in Mexico, challenges to the public policies'. *Journal of Chinese Sociology* 6(16): 1–17. doi.org/10.1186/s40711-019-0106-0

Muna, Ayesha Nadya, Diva Tasya Belinda Rauf and Ika Krismantari. 2020. 'Indonesia's rise in domestic violence during the COVID-19 pandemic: Why it happens and how to seek help'. *The Conversation*, 6 August. https://theconversation.com/indonesias-rise-in-domestic-violence-during-the-covid-19-pandemic-why-it-happens-and-how-to-seek-help-142032

Olivia, Susan, John Gibson and Rus'an Nasrudin. 2020. 'Indonesia in the time of COVID-19'. *Bulletin of Indonesian Economic Studies* 56(2): 143–74. doi.org/10.10 80/00074918.2020.1798581

Purnamasari, Ririn and Rabia Ali. 2020. 'High-frequency monitoring of households: Summary of results from survey round 1, 1–17 May 2020'. *Indonesia COVID-19 Observatory Brief* No. 3. World Bank, 26 June. https://openknowledge.worldbank.org/handle/10986/34740

Santini, Ziggi Ivan, Paul E. Jose, Erin York Cornwell, Ai Koyanagi, Line Nielsen, Carsten Hinrichsen, Charlotte Meilstrup et al. 2020. 'Social disconnectedness, perceived isolation, and symptoms of depression and anxiety among older Americans (NSHAP): A longitudinal mediation analysis'. *Lancet Public Health* 5(1): E62–70. doi.org/10.1016/S2468-2667(19)30230-0

Saputra, Antoni. 2020. 'Indonesian disability activism amidst the COVID-19 pandemic'. *New Mandala*, 15 June. https://www.newmandala.org/indonesian-disability-activism-amidst-the-covid-19-pandemic/

Sen, Amartya. 2000. 'Social exclusion: Concept, application and scrutiny'. *Social Development Papers* No. 1. Manila: Asian Development Bank.

Sumner, Andy, Chris Hoy and Eduardo Ortiz-Juarez. 2020. 'Estimates of the impact of COVID-19 on global poverty'. *WIDER Working Paper* No. 43. doi.org/10.35188/UNU-WIDER/2020/800-9

Suryahadi, Asep, Ridho Al Izzati and Daniel Suryadarma. 2020. 'Estimating the impact of COVID-19 on poverty in Indonesia'. *Bulletin of Indonesian Economic Studies* 56(2): 175–92. doi.org/10.1080/00074918.2020.1779390

Syakriah, Ardila. 2020. 'COVID-19 pandemic forces Indonesian mothers to do it all'. *Jakarta Post*, 21 April. https://www.thejakartapost.com/news/2020/04/21/covid-19-pandemic-forces-indonesian-mothers-to-do-it-all.html

United Nations. 2020a. 'Launch of Global Humanitarian Response Plan for COVID-19'. 25 March. www.un.org/sg/en/content/sg/press-encounter/2020-03-25/launch-of-global-humanitarian-response-plan-for-covid-19

United Nations. 2020b. 'The impact of COVID-19 on women'. *Policy Brief*, 9 April. https://www.unwomen.org/en/digital-library/publications/2020/04/policy-brief-the-impact-of-covid-19-on-women

Wisor, Scott, Sharon Bessell, Fatima Castillo, Joanne Crawford, Kieran Donaghue, Janet Hunt, Alison Jaggar, Amy Liu and Thomas Pogge. 2014. *The Individual Deprivation Measure: A Gender-Sensitive Approach to Poverty*

Measurement. Melbourne: International Women's Development Agency. www.individualdeprivationmeasure.org/resources/arc-report/

World Bank. 2015. *A Measured Approach to Ending Poverty and Boosting Shared Prosperity: Concepts, Data, and the Twin Goals*. Policy Research Report. Washington, DC: World Bank.

World Bank. 2017. *Monitoring Global Poverty: Report of the Commission on Global Poverty*. Washington, DC: World Bank. https://openknowledge.worldbank. org/handle/10986/25141

World Bank. 2020. 'Unemployment, youth total (% of total labor force ages 15–24) (modeled ILO estimate)'. World Bank, 21 June. https://data.worldbank.org/ indicator/SL.UEM.1524.ZS

Yusuf, Arief Anshory. 2020. 'Initial assessment from simulation with IndoTERM CGE economic model.' Bandung: SDGs Center, Padjadjaran University.

Yusuf, Arief Anshory and Andy Sumner. 2017. 'Multidimensional poverty in Indonesia: How inclusive has economic growth been?' *Working Papers in Trade and Development* No. 2017/09. Canberra: Arndt-Corden Department of Economics, Crawford School of Public Policy, Australian National University.

Glossary

AEC	ASEAN Economic Community
AFC	Asian financial crisis
ASEAN	Association of Southeast Asian Nations
automatic stabiliser	public revenue shortfall caused by reduced economic activity
Bappenas	Badan Perencanaan Pembangunan Nasional (National Development Planning Agency)
BKF	Badan Kebijakan Fiskal (Fiscal Policy Agency)
BLBI	Bantuan Likuiditas Bank Indonesia (Bank Indonesia Liquidity Assistance)
BLT Dana Desa	Bantuan Langsung Tunai Dana Desa (Village Funds Direct Cash Assistance; created for COVID-19 response)
BOS	Bantuan Operasional Sekolah (Schools Operational Assistance)
BPJS-K	Badan Penyelenggara Jaminan Sosial Kesehatan (Healthcare and Social Security Agency)
BPNT	Bantuan Pangan Non-Tunai (Non-Cash Food Subsidy Program; now Kartu Sembako)
DAK	Dana Alokasi Khusus (Special Allocation Fund)
DAK Fisik	Dana Alokasi Khusus Fisik (Special Allocation Fund for Capital Spending)
Dana Desa	Village Funds
DAU	Dana Alokasi Umum (General Allocation Fund)
DID	Dana Insentif Daerah (Regional Incentive Fund)
dinas	district local offices
DKI Jakarta	Daerah Khusus Ibukota Jakarta (Special Capital Region Jakarta)
DPR	Dewan Perwakilan Rakyat (House of Representatives)

DTKS	Data Terpadu Kesejahteraan Sosial (Integrated Database for Social Welfare); formerly Basis Data Terpadu, the Unified Database
FAO	Food and Agriculture Organization of the United Nations
FX	foreign exchange
GDP	gross domestic product
GFC	global financial crisis
IDM	Individual Deprivation Measure
IFAD	International Fund for Agriculture Development
IFLS	Indonesia Family Life Survey
ILO	International Labour Organization
IMF	International Monetary Fund
IMMP	Individual Measure of Multidimensional Poverty
IT	information technology
ITC	International Trade Centre
Jabodetabek	Jakarta and the surrounding metropolitan area, including Bogor, Depok, Tangerang and Bekasi
JKN	Jaminan Kesehatan Nasional (National Health Insurance)
Jokowi	(President) Joko Widodo
Kartu Prakerja	Pre-employment Card
Kartu Sembako	Staple Food Card (from *sembilan bahan pokok*, nine basic commodities, originally rice, sugar, cooking oil, meat, eggs, milk, corn, kerosene and salt); fomerly known as BPNT
KPK	Komisi Pemberantasan Korupsi (Corruption Eradication Commission)
MSME	micro, small and medium enterprise
NIK	Nomor Identifikasi Kependudukan (Population Identification Number)
ODP	*orang dalam pemantauan* (tracing surveillance)
OJK	Otoritas Jasa Keuangan (Financial Services Authority)
PDAM	*perusahaan daerah air minum* (local water supply company)
PEN	Program Pemulihan Ekonomi Nasional (National Economic Recovery Program)
Perppu	Peraturan Pemerintah Pengganti Undang-Undang (Regulation in Lieu of Law)
Perpres	Peraturan Presiden (Presidential Regulation)
PIHPS Nasional	Pusat Informasi Harga Pangan Strategis (National Strategic Commodity Price Centre)
PIP	Program Indonesia Pintar (Smart Indonesia Program)

PKH	Program Keluarga Harapan (Family Hope Program)
posbindu	*pos binaan terpadu* (community-based health promotion post)
posyandu	*pos pelayanan terpadu* (community-based integrated healthcare post)
prolanis	*program pengendalian penyakit kronis* (chronic disease management program)
PMT	proxy means testing
PSBB	*pembatasan sosial berskala besar* (large-scale social restrictions)
puskesmas	*pusat kesehatan masyarakat* (community health centre)
Rastra Program	Rice Program (from *beras sejahtera*, 'rice for the prosperous')
REER	real effective exchange rate
Rp	rupiah
SBN	*surat berharga negara* (government bonds/securities)
SUP	Surat Utang Pemerintah (special-purpose debt instrument)
Susenas	Survei Sosio-Ekonomi Nasional (National Socioeconomic Survey)
TNP2K	Tim Nasional Percepatan Penanggulangan Kemiskinan (National Team for the Acceleration of Poverty Reduction)
UNCTAD	United Nations Conference on Trade and Development
UNICEF	United Nations International Children's Fund
Unified Database	Basis Data Terpadu; now DTKS (Data Terpadu Kesejahteraan Sosial, Integrated Database for Social Welfare)
USD	United States dollar
VAT	value-added tax
WFP	World Food Programme
WHO	World Health Organization
WTO	World Trade Organization

Index

www.ingramcontent.com/pod-product-compliance
Lightning Source LLC
Chambersburg PA
CBHW050223270326
41914CB00003BA/542